D0989823

THE LIFE AND EVIL TIMES OF
NICOLAE CEAUSESCU

THE LIFE AND EVIL TIMES OF NICOLAE CEAUSESCU

JOHN SWEENEY

HUTCHINSON

London Sydney Auckland Johannesburg

This edition first published in 1991 by
Hutchinson

Random Century Group Ltd
20 Vauxhall Bridge Road, London SW1V 2SA

Random Century Australia (Pty) Ltd
20 Alfred Street, Milsons Point, Sydney, NSW 2061, Australia

Random Century New Zealand Ltd
PO Box 40–086, Glenfield, Auckland 10, New Zealand

Random Century South Africa (Pty) Ltd
PO Box 337, Bergvlei, 2012, South Africa

British Library Cataloguing in Publication Data

Sweeney, John *1958–*
The life and evil times of Nicolae Ceausescu.
1. Romania. Ceausescu, Nicolae *1918–1989*
I. Title
949'.803092

ISBN 0–09–174672–8

Photoset by Deltatype Ltd, Ellesmere Port, Cheshire
Printed and bound in Great Britain by Mackays, Chatham

TO ANNE

'Remember the absurd game of chess
where the mad knight moved villages
first sacrificing the horses,
and a thousand people hurried out to praise his game'
  From 'Absurd Chess', Mircea Dinescu

'Awareness always comes late, nearly always too late; we are dogged
by the curse of apathy, our hearts and minds sick with indolence.'
  From 'Incognito', Petru Dumitriu.

'Since a man can go mad I do not see why a universal system cannot go
mad too . . .'
  From 'Aphorisms', Georg Christoph Lichtenberg.

Interviewer: 'Did you have a good Christmas?'
Peter O'Toole: 'Not as interesting as the Ceausescus'.'

Contents

List of Illustrations

Photo credits: p.3 *top left* Reuters, *top right* Keystone, courtesy of the Hulton-Deutsch collection, *bottom* Associated Press Ltd; p.4 Keystone, courtesy of the Hulton-Deutsch collection (*both*); p.5 *top left* Ellen Stork-Elmendorp, *top right* Reuters/Bettmann, *bottom* Dod Miller; p.6 Associated Press Ltd (*both*); p.7 Associated Press Ltd (*both*); p.8 Dod Miller (*both*). Other photographs are courtesy of the author.

Acknowledgements

This book would not have been possible without the help of a great number of people, some of whom gave their time at no little personal risk. The Securitate are still around, and it is understandable that many Romanians sought anonymity when discussing the late dictator. To them, quiet thanks.

Any writer on Romania owes a great debt to the staff of Radio Free Europe, who logged the Ceausescu 'Years of Light' with great passion and, when suitable, splendid glee. They must know their greatest praise was the fear and loathing they roused in the dictator himself.

The following people shared their knowledge of Ceausescu's time with me. In Romania: Gabriel Adam, Cathy Adams, Ali Hadyar Yurtsever, Violeta Andrei, Gheorghe Apostol, Professor Andrei Bantas, Bogdan Mihalascu, Florin Bottez, Silviu Brucan, Pavel Campeanu, Nicu Ceausescu, Valentin Ceausescu, Mariana Celac, Sergiu Celac, Marc Champion, Vicky Clarke, Petr Clej, Corneliu Coposu, Gabriel Costache, Geoff Dowens, Mihnea Gheorhiu, Prince Serban Ghica, Rodika Gabrila, Mike Goldwater, the Canadian ambassador Saul Grey, Tony Horwitz, Dr Theodor Ionescu, Peter Jouvenal, Paul Lowe, Colonel Lucescu, Ion Maurer, Viorel Mazilu, Professor Iulian Mincu, Mira Olareanu, Alec Pattison of the British Council, Alec Russell, Mark Schoofs, John Simpson, Tira Shubart, Chris Stevens, the Dutch ambassador Coen Stork, Ellen Stork-Elmendorp, General Victor Stanculescu, Tibi Tomcianyi, and at the United States embassy ambassador Alan Green, Jr, his deputy Larry Napper, and Virgil Bodeen.

In the West: Richard Alexander MP, the Rt Hon. Julian Amery MP, Amnesty International, Hugh Arbuthnott, the late Lord Jock Bruce-Gardyne, Guy Bunclark, the Rt Hon. Lord Callaghan, Sir Kenneth Cork, the Rt Hon. Edmund Dell, Michael Dutfield, Richard and Elizabeth Germany, Robin Hoggard, the Rt Hon. Sir Geoffrey Howe MP, Robert Govender, Frank Haynes MP, Ivan

Helmer, Paul Holmer, Andrew Hunter MP, Dr David Husain, James Johnson, Michael Lanning, Maureen MacGlashan, Brian Mees, Sally Mills, Lord Newall, the Rt Hon. Dr David Owen MP, Dr Raj Patel, Ivor Porter, Mariana Procopiu, Robert Robinson, the staff at the library of the School of Slavonic and East European Studies, William Shawcross, Michael Shea, Sir David Steel MP, Lord Whaddon, Lucy Willis.

Thanks are due to William Heinemann for permission to quote from *Red Horizons* by Ion Pacepa.

A special thanks is due to my three interpreters, Andrei Razvan Debau and Razvan Constantinescu of Contact Romania and Ionna Draghici. Philip McKearney, the former British ambassador to Romania, read part of the manuscript, and Dr Dennis Deletant, senior lecturer in Romanian at the School of Slavonic and East European Studies, read the whole. One day the definitive scholarly work on the Romanian revolution will be written and Dr Deletant will be its author.

This book only exists because my newspaper, the *Observer*, sent me to cover the Romanian revolution at Christmas 1989 and then gave me time off in which to write it. I am indebted to the editor of the *Observer*, Donald Trelford, his deputy Adrian Hamilton, magazine editor Angela Palmer, Martin Huckerby, my secretary Ruth Fisher, Jeffrey Cane and his library staff, Mark Seacombe, who lent me his overcoat, and my friend Andrew Billen for his constant help and unstinting encouragement.

Thanks to my model of an agent, Imogen Parker, and Richard Cohen and Robyn Sisman of Hutchinson for their advice and enthusiasm. Finally, thanks to Sam Sweeney and Anne Patterson, who saw me off at Heathrow and welcomed me home when I got back.

Introduction: Christmas 1989

This is a horror story – a true one – about a monster who came to be president of a country. It starts at dawn on Saturday 23 December 1989 with a heap of corpses.

Eighteen bodies lay underneath an electricity pylon on white plastic sheets in the paupers' cemetery in Timisoara, naked to the gunmetal sky. The honey-sick stink of the dead hung in the air; nearby were the graves from which they had been disinterred. The bodies were soiled by the dirt from the graves, their nudity cold, pointless, obscene. On one woman's stomach lay a perfectly formed foetus, its skin stained an unnatural purple. At the sight of the foetus a middle-aged Romanian woman crumpled to the black earth and started to sob. Thirty paces away, inside a pink funeral chapel, lay the corpse of what looked like an old man, his feet bound by twisted wire: tortured? Nineteen corpses in all. The news agencies were saying 4,000, 40,000, 60,000 dead. Where were the rest?

And there was something strange – you could say unsatisfactory – about the nineteen. Eight corpses had stitches in their stomachs, perhaps from autopsies; some of the rest were so badly decomposed the flesh had rotted away from the bones. These dead did not look as though they had been killed the previous Sunday, the flashpoint of the Romanian uprising, when churchgoers in Timisoara physically defended their pastor, Laszlo Tokes, from threatened internal exile. They had been dead too long.

None of the dead had obvious bullet wounds. This conflicted with the story that had travelled to the West, despite the sealing of Romania's borders in the days that followed the Timisoara uprising, that the army and president Nicolae Ceausescu's secret police, the Securitate, had fired blindly into the protesting crowd, killing thousands of people. Most disturbing of all was the foetus with the purple stain, as if it had been a clinical specimen in a jar.

The paupers' cemetery was like a tawdry horror show at a funfair.

You left it sickened by the original impulse to see for yourself; troubled, too, by the doubtful authenticity of the exhibits. For the Romanians present it was proof enough of the evil they were fighting. The Niagara of emotions that thunders in a revolution is not best suited to the weighing of contradictory evidence. But from then on I did not completely believe anything that happened in the Romanian revolution, unless I saw it with my own eyes. And even then. . .

Timisoara was waking up to a street battle. Gunfire rang out, harmless when far off; electrifying when close to. Sight was almost completely useless in judging the danger. One learnt, astonishingly quickly, to listen hard, differentiating between the too close snap, the middle-distance crackle and the comfortingly far-off pop of gunfire. Truck-loads of troops, waving the Romanian flag with a hole in the centre where the communist logo had been torn out, roared across town. The army, which had now switched sides and was fighting for the revolution, was struggling to overcome the resistance of the Securitate, still loyal to Ceausescu. Edging uncertainly around the noisier gunfights, we drove to the city's main emergency hospital, stopping bonnet to turret with a tank. It waved its machine gun at us to stop; we stopped.

Inside the hospital, the first horror was an eighteen-year-old man so freshly slaughtered that the bloodstains on his shirt were still red. He had been shot in the back: we could see the exit hole, the size of a grapefruit, which the AK-47 bullet had made in his chest. Another eighteen-year-old had been shot in the chest and liver but still lived; a 23-year-old toymaker shot in the pancreas had a tube of something coming out of his mouth. The toymaker, Calin Marius, spoke a little English. In a too quiet voice, he said he had been gunned down outside the cathedral at nine on Sunday night.

The doctor in charge of the intensive-care unit was the calmest source of information in a city spastic with fear. Dr Aurel Mogoseanu said that the hospital had accepted 26 people dead and 200-odd wounded since the revolution had begun, with most people admitted on Sunday night and Monday morning; 30 were in intensive care. One of the dead was a three-year-old girl, shot in the heart. Another child, a four-year-old, had been shot in the abdomen, but was still alive. The doctor was joined by a colleague who did not wish to be named because he was still afraid of possible Securitate retribution. He said that at the beginning of the week the Securitate prevented the wounded from coming to the hospital; they had even blocked in the hospital's ambulances with a tank. In any case, the doctors had not seen anything like 4,000 dead. They had heard about the stomach stitches in some of the dead at the paupers' cemetery: it was a mystery to them, too.

So the Securitate had shot at least twenty-six dead, probably more, but not many more than, say, fifty. That was massacre enough. Ceausescu could hardly have gone on TV and said: 'Listen, we only shot twenty-six dead.' In the news vacuum created by the sealed borders, the rumours of the dead had spiralled uncontrollably. The irony was that Ceausescu had stayed in place all those years by fear and lies; and now he had been brought down in the same way. If he tried to tell the truth – that the massacre of Timisoara was much exaggerated – no one would have believed him. (A similar rumour, that a student had been killed by riot police, triggered the Czechoslovak revolution. By the time the people realised that no one had died, the communists were finished.)

Questions multiplied: where were the rest of the dead? Why the fake horror show? The answers were to come much later. Time, against us, prevented more thorough checking. The photographer Geoff Dowen and I had a deadline hours away, for the next day's *Observer*. From the hospital, we now had to cross town to the Timisoara hotel.

At every road junction gunfire seemed to ring out, but its direction was impossible to tell as it echoed off the seedy concrete blocks which made up the town centre. Out of habit, I found myself stopping at some red traffic lights until jeers from the passengers – Geoff, Tony Horwitz of the *Wall Street Journal* and Ali Hadyar Yurtsever of the Turkish service of the BBC – put me right. The streets were empty of traffic, apart from tanks – manned by the army, now the good guys – blazing their machine guns at Securitate snipers, at shadows, at anything that twitched.

We drove up one street to find it blocked by two tanks. Again, there was no knowing who was shooting at whom. We got out of the car. Geoff and Ali ran ahead to snap the firefight while Horwitz and I took in the scene from behind a tree. I picked up some spent AK-47 bullet cases. They clinked in my coat pocket like loose change. Semi-automatic fire burst out, very close. Geoff and Ali doubled back, breathless. We got in the car, took a side road, turned into a main road and edged along slowly. A knot of people, pressed against shop doorways, shouted at us to stop. One woman waved a handkerchief. Sorry, but there was a deadline to catch. The BMW crept onwards.

Snap-snap-snap. The tracer bullets spat out from the right. They were closer than anything so far, so close that Geoff and I saw the thin jet streams of the bullets a few feet in front of the car's bonnet. The noise was sharper and louder, too, a crack rather than a bang: we were hearing it before the echo. It could have been the Securitate; perhaps it was the army. It did not seem a good time to ask. Snap-snap-snap. Reverse. Where was reverse? Was it up and over to top left? Or was it down and over to bottom right? Snap-snap-snap. 'Get the fuck out of here!' someone shouted. Snap-snap-snap. I found reverse at last and floored the accelerator. The car slewed backwards round a corner and we were, sort of, safe.

There were no phone lines out of Timisoara, so Ali and I drove to Yugoslavia to file our copy. The journey to the frontier should have taken half an hour, maybe less, but it was made longer and tenser because we had to negotiate a dozen or so citizens' roadblocks, searching for the Securitate, now called 'terrorists'. At the roadblocks, or 'controls', a frenzied crowd would race up to the car waving sticks, coshes and the occasional elderly gun. The sight of a press card and a few words of English – 'Press' or that lovely white lie 'BBC' – changed everything. The suspicious faces eased into smiles, we were clapped and cheered away, until the next roadblock, a few hundred yards on.

Yugoslavia was pleasantly dull. On the road to Timisoara, back in Romania, we switched on the local radio to hear martial music punctuated by an excited announcer speaking the same stock phrase. Two lads on the road confirmed in halting French that Nicolae Ceausescu and his wife Elena had been arrested. Ali and I hugged each other, we cracked open a bottle of beer and toasted the end of the revolution.

No one had told the Securitate. The gunfights crackled throughout the night, mainly distant, but enough to keep us on edge. At five o'clock on Christmas Eve morning, Ali and I picked our way past the sleeping soldiers, sprawled like King Arthur's knights on the staircase and in the lobby of the pitch-black hotel, and headed for Bucharest.

Just before Buzias we were stopped by a roadblock. Rumours fly in a revolution: one was that Ceausescu drank the blood of newborn babies; another was that the killers were not true Romanians but specially trained Libyan terrorists. I did not look Libyan, but Ali did.

As we drew up, I yelled *'Pressa Inglesa'* as I had done a dozen times before. One of the men at the back of the group started shouting, his voice incoherent with fear. His mood infected the others. When they saw Ali's Turkish passport, they pulled us out of the car, motioned 'hands up' and pressed their Kalashnikovs against our backs. They shone torches in our faces while others searched the boot. Ali started to protest, then he shut up. Another man was shouting in German, a language I do not understand.

It was very cold. My arms started to ache. The whole thing was so bloody ridiculous. I even had an unlit cigarette in my lips, like a Hollywood cliché. I started to say that I was a British journalist; if they would let me get my passport from my inside pocket I could prove it. I tried to reach for it, but the action prompted a new frenzy of shouting. I heard the rough catarrhal sound of a Kalashnikov being cocked and felt a fresh dig at my spine. 'I am a British journalist,' I repeated in a pained, sulky voice.

'Shut up, Mr John.' This was Ali. 'They are saying in German, "Shut up or we shoot." '

I shut up.

We must have stood there, with our hands up, for about half an hour before they realised they had been mistaken and apologised for treating us as terrorists. We drove off, shuddering from the cold and the scare. Only later did Ali realise that they had kept his Romanian visa form; but neither of us felt like turning back.

Buzias, Lugoj, Caransebes, Orsova: we overtook horses and carts; in the wooden villages people stared at our expensive foreign car as if we were men from the moon. Through the Transylvanian Alps there were bonfires blazing in each village, surrounded by knots of men standing in shabby black suits. At one of these bonfires we were given a slug of *tsuica*, the Romanian plum brandy, from a boozy-breathed old man who said 'Ceausescu' and did a handcuffs mime. And the fire? The old man said: 'Christos.' It had been easy to forget that this was Christmas Eve.

Just past Orsova, we crossed the Danube to buy petrol in Yugoslavia. On getting back into Romania, a shifty-faced fathead of a border guard with a lot of scrambled eggs on his shoulders – who had been barring the world entry on Ceausescu's orders two days earlier – turned up the revolutionary music on the TV. 'I like this music,' he said and smiled, convincing no one.

At a shipyard on the Danube a painter dangled from a harness held by a spindly crane. He was whiting out the words 'Nicolae Ceausescu' on a huge hoarding written on a factory wall. On the way to Bucharest all the billboards praising Ceausescu had been knocked over and some set on fire.

On the outskirts of Craiova, a revolutionary at the roadblock told us not to go any farther. Why? He did a fair impression of Jimmy Cagney cradling a tommy gun: 'Rat-tat-tat.' And Slatina? 'Rat-tat-tat.' Pitesti? 'Rat-tat-tat.' Bucharest? 'Rat-tat-tat, rat-tat-tat.' He let us go on when we told him we had come from Timisoara. What was it like there? There was only one possible reply: 'Rat-tat-tat, rat-tat-tat, rat-tat-tat.'

We arrived in Bucharest as dusk fell. Two steely, middle-aged toughs flagged us down on a quiet street. Like the rest of the country it was unlit and gloomy because of Romania's energy crisis. They didn't look like revolutionaries: they were too old and severe, too controlled. They said they were engineers. They demanded that we unload our baggage out of the boot. My instinct was to refuse, but Ali, whose policy was to comply with every request with a punctilio just short of parody, did as he was told. The man in glasses grabbed hold of our press cards and would not give them back. We started shouting at each other. Then the other man questioned Ali. Why did he not have the serial number of his typewriter written on his passport? (Ceausescu had decreed that every typewriter face in the country was registered with the police, which meant the Securitate, to prevent the circulation of samizdat publications.)

The alarm banged in my tired head that these two 'engineers' might only be playing at being revolutionaries; after all, a foreign press card would come in handy for a secret policeman on the run. The street was empty, in deep shadow. It was getting very creepy. On cue, like the Sixth Cavalry, a truckload of students came swinging by, waving the now familiar Romanian Polo-mint flag. I shouted 'BBC' at them and at that magic abracadabra they stopped and tumbled out, bawling and chaotic but assuredly the good guys. They played 'roadblocks' with us, but we didn't care. In the confusion a plastic bag full of liquor, cigarettes and chocolate was stolen, but we got our press cards back. A moment later the 'engineers' had melted into the night.

When Ali and I staggered into the lobby at the Bucharest Inter-Continental, we hugged each other like lovers. It was crawling with journalists, some old friends, some old enemies. From what they told us, the fighting in Bucharest had been severe, far worse than in Timisoara. No one knew how many Romanians had lost their lives in the uprising.

The journalists' body count was more precise. In Bucharest earlier that day a French TV producer had been killed by an army tank. He had been standing behind it, sheltering from Securitate sniper fire, when it reversed suddenly and crushed him. That morning an American journalist had been shot in the back going into the main hospital in Timisoara, the one we had visited; a French journalist had been shot while driving through Timisoara. A few days later, the British photographer Ian Parry was killed in a plane crash shortly after take-off from Bucharest. Only hours after we arrived, a press convoy coming into the capital's outskirts was shot up by Securitate snipers; a Belgian journalist was killed, a Turk shot in the head was in coma. The Turk was a friend of Ali's.

But that was later. For the moment, it was hard not to get roaring drunk on 100 per cent proof revolutionary spirit. Difficult, though, to find something decent to drink. The British embassy had decamped to the basement of the American embassy because of Securitate sniper attacks. There, a bottle of eggnog was liberated. While it was being drunk, the family of the British ambassador, Michael Atkinson, described sheltering in the basement of their home while they heard men stomp about above, firing their guns. They had to flee when whoever it was – Securitate? – set fire to the place.

After the eggnog I wandered around Bucharest, half-cut, listening to the gunfire. The square in front of the Central Committee building, where Ceausescu had made his last, stumbling speech before his helicopter took him away, was littered with tanks and armoured cars, residue of the battle that day. The old Royal Palace was a pockmarked ruin; every building had its bullet acne, and some had been blasted into rubble. Here and there flames still licked at windows; roofs glowed a dull red. Despite the gunfire, people seethed around, shouting, singing snatches of songs. Small bonfires illuminated their faces, some black with dirt, others the colour of whey, all exhausted, but with eyes alive, sparkling, reflecting the fires. Shards of glass and spent bullet cases crackled underfoot.

The songs died and the crowd flattened – me too – when an army gunner started blasting away from a window inside the Central Committee building, pointlessly. There was no answering fire. The sniper he was furiously exterminating existed only inside his head. A student came up: 'You must understand what a mind-fuck Ceausescu has been for us.'

On Christmas morning I went looting in the Central Committee building itself. Ceausescu's office on the first floor looked like a saloon bar in a John Wayne western after the brawl. The windows had been shot to pieces by the army, the floor was peppered with spent bullets, broken glass, fallen masonry. A hodgepodge of revolutionaries acted out their own overwritten scripts, declaiming, shouting, waving guns around, overlooked by a bemused Michael the Brave, for ever riding his white charger from within Ceausescu's favourite painting.

Soldiers stood around, gawking at the revolutionaries, their French-style First World War helmets lending the scene a period touch. The building had been ransacked. Desks and chairs had been tipped up, typewriters upended, cupboards smashed open in the search for loot. Anything of conceivable value had already been stolen, leaving only the detritus of Ceausescu's Great Era behind: his *Collected Works*, for example, all twenty-seven volumes of *Romania on the Way of Building Up the Multilaterally Developed Socialist Society*. In one room, not far from Ceausescu's office, there was a paper bag bursting with tinny fake-gold and red badges, commemorating the 9th Party Congress, decorated with the hammer and sickle. As I put the bag into my pocket, the badge pins pricked my hand. In another room there was a stack of photograph albums, including one picture of some unnamed Chinese notable in a Mao suit and Ceausescu himself, standing erect at an airport greeting ceremony. It is a photograph of quiet, understated menace. I ripped it out and stuffed it inside my coat; it is on my desk as I write.

I flicked through some more albums. All the pictures were of the man the Romanians called Him. There was one taken at some shipyard on the Black Sea, a boat's hull in the background; in the foreground stood a Sixties fish-finned gas-guzzler with a radiator grille like a killer whale's mouth, packed with chrome teeth. He was there again, a small, quick man with a shock of silvery hair, standing in a black suit, surrounded by heavy-jowled trusties: the gangster president.

There wasn't that much left in the old Royal Palace, opposite the Central Committee building. The grand marble staircases were carpeted with down from feather mattresses, splinters from smashed windows and the now ordinary scattering of spent bullets. But there was one exciting find in the palace's vast attic. Erected on a special platform stood a city of white styrofoam, testament to the grandiose, banal rebuilding of Bucharest that Ceausescu had half completed. Here the real Bucharest, a higgledy-piggledy, untidy place built up over the years by a multitude, had been wiped clean. A Romanian journalist and I stood on the model city and had our picture taken, not caring how many styrofoam blocks we squashed underfoot.

There were more corpses to see. Inside a small Orthodox church near the Inter-Continental lay the body of a student, his coffin crowded round with weeping women. He had been shot dead on the Thursday or the Friday. His face was going bottle green. The incense in the church was thick; even so, it did not wholly blanket that too familiar smell of the dead. In the street a newspaper lorry trundled by, with two men throwing copies of the launch editions of real newspapers on to the cobbles – the first honest news Romanians could read for more than four decades. People ran after the lorry, snatching the newspapers from the air, as the hungry snatch at bread.

That night, while eating a disgusting Christmas dinner at the Inter-Continental, I heard that Ceausescu and Elena had been executed by revolutionary forces. Misgivings came later; at the time it seemed like a fitting Christmas present for the Romanians. The announcer on Romanian TV celebrated the news by saying: 'This Christmas we have someone new on television.' He then placed a grinning Father Christmas on his desk.

Ceausescu was dead, but unanswered questions remained. Where, now, were the Securitate? How many people had been killed? What was the explanation for the too-long dead of Timisoara? How had he remained in power for so long? What sort of man was he?

Outside the church by the Inter-Continental a woman stopped me, tears streaming down her face, her voice brimming with hysteria. Someone translated: 'Why did you in the West support him?' I had no answer to give her.

Pawn

Truth, in the time known to Romanians as 'Our Great Era', always came with at least one layer of varnish. The further back one goes, the more lacquered the evidence. Even now, after the revolution, it is impossible to strip down to the original bare wood. Take the two-room peasant's cottage where Nicolae Ceausescu, the third of ten children, was born on 26 January 1918. It still exists, set back from the road which runs through the village of Scornicesti, then a dull backwater in Olt Valley, less than a hundred miles to the west of Bucharest.

Not long before the revolution, the cottage was completely renovated to make it – the birthplace of the Leader (as we would say in English) or Führer (as Romania's ethnic Germans would say) or Conducator (as the Romanians had to call him) – a more fitting shrine. The old, rotten wood was replaced with new timber, the mud walls rebuilt and covered with woodchip wallpaper, itself coated with whitewash, giving it the appearance of a newly opened Indian restaurant. A vast brick stove still dominated the pygmy kitchen. Straw had been scattered on the floor, perhaps to reinforce the ideologically correct line – which also happened to be true – that the infant Ceausescu was born, like Jesus, to a family of straitened circumstances. It is more difficult to touch up a garden, and the old Ceausescu backyard seemed a pleasant spot, with vines and cherry trees giving shelter against the sun and a modern bench-swing where perhaps Nicolae and Elena had once sat.

The locals in Scornicesti had got to the old house and wrecked it. They had torn down the Ceausescu photographs and hagiographic goo which commemorated the early years of the dictator. All that was left was some rotting potatoes in a small outhouse and a pile of back copies of *Scinteia*, the official newspaper of the Romanian Communist Party. The newspapers smelt musty; one had to brush off the cobwebs to read the print. One front page, dated 12 April 1988, showed

Ceausescu and Elena on a state visit to Australia. Posed with the Australian prime minister, Bob Hawke, and his wife, and the country's governor-general, Ninian Stephen, and his wife, they stood at the centre, as rigid as if they had been rivet-gunned into the floorboards.

The stiff Ceausescu is a constant feature of *Scinteia*'s front page photographs over 1988 and 1989: Ceausescu speechifying to massed crowds waving banners and his photograph on poles in front of the Central Committee building in Bucharest; a Ceausescu portrait staring dully out of the paper above reams and reams of his printed philosophy; Ceausescu receiving floral tributes from children. The youngsters were specially selected offspring of the Securitate, cleansed, quarantined and disinfected for three days before touching the hand of the dictator, who then washed his hands in alcohol: a common despot's tic.

In the 1960s in Bucharest Ceausescu's father, Andrutsa, won a kind of fame for his drinking bouts, which reduced him to the state of an incoherent wino, but one who was allowed to wallow, unmolested, in his own degradation thanks to his son's position. The strain of alcoholism in the Ceausescu family seems to have skipped a generation and passed on to Andrutsa's grandson, Nicu Ceausescu, who is – so they say – slowly dying of cirrhosis of the liver and a varicose oesophagus. Like Nicu, Andrutsa chafed at Nicolae Ceausescu's severe regime. He once told his drinking pals in a pub in Bucharest's Dorobantsi Square not to swallow his son's grandiloquent speeches: 'He tells nothing but lies.' The next day the whole pub vanished, to be replaced by a dairy-food outlet.

Ceausescu's mother, Alexandra, who lived to a great age, could neither read nor write. She clung to the peasant's religious certainties despite the official atheism of her son's regime. When Andrutsa, a bully as well as a drunk, died in 1971, Alexandra is said to have insisted upon, and got, a church funeral for him. Alcoholic and devout Christian – little more is known about Ceausescu's parents.

The sparse information that is available about his early life comes from the official hagiographers. The Romanian versions are crude and raw; the foreigners' a touch more subtle. In these we learn that the Ceausescu children worked in the fields to earn a little extra; that one farmer remembered Nicolae for his 'great spirit of organisation'; that a local landowner once remarked of Nicolae: 'I'm sure that given the chance this child could develop a great flair for organisation.'

Nicolae's sister Elena is said to have remarked that as a child he was 'never violent' and suffered hardships 'with the best humour'. The young Ceausescu often went to school barefooted and had to borrow books from his friends; even so he was always first in his class. One biographer quotes a teacher who describes him as 'an attentive, disciplined pupil, gifted with a very broad memory, brilliant in mathematics and, in addition, a very good comrade.'

The varnishmen should not be lightly dismissed as irrelevant. Their paeans of praise were picked up and played back to the Romanian public as evidence of the high esteem their president enjoyed abroad. It was all part of the sorcery of power which Ceausescu mastered so well. How would the Romanian public know that Donald Catchlove, Robert Govender, Andrew Mackenzie and Stan Newens, a former Labour MP – billed as 'important writers' in the Romanian press – were, compared to, say, Graham Greene, relative unknowns?

The dictator also featured in a volume of the Leaders of the World series published by Pergamon Press, entitled: *Nicolae Ceausescu: Builder of Modern Romania and International Statesman.* The general editor of this series was Robert Maxwell, the well-known British publisher. The book ends with an interview between the dictator and Maxwell. At the end of the interview Maxwell says:

Mr President, I feel dutybound to express my deep gratitude for the time you have given to answering my questions, for this interesting, frank and comprehensive talk. I wish you good health and power to continue your constant, tireless activity for the good of your country, for the success of peace and detente worldwide, for understanding and collaboration among nations.

None of the hagiographers care to analyse the Securitate. To write anything about Ceausescu without discussing his secret police is like Hamlet without the Prince, everybody else and the skull.

No word appears in the hagiographies about Ceausescu's most distinctive trait: his stutter. All his life he struggled to overcome this speech defect, which was first publicly noted in prison with fellow communists, and later at party meetings where he had to conquer it to speak. In all the conversations with the world's eminent people, the single most remarked aspect of the man was his stammer. He overcame it by moving his head backwards while drawing his lips sideways. The effect was an ugly and sometimes frightening leer.

One man who knew the stammer all too well was Sergiu Celac, Ceausescu's chief English-language interpreter for the Seventies, until he was fired from his position in late 1978. He had too close an association with the dissident mathematician Mihai Botez, who eventually had to flee Romania. Celac is now Romanian ambassador to the Court of St James's. A witty and urbane man with exquisite manners, Celac is reluctant to do his impression of Ceausescu's stammer because 'it is impious to mock the dead'. Pressed, however, he performs a brilliant impersonation of Ceausescu, his hand chopping the air like a break-dancing robot, his mouth gulping for the resisting words until, after a series of percussive false starts, they come too fast out of his mouth. Celac said: 'Sometimes he would sustain an hour-long discussion without a stammer. Emotion played a role in it. His stammer became especially noticeable when he was nervous or angry. And coming out of the stammer, he would make a grimace.'

Worse than the stammer was his body language, which, according to Celac, was all wrong. 'He was very awkward, not at all smooth. It was common knowledge that he had an asymmetry between word and gesture. His gestures were an odd counterpoint to his movements.' Here Celac illustrated his point by bringing down his hand on the wrong beat of the words. 'It was out of sync.' One of the consequences of the revolution is the falling into disuse of what Celac calls 'an enormous treasury of folklore mimicking him. It was a staple provider of laughs to imitate him or her. Actors used to learn whole speeches for private parties, but they never wrote these down, of course.' Ceausescu's lack of rhythm must be the explanation for one of the most distinctive absurdities of an absurd era: the staccato hand-clapping, as regular as the ticking of a metronome and therefore odd, with which the Communist Party apparatchiks applauded him at congresses and big meetings.

Another trait acquired in his early days was his accent: coarse and unsophisticated to the ears of the Bucharest bourgeoisie. His tongue could not get round seemingly simple phrases like *tutulor*, a form of address meaning 'to everybody'. When Ceausescu said it, it sounded like 'everyboggy'. It is hard to put across to those who have not heard Romanian, a language waggishly described by the BBC's John Simpson as a 'mixture of dog Latin and Esperanto', just how uncouth Ceausescu sounded. To American ears, one must imagine a New Jersey drawl; to British ears, one should think of a Wolverhampton whine: provincial, but not interestingly so.

Ceausescu's elderly contemporaries who still live in the gentle undulating Olt Valley, after more than four decades of burying any damaging, embarrassing or even just humanising recollections about the young Nicolae, are generally unwilling to disinter them. The Oltenians prospered from Ceausescu's favouritism towards his own region, and perhaps now share a communal shame at the comparative riches that came their way. Olt County was consistently ascribed the best agricultural figures in the country; Olt was chosen as the most suitable site to produce a new small, family car in cooperation with the French car giant, Citroën, called the Oltcit. The valley was even credited with being the fount of the origin of species: Romanian palaeoethnologists claimed they had discovered the remains of the oldest, pre-Palaeolithic hominid, a primate on the cusp of ape and man, in Europe in the Olt Valley in 1981. They called him *Australanthropus Olteniensis.*

Ilie Manea, the mayor of Scornicesti, which by 1990 was no longer a village but a town of 13,000 people, told one journalist that when Ceausescu did make visits, 'They would never announce his coming. Around 500 Securitate would converge on the town, and on the surrounding hills and forests, and the mayor's and local police's only job was to find enough people to make up a cheering crowd.' A Scornicesti teacher told Philip Jacobson of *The Times*: 'It's true that the town did well from the connections of the Ceausescu mafia. But that always made us very ashamed in the company of other Romanians. There were often nasty jokes about people from Scornicesti, especially after Ceausescu announced that the workers here were the best in the land.'

A Scornicesti resident called Florea Ceausescu, who claimed to George Jahn of the Associated Press to be the dictator's cousin and not his brother of the same name, was equally venomous: 'He was a cruel man, who worked only for his own people and had no feeling for outsiders.' Florea said that when Ceausescu made his fleeting return visits to his home town he showed no interest in his neighbours and 'we had no chance to talk to him because he was always surrounded by bodyguards'. Florea remembered young Nicolae as moody but sure of himself: 'Even as a youngster he had the feeling he would lead the people,' a recollection creepily in tune with the hagiographers' line about 'flair for organisation'. Florea added: 'He would play with us for a while, and then he would suddenly stop for no reason and say "I've had enough." He was a little strange. He never laughed, he was serious all the time.' Jahn noted an uncanny resemblance between Florea and his infamous cousin, to which he retorted: 'I will change my name. Everyone will now say that we are all bad.'

Some relatives were more equal than others; the closer to Ceausescu himself, the warmer their place in the sun. Alexandra Ceausescu bore ten children, three girls and seven boys, though one boy died at an early age. The youngest brother was also called Nicolae: his parents had more children than they knew names. Each sibling later became a tentacle of the Ceausescu family octopus which kept tightening its grip on Romania. The family likeness is striking among the boys, in particular the second Nicolae, Nicolae Andrutsa. The closeness in looks between the two men is one explanation for the virulence of the rumour, during the revolution, that it was not the dictator who had been killed, but a double. In 1983 Nicolae Andrutsa was brought into the Ministry of Interior with the rank of lieutenant general. At the time of the revolution he was in charge of the Securitate training school in Baneasa. He was accused of personally shooting anti-Ceausescu demonstrators in the days before the dictator fell.

Brother Ilie was the dictator's man in the army. He rose from Scornicesti with no academic qualifications to become a professor of history at the military academy in Bucharest and an author of a brace of stodgy books about military theory. At least, his name appears on the spine. Come the revolution, he was deputy minister of defence and head of the Higher Political Council of the Romanian Army, also with the rank of lieutenant general. Although nominally number two in the army, there is some evidence to suggest that it was he who had the real clout. In Ceausescu's Romania, proximity to the man at the top was the key to power, not your title. According to a report in the *Washington Post*, brother Ilie, with brother Marian, operated a clandestine arms bazaar from an office in Vienna, selling Soviet-made mobile rocket launchers, radar equipment and other weaponry to the CIA for a total of $40 million throughout the Eighties and selling Western military technology to the Soviets. Brother Marian committed suicide in late December 1989.

Brother Florea worked as a journalist on the party newspaper *Scinteia* in the vast Stalinist wedding cake called Casa Scinteii, or Spark House, on the outskirts of Bucharest. Brother Ioan, trained as an agricultural scientist, was at the time of the revolution a member of the party's Central Committee and first vice chairman of the State

Planning Committee. The titles are muddy. In colloquial English, brother Ioan was 'a big cheese'.

Nicolina was the eldest in the family, and like Nicolae took to politics early on; the youngest daughter, Maria, became vice chairman of the Romanian Red Cross and the middle daughter, Elena, married a local party hack, Vasile Barbulescu. Awarded the Order of Labour of the First Class in 1983, Elena Barbulescu was a school inspector in the Olt Valley, though not a fastidious one. Gratiela Simion, a nurse at the pitifully ill-equipped Slatina Orphanage in Olt County – stuffed to the gunwales with unwanted children thanks to the Ceausescu's birth-promotion campaign – recalled one of her two visits in the five years running up to the revolution in unflattering terms: 'She put her handkerchief over her nose. She didn't like the smell, or the way the children looked. We tried to do something about it, so that these children could have better conditions. They categorically refused to take us on. They actually told us to get lost.'

Elena Barbulescu's husband was first secretary of the Olt County's party committee. Previously he had been chairman of the collective farm in Scornicesti, itself the darling of the Romanian press. The official titles are too austere to convey the reality of the family members' breath-taking luxury. The Barbulescus, for example, lorded it over the Olt Valley, from their modern, wooden villa, which loomed over the old family-home-cum-dictator-shrine in Scornicesti.

Through the windows, some of them broken, one could see that the revolutionaries had expressed their long-suppressed hate by smashing this place up too. Once a small temple of Our Great Era kitsch – dreary and contemptible by the standards of Western décor, fabulously lavish to a Romanian – it had now been reduced to a pigsty by the mob. Floorboards, tables, chairs, bookcases and cupboards had been up-rooted and then thrown on the floor in search for Barbulescu gold. Even the wooden slats of the in-house sauna had been broken, probably to little avail. Upstairs a great library of Ceausescu works, praising him, had been thrown higgledly-piggledy on the floor. A muddy bootprint was stamped across a photograph of Ceausescu in a black fedora, standing in a cornfield with a gang of his courtiers. The photograph was in an enormous book called *Homage*.

As an example of unctuous prose poured onto the dictator by Romanians and Westerners, be they monarchs, diplomats, politicians or businessmen, *Homage* is without equal. Printed in 1978, in many ways Ceausescu's *annus mirabilis*, it was produced to celebrate

Ceausescu's sixtieth birthday and forty-five years of courageous revolutionary activity. The contents, written in English as well as Romanian, Russian, German, Spanish and French, give a flavour of the style.

Imposing Acknowledgement of the remarkable contribution made by Comrade Nicolae Ceausescu to enriching the treasure of revolutionary thinking and practice. . . . High consideration and valuation of the general secretary of the party, Romania's President, for his tireless activity devoted to peace and collaboration among peoples. . . . Profound respect, devotion and gratitude to the general secretary of the party, the country's president, Comrade Nicolae Ceausescu. . . . Heartfelt messages of the capital and the homeland's counties addressed to the beloved Leader. . . . Profound love and esteem to Comrade Nicolae Ceausescu for the prodigious activity carried out for the good of the country and the people.

Faced with the banal, monotonous language of the Ceausescu personality cult, the reader is liable to skim such passages. The temptation should be resisted. To understand the extraordinary fact of Ceausescu's monolithic power, and the otherwise incomprehensible lack of resistance to it, one must try to experience the sheer dead weight the Romanians bore day in, day out. During the twenty-four years of his reign, their thoughts were blunted and restricted by what George Orwell might have called 'Homagespeak'.

Homagespeak, over the years, seeped into people's minds, leaving even the bravest dissidents still unwilling to utter his name months after his execution. No one in Romania dared to mouth the word 'Ceausescu' in an angry, mocking way, not even the political prisoners, in the same way that devout Catholics in Spain never articulate the word 'Devil'. As Saul Bellow noted in his glitteringly shrewd novel *The Dean's December*, which contrasts the 'moronic inferno' of Western cities like his native Chicago with the 'peculiar psychoses of penitentiary societies' like Romania, it was the practice in Bucharest to refer to Ceausescu as just 'Him'.

The Romanians were trapped, so it is not surprising that some people sang his praises in *Homage* – including Ion Iliescu, then a high-ranking member of the *nomenklatura*, today Romania's president. But the contributions to *Homage* from various Western presidents, prime ministers and political leaders, translated from the Romanian, make for curious reading. Here are tributes from president Jimmy Carter; prime minister James Callaghan; Gordon McLennan, then general secretary of the Communist Party of Great Britain; Ian Mikardo, then a serving Labour MP and member of the party's National Executive Committee; Baroness Elles, then president of the International Department of the Conservative Party of Great Britain; Edward Heath, former prime minister and leader of the Conservative Party; and Julian Amery, a Conservative MP and former Foreign Office minister. There are telegrams from the former French president Valéry Giscard d'Estaing, Queen Juliana of the Netherlands, King Juan Carlos of Spain, King Carl Gustaf of Sweden and Emperor Bokassa.

And dozens of photographs, too, of Ceausescu signing a summit declaration with Leonid Brezhnev, general secretary of the Communist Party of the Soviet Union; smiling thinly at president Tito of Yugoslavia; sitting across a table from Pol Pot, leader of Cambodia's murderous Khmer Rouge; grinning – a rare capture, this – at Cuba's Fidel Castro; standing upright in the traditional, rivet-gunned pose with the Marcoses of the Philippines; inspecting the troops with King Hussein of Jordan; in the shooting gallery with the Shah of Iran, and again with emperor Hirohito of Japan; greeting Pope Paul at the Vatican; sitting on a bench with Canadian prime minister Pierre Trudeau; side by side with the leader of the PLO, Yasser Arafat; holding his hands out in the fisherman's 'it was this big' pose with Mrs Thatcher; standing on a White House balcony with president Carter, and smiling grandly with Her Majesty the Queen of England in a state landau, the Duke of Edinburgh and Elena trotting on behind. The strange boy with the stammer from Scornicesti had made good.

By the tumble of books in Barbulescu's house lay a child's orange rubber ring, which would not inflate. It must have been punctured.

Pawn to King Four

Was it the monster or was it the swamp? Ceausescu or Romania? The dictator's eldest son, Valentin (the stress is placed on the last syllable: 'Valenteen') Ceausescu, relaxed on a pastel-shaded sofa in a quietly tasteful flat in the centre of Bucharest. Books and a few abstract paintings lined the room. He took a sip of the Dimple whisky in his glass, savouring his recent release from prison in autumn 1990. 'I think the swamp has something to do with it.' He paused to consider his words.

A physicist of high standing – a genuine one, not a confection of the sycophants – a former student of Imperial College, London, and fluent English-speaker, Valentin is the Good Prince in the Ceausescu fairy-tale-cum-horror-story. He spent most of his adult life at a calculated distance from his parents and their deeds, partly because his mother did not approve of his first marriage, partly because he disliked his father's 'fanaticism'. He did not gorge himself on the lees of power, as his brother Nicu – the Bad Prince – so infamously did, but lost himself in his family, friends and work at the Central Institute of Physics in Bucharest. 'I took a conscious decision at the age of seventeen that I could not speak out because I had a privileged position. It's difficult to talk about it now, after all those years. It was a kind of internal exile,' he said.

For nearly all Ceausescu's time, Valentin kept this distance, holding his tongue while the rest uttered Homagespeak. So his criticisms of the Romanian people for their lack of resistance to his father are all the more striking. 'I was furious with the people towards the end. Absolute power corrupts absolutely, but submission corrupts too. Where were the dissidents? There was no movement.'

There is no easy answer, but the ugly history of the country which Valentin's father crossed in 1929 at the age of eleven, forced to leave home for Bucharest because of the family's poverty, provides part of the explanation. A look at the map helps, too. Romania then had roughly the same shape as it does today: that of a Rorschach test, a blob of ink flicked at the map of eastern Europe. It is made up of three old principalities: Wallachia, at its centre the modern capital, Bucharest; Moldavia, with its capital Iasi, very close to the modern border with the Soviet Union; and the rocky heartland of Transylvania, its 8,000-foot peaks of the Carpathian Mountains providing a natural fortress. Wallachia and Moldavia, known jointly as the Regat or Old Kingdom, form a rough, backwards L. Wallachia, the foot of the backwards L, runs down from the Carpathians to the only natural frontier in the territory, the Danube, which bumps along the bottom of the map until it spreads into a swampy delta that opens on to the Black Sea. Moldavia, the upright stem of the L, is bounded today by the river Prut. Only Transylvania, geographically at the centre of the ink blob, is defendable; the rest of the country has always been easy meat for invaders. The early rulers of what is now Romania kept going, against the grain of geography, by a blend of deception and savagery. It is a rich country, but never a particularly happy one. A character in Olivia Manning's *Balkan Trilogy* – a required treat for anyone interested in Romania – says:

You know the story that Romanians tell about themselves: that God, when He had given gifts to the nations, found He had given to Romania everything – forests, rivers, mountains, minerals, oil and a fertile soil that yielded many crops. 'Hah,' said God. 'This is too much', and so, to strike a balance, he put here the worst people he could find. The Romanians laugh at this. It is a true, sad joke!

Its large ink-blob shape is relatively new. History only once saw Romania as we see it, during the much-sung reign of Michael the Brave, whose picture on a white charger hung in Ceausescu's office in the Central Committee building. Michael the Brave welded the three principalities into one in 1600. A year later he was dead, and the union vanished. Union was the bold exception to the rule. For most of its history Romania has been divided, skewered and kebabed by a succession of foreign invaders and masters, some of whom were unspeakably nasty. Cruel as Ceausescu's time was, it was not without precedent in his country's history.

One of the most frequent clichés about Romania, worn smooth with constant use by journalists over the years when they had little else to go on, is that the country is a 'Latin island in a sea of Slavs'. The received version in Romania is that the country speaks a Latin language – albeit a bastard variety, full of Turkish squiggles – thanks to the lasting influence of the Roman legions, who vanquished the local tribe, known as Dacians, in AD 107 under the emperor Trajan. The Dacians were a sub-branch of the Thracians, who, according to Herodotus, the leading journalist of his day, were 'the bravest and most righteous' of the lot. (The Thracians were supposedly linked to the Illyrians of Albania, a proposition based on some linguistic evidence.)

It was a rich victory over the Dacians. The emperor commemorated it by constructing a triumphal column in Trajan's Forum in Rome. The figures depicted on the column wear the same clothes as worn by Romanian peasants when Ceausescu was a boy. There was so much booty in Transylvania, principally gold, that Trajan was able to cancel all taxation in the Roman Empire for one year and make a gift of 659 denarii to each citizen.

The Romans proper stayed only 160 years, retreating to the south of the Danube as the Goths, the first of the migrant hordes, overran them. Nevertheless, this one and a half centuries was enough for the Dacians to be thoroughly Romanised and, therefore, somehow more civilised than the surrounding neighbours. Such is the 'Daco-Roman Continuity Theory'. This theory goes on to explain that the Romanians preserved their language in the mountain fastnesses of Transylvania, coming down to repopulate the flatter land towards the Danube when it was safe to do so. In this way the modern Romanians can trace themselves directly back to the emperor Trajan's men. Moreover, the Continuity Theory – if true – establishes a title to Transylvania, a territory also claimed by their Hungarian, or Magyar, enemies to the west. The Hungarians, of course, do not accept the theory.

There is a barely submerged strand of racial superiority to the Continuity Theory, a strand which Ceausescu when dictator teased out to its full, fascist length. The evidence is not favourable towards the racial purists who support the Continuity Theory. Although blessed with a resilient Latinate language, the Romanians absorbed a succession of conquerors, the Goths in the third, fourth and fifth centuries, the Huns also in the fourth and fifth centuries, followed by the Avars, Slavs and Bulgars in the sixth and seventh centuries, the Magyars, or Hungarians, in the ninth and tenth, the Pechenegs in the tenth and eleventh, the Cumans in the twelfth and thirteenth, and the

Tatars (or Mongols) in the thirteenth. The few details we have of these invaders, who, with the exception of the Baltic Goths, came rolling in from the steppes to the east like surf, are all pretty grim. Take, for example, Krum, one of the first khans of the Bulgars. He and his noblemen used to sup out of the skull of the captured emperor Nicephorus, which had been split into two and lined with silver. The Tatar raids scourged so deep that the locals who lived near the Buzau pass in the southeast corner of the Carpathians still referred to it as the 'Tatar pass' in the 1930s.

The Romanians, not without good reason, moulded themselves to the shape of the last bottom that sat on them. The Romans' language stayed, but the 'purity' of the Dacian race became a little threadbare, if not an empty boast, through the generations of different migrant invaders. A casual glance at the rich variety of faces on a Bucharest street – swarthy, Teutonic, Tatar-eyed, Gypsy, and so on – punctures the notion of Daco-Roman purity.

And facts? There are hardly any to bring to bear. The Tatars burnt all the paperwork, along with abbeys and castles and churches in the thirteenth century. This absence of evidence, as Patrick Leigh Fermor dryly points out in his classic travel tale *Between The Woods and the Water*, about his journey through Transylvania before the Second World War, has not proved a bar to the fierce prosecution of the argument: 'Theories can be evolved in a void. . . . The interpretations are as different as the work of two palaeontologists, one of whom would reconstruct a dinosaur and the other a mastodon from the same handful of bone-fragments.'

Although Transylvania belonged to Hungary for about a thousand years, apart from the odd tidal wave of Turks to and fro, the crucial point is that there are now and have been for a long time several million more Romanians in the former principality than Hungarians. In feudal times, which in this part of the world lasted until the early twentieth century, this arithmetic mattered less. The Romanians were, largely, the serfs and the Hungarians the masters. Come the pressure for equality, which exploded in feudal Russia in 1917, then the numbers game would always work in favour of the Romanians. The unsolvable rub is that the Transylvanian Hungarians are not a peripheral, minuscule minority, but number some 2 million-odd people, living in a dense mass 200 miles east of their compatriots, completely surrounded by many more Romanians. The battle about Transylvania, and the old, dusty historical controversies thrown up by it, matter to the Ceausescu story, because Romania's Hungarian minority suffered badly under him and articulated their plight early on. For too long, complaints about human-rights abuses in Romania were written off by the West as 'Hungarian propaganda'.

To the southwest lies Yugoslavia, and yet more Slavs. The two countries are separated by the Danube, bloated by a banal dam, drowning the famous Iron Gates, which Ceausescu and Tito had laid across the river. Towards the end of Ceausescu's era the very brave would be so desperate to escape that they would try to swim across, dodging the border guards to land, exhausted, on the Yugoslav side. Not a few were ordered to go back, at gunpoint, to face imprisonment, torture and worse. The Romanians and the Yugoslavs have, by and large, been friendly neighbours.

To the north and east Romania is overshadowed by Russia, an old and pitiless enemy which has too often masqueraded as an ally. One of the characters in Olivia Manning's *Balkan Trilogy* says: 'The friendship of Russia has been more disastrous to Romania than the enmity of the rest of the world.' And this was written about prewar Bucharest, before the wholesale Soviet takeover of the country from the mid-Forties on.

To the south lie more Slavs in Bulgaria, and farther off to the southeast there is Turkey. The Sublime Porte held Romania in its decadent, perfumed palm for hundreds of years. The last invasion took place in 1710, the last raid by the Turco-Tatars was launched in 1788, though it was not a shining example of the genre. The Turks' nominal control, effectively under a gang of seedy Greek appeasers known as the Phanariots, continued well into the nineteenth century. While the British were passing the first of the parliamentary reform acts, the Romanians were still under the sultan's podgy thumb. The Ottoman Empire lingers in hard-to-define ways: gestures, smells, attitudes. Coffee is drunk Turkish-style in Bucharest, dark, impossibly sweet and disgustingly gritty. Baksheesh oils many a transaction with government officials: a packet of Kent cigarettes will normally secure entry to one of Ceausescu's many villas from the guards on the gate, placed there to stop anyone from entering; a few dollars more buys you a conducted tour.

The cultural difference between the Old Kingdom, made up of Moldavia to the east and Wallachia to the south, ruled, sort of, by the Turks, and the lands to the north and west on the European side of the Carpathians, which lived under the double eagle of the Austro-

Hungarian Empire, is too sharp to be ignored. The Hungarians are fond of whispering: 'Europe stops at the Carpathians, you know.' Perhaps it is significant that the revolution was ignited in Timisoara – part of old Austro-Hungary – and not in the former Turkish suzerainty.

Submission to power – the Romanian quality Valentin Ceausescu so despaired of – is summarised in a Romanian proverb: Kiss the hand you cannot bite. At times, faced with this submission and the callousness and cruelty of Ceausescu's apparatchiks towards the weak and the wretched, it is tempting to conclude that everything is a continuum of the 'Oriental' outlook brought to Romania by the Turks.

But the Wallachians, forerunners of the Romanians, could be crueller than the Turks. In June 1462 a great army led by Sultan Mehmet II, the conqueror of Constantinople, crossed the Danube into Wallachia. They advanced across scorched earth through a country-side empty of people, food and water. On the night of 17 June the Turkish camp was raided. Their demoralisation increased as they approached the old capital of Tirgoviste only to gag in repulsion at what they saw. On the route to the capital a new, stark forest had been planted. It was over half a mile long by two miles wide. Instead of trees, the bodies of 20,000 Turkish and Bulgarian soldiers, slain the year before, lay rotting in mid-air, spiked through their rectums. Leigh Fermor writes: 'The Sultan, whose aquiline features and snowy globular turban we know from Bellini's painting and the ingraving by Pisanello, had been brought up on blood, like a falcon: he recoiled in horror . . . and burst into tears.' This was the work of Vlad the Impaler, or Vlad Tsepesh; son of Vlad the Dragon, Vlad Dracul. The Romanian for 'son of the Dragon' is Draculea.

The Impaler was a monster, made infamous by the new technology of woodcuts, the tabloid newspapers of the day, published by his Saxon enemies. The Saxons were, and still are, another minority in Romania, having sailed down the Danube from Germany, concentrating their numbers in Transylvania's semi-independent market towns of Kronstadt, now Brasov (and, for a time after the communist takeover, Stalin), and Hermannstadt, now Sibiu. The woodcuts were dispatched to the far corners of a horror-struck Europe. The forest of impaled, rotten corpses which made the conqueror of Constantinople weep was the *coup de théâtre* to top a career spattered in blood.

The Impaler spent his childhood as a hostage in the Turkish court, where his paranoia was first nurtured. Submission to the Turks was one thorn; another the unruly boyars, or nobles, who did not take warmly to the central authority of the Wallachian princes, or hospodars. One reason was that the princes were only jumped-up boyars, paying a tribute to the Turks for the privilege of the title. So it was perfectly in keeping with the spirit of the times that the boyars buried alive the Impaler's father and his elder brother, Mircea. To crush the boyars and subdue the Saxons, the Impaler acted with a blend of cunning and ferocity which gives any student of modern Romania a feeling of *déjà vu*.

The Impaler eradicated crime by punishing virtually every trans-gression with death: and that meant death by impaling. The terror of him was so great that he could leave a golden cup beside a lonely fountain where 'whoever would like to drink water' could use it. No one dared steal it. He invited the boyars for Easter lunch in 1459. Those who were unsuspecting enough to accept were seized and impaled. He invited the poor, the crippled and the unemployed to a similar feast at Tirgoviste, asking, compassion in his voice, if they wished to be rid of life's sufferings. When they said yes, he burnt the lot of them.

The following year the *Chronicon Mellicense* informs us that, after a successful raid against the Saxons, he dined in a garden among a copse of skewered foes, using a holy icon as a plate. Once, when questioned by a peasant who asked him how he could possibly eat when he was breathing in the stench of so many corpses, Vlad chose to impale the wretched peasant on a particularly high pole so that he 'could breathe cleaner air'.

He then turned his attentions to the Turks. He made his displeasure known by defaulting on two payments to them, and then, when two plenipotentiaries from the Sultan arrived, demanding payment, the Impaler, in turn, demanded that they doff their turbans. They refused. He had their turbans nailed to their heads. Mehmet invaded; the rest is woodcut history.

He died, killed perhaps, in not so clear circumstances in 1475. His head vanished – one story suggested that it was sent as a gift to the Sultan – but the Impaler's headless corpse was buried at the island monastery in Snagov, a stone's throw from the villa where Ceausescu was to have spent Christmas 1989, had not his plans changed.

Under Ceausescu, the stories of Vlad the Impaler's bloodthirsty campaigns were played down as black propaganda dreamed up by the anti-Wallachian Saxons and the upstart boyars who opposed him. He even appeared on a stamp in 1959 and was 'fully rehabilitated' on the occasion of the 500th anniversary of his death in 1976. The party's historians declared him 'a hero of the struggle for freedom and independence' and placed him in the Communist pantheon.

The Impaler is by no means the only sadist who features in Romania's past. Just as nasty was the Blood Countess, Elizabeth Bathori of Cachtice. She was born in 1560. Perhaps inbreeding was the cause of her terrifying rages. Brought up with a healthy contempt of peasants, she took this, eventually, too far: beginning with sticking pins into servant girls – always peasants, and always girls: she was a lesbian – then forcing them to lie naked in the snow, and finally biting chunks of breasts and necks off. This unsavoury habit may be the origin of the legend that she bathed in blood to keep her skin white. Eventually her accomplices, including a dwarf called Fizcko, were tried in camera, but her part was hushed up, so that 'the families which have won such high honours on the battlefield shall not be disgraced . . . by the murky shadow of this bestial female'.

The Dracula myth is still believed in the Balkans. It has its roots in the region's folklore, myths that were told and embellished around the flickering fires centuries before Bram Stoker's *Dracula* (1897). Vampires, known as *vampir* in Hungary, *upir* in Poland and Russia and *strigoi* in Moldavia and Wallachia, are the undead. Although the details vary from place to place, the central feature of a vampire is that it does not decay after death. They cannot show themselves in daylight, but emerge from their graves at night to suck the blood of the living.

It is easy to scoff at such stories as peasant superstition. But the drinking of the blood of victims, more repugnant even than Khan Krum supping from the emperor's silver-lined skull, is not just a thing of the past. During the civil war in Russia a Baron von Sternberg-Ungem believed himself to be a reincarnation of Genghis Khan and drank the blood of the communists. In 1980 an American psychopath shot his grandmother in the head and then sucked the blood out of the bullet holes because he thought himself to be a vampire. In 1986 a man in Titusville, Florida, accused of kidnapping a teenage girl, was also charged with robbery because he was suspected of drinking her blood after claiming to be a vampire.

There is a very plausible medical explanation for vampire symptoms. In 1985 Dr David Dolphin delivered a paper to the

American Association for the Advancement of Science arguing that a rare genetic disease, erythropoietic porphyria, could be responsible for the myths. The disease, which affects one person in 200,000, has a devastating effect on the body. The skin becomes extraordinarily sensitive to sunlight, so that even mild exposure leads to disfigurement. The nose, fingers and lips fall off, leaving the teeth sticking out of the gums in a fearful, animal-like manner: the classic Dracula face. Avoiding sunlight, sufferers venture into the open only at night. Among the known cures for the disease is an injection of the blood product haem, which victims of a past age may have acquired by sucking blood from their loved ones. In Dr Dolphin's view, sufferers may have instinctively sought out blood by biting humans. As watchers of horror movies know, the results of a vampire bite are immediate. The bitten becomes a vampire too. Dr Dolphin can explain this as well. Given that the disease is genetic, many of the victim's brothers and sisters may have had the same defective DNA, but with dormant symptoms. The shock of a bite from the first sufferer may have led the sibling to develop symptoms. And garlic, the traditional defence against vampires? According to biochemical evidence, about the worst thing for porphyria sufferers is the smelly garnish.

During Ceausescu's time rumours washed around Bucharest that the dictator was a vampire. These stories were given more credence in the heat of the revolution. But even afterwards, Ceausescu the bloodsucker was 'a fact' in many conversations. The English traveller Peter Scott heard the following from an otherwise wholly sensible, middle-class Romanian couple with whom he was staying in the summer of 1990: 'Births were officially registered three days later than the actual date,' they told him. 'So that if a baby was actually born on 6 August, then officially the date of birth would be 9 August. In those three days, the baby was drained of some of its blood, which was given to Ceausescu to make him strong. If the baby survived its loss of blood and lived to the third day then everything would be all right. But if the baby died it did not matter – because it had never, officially, been alive.'

Ceausescu, the Impaler and the Blood Countess would stand out in any company, but the flow of Romanian history has always been a gory one. Transylvania, Moldavia and Wallachia were on Christianity's raw frontier with Islam: when war was not ravaging the countryside, the princes had to reap savage taxes from their peasants to pay off the Turks in a Balkan version of Danegeld. Periodically, the peasants rebelled. The Bobilna peasant uprising in Transylvania in 1437 was put down with savage ferocity by the noblemen, with the luckless leaders mutilated, then hung in front of the mob. The Magyar nobles tightened the screw on the Vlach peasants, barring them from citizenship and right of residence in the Saxon or Magyar towns, only allowing that they would be 'merely tolerated by grace'. Another peasant rebellion took place in Transylvania in 1514, ending when its leader Gheorghe Doja was captured. He was bound naked on a red-hot iron throne while his flesh was ripped out by tongs and fed to his followers, who were compelled to eat the flesh while Doja was still, just, alive.

Another uprising took place in Wallachia in 1655, when a mob of peasants ransacked the homes of the boyars in Bucharest, Tirgoviste, Ploiesti and Buzau. The revolt was put down with the customary brutality.

There was something of an intermission in Wallachia during the reign of Constantine Brancoveanu, 1688–1714, when a minor cultural renaissance took place, before the Sultan ordered him to Constantinople. On arrival the old man was tortured in front of his children, then invited to save himself on the payment of a colossal sum of 10 million piastres. It was beyond his resources, so the Turks executed him, his two sons and his son-in-law. Their bodies were thrown into the sea, their heads exposed for three days above the great gate of the Seraglio.

After Brancoveanu, the Turks gave up appointing native princes, choosing Greek merchants from the Phanar, or lighthouse, district of Constantinople, who became known as the Phanariots. The Phanariots, with names like Ghica, Cantacuzene, Rosetti and Duca, were, effectively, the Sultan's bailiffs. Paintings of the Phanariots of the time show chubby panjandrums, resplendent in plumed turbans, aglitter with diamonds, rubies and other gems.

The running of Moldavia and Wallachia from the early eighteenth century became, then, a mercantile transaction: to recover the money made over to the Sublime Porte for the privilege of power, it was necessary for the Phanariots to sink their teeth deep into Moldavia's and Wallachia's riches. One Italian ambassador wrote that 'the land sweated blood'. An eighteenth-century historian observed: 'What is remarkable about these despots is that all their riches, money, jewels, hoards and furnishings, are always in trunks and travelling coffers, as if they have to leave at any moment.' It was, in fact, only good business sense. The Phanariots employed agents at the Sublime Porte called Bash-Kapukihayas. If a prince was outbid at Constantinople, his Bash-Kapukihaya would tell him quickly, so that he could ransack the national treasuries and make off before the new prince arrived.

The Phanariot princes required submission from the boyars. The boyars had to carry the current Greek prince around in their arms, from room to room to bed. During the prince's siesta, all traffic, church bells and loud voices were stilled. Again, the student of Ceausescu feels the hairs at the back of the neck standing up. Ceausescu's small villa at Snagov lay close to the small town of the same name. Towards the end, when the old man was ailing, silence was enforced. Cocks, dogs and church bells – it is a Romanian tradition to ring the church bells when someone in the village dies – all were outlawed for fear of waking the sleeping dictator.

Paula Martin, a pleasant 68-year-old grandmother whose cottage backed on to the villa, occasionally heard the Ceausescus through the fence; once, even, she heard Nicu and Elena have a row about Nicu's unsuccessful marriage. She recalled: 'We had to sell our cocks because they were not allowed. There were no church bells, and no hammering either, or chopping wood, in case we woke him up.' Dumitru Ion Ionitsa, a boatman on the lake, said: 'My daughter played the radio a little loud one night. After a short time a man from the Securitate came round and switched it off.'

The boyars took out on the peasants the indignities – both psychological and material – they had to endure from the Phanariots. The people had to bear a ferocious weight of taxes. Daniel Chirot in *Social Change in a Peripheral Society: The Creation of a Balkan Colony* (1976) provides a list of the heavy burdens a Wallachian peasant faced:

By the end of the eighteenth century, the taxes levied on the ordinary villager included: a head tax, levied four times a year, but up to 12 times a year when the Treasury needed it; a hearth tax, levied twice a year; a tax on cattle, sheep, pigs, vines; a tax on smoke, from the household chimney, and on cellars; a tax on pasture grass; a 'flag tax' upon the accession to the throne of a new prince, and another tax three years later if the same prince was still on the throne; a tax on soap, on all goods sold in a marketplace, and on bridge tolls; a salt tax; and a tavern tax. Numerous others have not even been recorded because taxes were farmed out and the tax-farmers collected what they could without always keeping careful receipts.

The 'flag tax' was particularly onerous, as there were more than seventy coronations in Moldavia and Wallachia between 1711 and 1821. The peasants knuckled under, but minted a new proverb: 'Madmen rejoice when the rulers change.'

In Transylvania, reforms were in the air, thanks to Joseph II of Austro-Hungary. The burden of taxation, though harsh, was not quite so grindingly savage as suffered in the lands under Phanariot rule. In 1784 a great peasant rebellion broke out in the principality, led by Horea, Crishan and Closhca. The peasants were ignited by their attempts to achieve the better status of the serfs who lived on the military frontier, who were let off some onerous taxes because of the possibility that they might be called on to fight. But as the revolt snowballed, the peasants began to question the feudal order – they had to seek permission to move house, to marry and to practise a trade –by burning down mansions and roasting their overlords. Atrocities were widespread, but eventually the rhythm of Romanian history established itself. The peasants were crushed. Horea and Closhca were disembowelled alive and died on the wheel; Chrishan committed suicide.

The French Revolution detonated in 1789, sending the aristocracy across Europe into frenzy. In 1814 three Greek merchants founded a secret brotherhood, the Etairia, dedicated to overthrowing the Turks throughout the Balkans. The long-suppressed hatred of Phanariot rule finally exploded in Wallachia in 1821, with a revolt allied to the Etairia, led by Tudor Vladimirescu, who won from his admiring supporters the nickname Prince Tudor. His call to arms was graphic: 'How long shall we suffer the dragons that swallow us alive, those above us, to suck our blood?' He sent a message to the Turks, explaining that he was faithful to the Ottoman Empire but repelled by the Phanariot princes who 'robbed and flayed us so that we are left only with our souls'. The revolt followed the familiar pattern, ending with Vladimirescu's torture and death. But it did pressurise the Turks into ending Phanariot rule; moreover, it introduced a new actor into the play who so far had been waiting in the wings: Russia.

As the nineteenth century wore on, the influence of the Sublime Porte was replaced by that of Moscow. The Russians guaranteed Moldavia and Wallachia in 1829, after one of a series of Russo-Turkish wars. But the shockwave from the French Revolution continued to ripple across the Balkans. Its ideals were the goals of a small knot of revolutionaries – Nicolae Golescu, Ion Bratianu, Nicolae Balcescu and Mihail Kogalniceanu – who campaigned for unity between Moldavia, Wallachia and Transylvania and surged for control of the country in the Europe-wide revolutions of 1848. Instead, the Russians invaded to back the established order in the Old Kingdom and the Habsburgs reinforced their rule in Transylvania with no little brutality.

The unification of Moldavia and Wallachia finally came in 1859, when both national assemblies elected the same prince, Alexandru Ioan Cuza. But political infighting forced his abdication in 1866, making way for King Carol I, the first of the Hohenzollern dynasty, specially imported from Germany to escape the old problem of faction-fighting among the boyars. When the young King arrived in Bucharest, he asked: 'Where is the palace?' He was shown to an unkempt job lot of outbuildings, a tatty guardhouse and a group of pigs, snorting in the mud.

The Hohenzollerns are treated with great nostalgia by many Romanians today, and not without reason. Yet the conditions of the peasants did not change very much. Ten years after the last vestige of Turkish rule finally ended in Romania with the Berlin Treaty of 1878, there was another peasant revolt. Crushed, of course. The economy improved; good crops and Western investment in Romania's booming oil industry meant that by the turn of the century the country was easily the most prosperous in the Balkans, Bucharest 'the Paris of the East'. An old Greek beggar was quoted by Leigh Fermor, in his book *Roumeli* about a long sojourn in Moldavia, to the effect that in his day, before the First World War, the gentlemen of the road would always cross the Danube into Romania: 'Romanians were more prosperous and more open-handed, the place teemed with cattle and fowl and livestock of every kind, even buffaloes that the Romanians used for ploughing.'

But still the countryside simmered. The great Romanian peasants' revolt, the *raszcoala*, took place in 1907, shattering the cosy world of the Romanian aristocracy with its savagery, frightening people otherwise well-disposed towards its aims with the peasants' incoherent cruelty and raw anti-Semitism. It was put down by General Alexander Avarescu, commanding an army of some 120,000 soldiers, with matchless violence. Villages were destroyed and one estimate reckons that at least 10,000 peasants were slaughtered in three days. No one precisely knows the details, because the relevant files were secreted away in the Ministry of the Interior.

The country stayed neutral for the start of the First World War. Caroll
was torn between his loyalty towards his Hohenzollern, German, blood
and his people's overwhelming sympathy for the French, Allied cause;
the dilemma was resolved, for him, by his death in 1914. His son,
Ferdinand I eventually sided with the Allies in 1916. It proved, at first, to
be a disastrous decision. A Russian guarantee to help the Romanians
fizzled out. The Tsar's generals could not deliver their men, who began
to drift away from the war, prey to the new Bolshevik propaganda.
Romania's English-born queen, Marie, wrote in her diary for 13 July
1917: 'Misfortune pursues us; if the Russians will not fight we can be
invaded in a few days. . . . The Russians cut our throats.' The Russian
collapse allowed the Central Powers, including the hated Hungarians, to
surge in, forcing the Romanian court to quit Bucharest and be bottled up
in a tiny enclave in Moldavia. The worst was to come. The Russian
revolution completely cut off any help. The King signed an ignominious
peace treaty with the Central Powers in May 1918. However, the rout of
the Germans on the western front in the autumn threw Romania's
submission into reverse.

With the war over, Romania, on the side of the victors, won
Transylvania from the Hungarians at the Versailles Peace Conference.
Moreover, the debris of the Austro-Hungarian Empire offered up
most of Bukovina, a chunk of the Carpathians at the top centre of the
modern map. The Romanians got back Bessarabia, the Romanian-
speaking land between the rivers Prut and Dniester, from the
Russians, who, fighting their own civil war after the October
revolution, were in no position to argue. From Bulgaria, which had
also sided with the Central Powers, the Romanians won a sliver of the
southern Dobruja, the low-lying land abutting the Black Sea, and two
thirds of the Banat, the other third going to Yugoslavia. Romania
more than doubled, from roughly 53,000 square miles to nearly
114,000. It became the fifth largest country in Europe, after France,
Spain, Germany and Poland, with more than twice the prewar
population. It was a great victory at the conference table, won chiefly
by the charm of Queen Marie, whose fame was toasted by the
Algonquin wit Dorothy Parker:

> Oh, life is a glorious cycle of song,
> A medley of extemporanea;
> And love is a thing that will never go wrong;
> And I am Marie of Romania.

The Romanians had fought and lost everything; and then won it all back, and more, without a shot being fired. With the old principalities united, as they had been only once before in 1600 under Michael the Brave, the future looked bright. The Hohenzollern dynasty seemed secure, the Romanian aristocracy entrenched, the politicians bickered and intrigued as they always had. The glittering balls went on through the night in the palaces of the boyars; the peasants lived and died, unregarded. It was a world of rigid social certainties, unshaken in its self-belief. But the strange, jerky-limbed boy who arrived in Bucharest in the year before the Wall Street Crash was, one day, going to destroy it all.

Knight

The most intriguing information we know about the dictator's early life is to be found in the files of the old monarchist police:

My name is Nicolae Ceausescu. I was born in 1918, in the village of Scornicesti in the Olt region, and I am a shoemaker by profession. I arrived in Bucharest in 1928, and took a job in the shoemaking workshop of Alexandru Sandulescu at 89 Victoria Street. I worked there until 1932, and I am now employed at the Rusescu workshops, run by my brother-in-law, at number 15 Serban Voda Street. . . .

The statement goes on to admit that Ceausescu accepted 400 lei, a sizable sum in 1934, from 'a tall, well-built, fair-haired man' in return for creating a disturbance at a trial of striking railway workers. If the statement is true – Ceausescu later of course denied making it – the implication is that communist agitators like himself made trouble for money, not out of conviction.

He was first arrested on 23 November 1933, as a voluble supporter of the still outlawed Communist Party, for distributing leaflets that threatened 'the security of the state'. The police let him go because he was only fifteen. But by this age he had absorbed Marx, Lenin and Engels and was spouting them out to all who would listen. The first documented report of Ceausescu as a left-wing activist came earlier that year, in June 1933, when he represented the 'democratic' youth of Bucharest at a meeting set up to organise resistance to the growing threat of the mystical, anti-Semitic, thuggish bully boys of the Iron Guard, Romania's green-shirted version of Hitler's Brown Shirts. Ceausescu stood out at the meeting because of his youth and because he spoke so quickly. His words were later described as a 'turbulent, Carpathian torrent'.

The commonplace that cobblers are often left-wing turned out to be true in the case of one of Ceausescu's first employers. The young, under-educated but plainly bright teenager picked up his Marxism from the talk at the shoemaker's and swallowed it whole. His adherence to Marxism, or at least its rhetoric, would be lifelong and held with the passionate intensity of a religious convert; his understanding of its intellectual structure was thin and dully uncritical. Ceausescu never benefited from what the poet John Betjeman once described as the only worthwhile function of university – 'the gentle mockery of good friends'. If ever a man needed that, it was Nicolae Ceausescu. For people who witnessed 1989, Marxism seems self-evidently bankrupt, but in the early Thirties, with the Great Depression battering capitalism and millions of people starving in the United States, in much of Europe and in Romania, too, its appeal was shining. Faced with the near collapse of the liberal democracies, a Romanian teenager of peasant stock could be forgiven for believing it was better than what seemed to be the only alternative: Nazism.

The Romanian Communist Párty before the Second World War numbered less than 800 members out of a population of some 20 million, because many Romanians distrusted its pro-Soviet stance. The RCP's official policy, drawn up by the Comintern in Moscow, was that Romania should hand back Bessarabia, the land beyond the Prut stretching to the Dniester, which had been lopped off during the turmoil that followed the October revolution. The proposal to hand back Bessarabia made the party appear the tool of the Russians. Moreover, many of the RCP's members were not Romanian but belonged to the country's many ethnic minorities: German, Hungarian and Jewish. Ceausescu, pure Romanian, was something of an exception amid the party's rising stars. He was formally recruited to the party by Vasile Dumitrescu, later Romanian ambassador to Switzerland, when he was only fourteen years old.

Hugely more popular, enjoying the support of at least one million Romanians, was the Iron Guard, led by Corneliu Zelea Codreanu. It enjoyed the material and spiritual backing of the German Nazis and the Fascists under Mussolini, and combined Jew-baiting with apocalyptical orthodoxy, appeals to Romanian nationalism with a samurai's reverence for violent death and suicide. Codreanu used to dress in brilliant white, riding into muddy, provincial villages with an icon in one hand and the reins in the other. The peasants thought him a reincarnation of the archangel Gabriel, but he lacked the angel's immortality. He was murdered shortly before the war. But even after death, he exerted a sick, pseudo-religious, fascist influence on the

Romanians, accentuating their own shaky nationalism by attacking 'international Jewry'. There was a political edge to his anti-Semitism. The King's mistress, Elena Lupescu, was Jewish, a fact Codreanu and his successors played on to the unease of Carol II.

Paranoia appears to be the occupational disease of any Romanian ruler, and Carol II was no exception. Like Ceausescu, he knocked down buildings near his home – in this case, the Royal Palace – to make a clear field for machine-gun fire. Hannah Pakula's absorbing biography of his mother, Marie, *Queen of Roumania* (1984), describes a man trapped in a web of suspicion, spiteful and weak by turns. He cut off the allowance his father had willed to his mother. His spies followed her, and whenever she re-entered Romania her luggage was sent to the Palace for inspection. His vendetta against his wife was so ugly that she was forced to flee the country; another forced exile was Prince Stirbey, his mother's lover; a third Carol's own brother, Prince Nicolas. In a desperately sad letter written in July 1932, Queen Marie – who was greatly loved in Romania for her role in winning back Transylvania in Versailles – told her cousin, King George V of England: 'Lately I have been living in a world I no more understand and which has become very lonely.' Replying from Cowes, George wrote back: 'I cannot help thinking he is mad.'

Even so, many Romanians look back to those edgy years under Carol II with a poignant regret. Virtually any description of life under the monarchy makes anyone who knows Ceausescu's Bucharest wince with regret for the good old days. Architecture, cuisine, culture, press freedom, prison conditions, freedom to travel, to go to church: all seem to have been better before the communists. Only the quantity of whores in Bucharest appears to have remained constant.

The murderous assaults of the Iron Guard on Jews, the King's increasingly nervous isolation from his people, 'the pedantic, boring cry', in W. H. Auden's phrase, of the 'fashionable madmen' in Berlin and Rome were the alarums off as the tiny and unimportant playlet of the ups and downs of the Romanian communist movement were acted out in the Thirties. In June 1934 Ceausescu, now sixteen, was sent by the party to Craiova, a town about sixty miles to the west of Bucharest. There, a group of communist railway workers who had staged an unsuccessful strike the year before at the Grivitsa locomotive factory were about to go on trial. Among the accused was Gheorghe Gheorghiu-Dej, later to be the first secretary of the Central Committee of the Communist Party and effective ruler of communist

Romania, and Chivu Stoica, another prominent figure in the postwar Politburo. Other important communist figures on trial included Gheorghe Vasilichi, Dimitri Petrescu, Marin Florea Ionescu and Constantin Doncea. Ceausescu's role was to drum up support for the accused, gather signatures for a petition against the trial and generally agitate against the state's political persecution of the communists.

As the verdicts were called out, a counter-demonstration started outside the courthouse. The police moved in and arrested four men: one of them was Nicolae Ceausescu. In the official myth handed down by the hagiographers, Ceausescu told the investigating police that he denounced the 'regime of economic exploitation and repression of freedom'. It was then, too, that the statement about the 400-Lei bribe was either made or fabricated.

It was probably a police frame-up. From then onwards Ceausescu was continually being harassed and arrested, released and picked up again. Several times he was ordered to leave Bucharest for his home village and told to stay with his parents; later he was imprisoned. He repeatedly broke the Scornicesti detention orders and returned to Bucharest. This suggests that Ceausescu was nothing other than he always claimed to be: a committed communist. His son Valentin had a lot of time in prison after the Romanian revolution to ponder the question of whether his father was 'mad or bad or both'. He said: 'The new kind of politicians lie all the time. But my father was one of the old kind, more of a fanatic. He was driven by some kind of fanaticism. This belief that you can do good. It's a sort of madness.'

Rumours in Bucharest, after his accession to power, that Ceausescu started out life as a thief and police agent provocateur do not square either with Valentin's reading of his father or with the evidence of his persistent arrests. A man interested in 400-Lei bribes would not so masochistically follow the stony path of the communist movement in the Thirties. Many more lucrative careers of crime were open.

On 26 August 1934 Ceausescu was again caught, this time giving out communist literature, but released on interrogation. A few weeks later he was once more picked up and taken into custody. He had, according to his hagiographer Catchlove, been taking part in a debate on the theme: 'Having defeated the fascist danger, how are we to prepare Romanian public opinion for equal rights for all the people of the country?' He was accused of attending a political meeting that had been held without the sanction of the police or the army. Again, his youth ensured an early release from detention. But his identity card was stamped 'dangerous Communist agitator'. For an ambitious revolutionary, it is hard to imagine more exquisite stigmata. He was ordered home again, accompanied by an armed guard. Catchlove takes up the story of the young martyr:

Handcuffed and on foot, he was led from police station to police station. At night he slept on a police cell floor, still chained and with little food. The journey from Bucharest to Scornicesti, about 90 miles, took some ten days. His sister Elena remembers him arriving in the village in a filthy, bruised and near-starving condition.

According to *The Youth of a Hero* by the court writer Petru Vintila, published in 1980, it was on this trip back to Scornicesti that Ceausescu first clapped eyes on the woman who was to be his queen – Elena, also known as Lenutsa, Petrescu. Vintila slaps it on thick, in the manner of Mills and Boon: the young woman is described as having 'fine and delicate features' that were enhanced by the 'unusually deep shadow of her black eyes' and her 'lively, almost childish' and 'charming' expression. On seeing the young Ceausescu in handcuffs, the 'beautiful girl', called 'Snow White' by the sergeant who was guarding him, took an apple and a couple of walnuts from the basket she was carrying and presented them to the young revolutionary, who was overwhelmed by her 'fascination'. After Ceausescu had explained to the two women that he had been put into fetters for 'being strongly dissatisfied with the rich and with injustice in the world', his future mother-in-law presented him with five Lei for the cause of communism.

Fed up with life in Scornicesti, Ceausescu returned for a clandestine life in Bucharest, proselytising the communist cause. The early years of being on the run from the King's secret police forged his outlook. More forcefully than Marxism or Leninism, a conspirator's distrust of other people sank into his mind. For the rest of his life he never regained trust or a sense of safety or repose. From teenager to the old, sick president at the end, he exuded the restless paranoia of a hunted man.

He avoided arrest for a year, working as the secretary of the Union of Young Communists for the district of Prahova, north of Bucharest. His elder sister, Nicolina, who had become involved with the communist movement before him and was therefore something of a role model, provided his only contact with his parents. He was finally picked up again in 1936 during a police raid on a secret meeting of another communist organiser, and was held for a time in the prison at Brasov, awaiting a mass trial of communists and anti-fascist cadres. The police indictment read:

Nicolae Ceausescu, 18 years old, living in Vasile-Lascar Street, Bucharest, is a communist and anti-fascist propagandist and activist, well known for some time to the police and the Ministry of Justice.

During the trial Ceausescu's impulsiveness got him in trouble yet again. A communist sympathiser called Vladislav Tarnovski (whose Russian name is one example of the influence of non-Romanians in the RCP) so angered the judge, Colonel Gheorghe Radu, by shouting out a protest about the treatment of the detainees that he was expelled from court. As the judge ordered Tarnovski out, Ceausescu jumped up and bawled: 'Then we are all in solidarity with Tarnovski.' The judge added in his report that Ceausescu made offensive gestures to the bench and was 'in other ways showing a disrespectful attitude to the court'. For the interjections Tarnovski was given fifteen days, but Ceausescu, the greater irritant, six months in prison.

A reporter from the left-wing *Free Word* newspaper, Eugen Jebeleanu, managed to secure an interview with Ceausescu inside Brasov prison, access which journalists would not enjoy in later years under the communists. The Jebeleanu piece was the first independent description of Ceausescu, and he paints an attractive and sympathetic young man:

A guard brings the two prisoners, and they come forward smiling, with frank, open faces. They are still children. Ceausescu is 18 years old, and he is a shoemaker. He tells us why they were sentenced, he and Tarnovski, and what the interjection was all about. . . . Ceausescu is a child, but a child with a surprising intelligence and maturity. He is small and thin, with tiny, darting eyes, like two agile peppercorns. He speaks clearly, if a little too fast, as though he wanted to say, all in one go, everything that he knew. He is 18 years old, but he has seen and suffered as much as any 80-year-old. 'Beatings! And some. The guards don't play about.' He tells it very simply, as though it were a natural thing, sometimes making short gestures, with three fingers together, drawing circles around his own phrases. . . . Young and generous heart, who can wonder that he got six months?

The article has since entered the Ceausescu myth; Jebeleanu later became a court poet under the dictator's regime.

On 6 June the court sentenced Ceausescu to a further two years for his illegal activity as a communist youth organiser. Most of the regime's political prisoners were sent to Doftana, a horseshoe-shaped prison known as the 'Romanian Bastille', built on the site of an old salt mine. A carapace of mythology has concreted itself around the 'Doftana slaughterhouse', as the communists called it. By the standards of Western Europe, it does appear a fearsome place; by what was to come later, in the late Forties and early Fifties, not so bad. An official report, quoted in Catchlove, declared:

The condemned would prefer to enter any other prison than this. To be sent to Doftana constitutes the most terrible punishment, since they find themselves in a place without any contact with the outside world, where revolt is known to be out of the question, and where it is possible to keep a constant surveillance on every individual day and night.

The French writer Henri Barbusse reported on conditions inside the prison:

The inmates are chained by the feet and hands and three times a week are given bread and water. In the prison there is a special 'H' section, where they put difficult prisoners. There, they are confined in an area nine feet by three, without air, without a bed, without table or chair, without any sort of sanitary installation. The food is inadequate and barely edible anyway. . . . The prisoners, beaten on the soles of their feet, are usually unable to walk when they are returned to their cells. And when they become ill, they are left to die.

Anyone familiar with the strand of cruelty in Romanian history will be unsurprised that Doftana was a pretty grim place. But a prison newspaper was published in a clandestine fashion, so the regime inside Doftana can't have been quite as ferocious as the communist propaganda later made it out to be. According to one old communist who made a study of the early years of the party, there was a library at Doftana which had books in seventeen languages. When the Jewish industrialist Max Auschnitz arrived in Doftana in 1937, he was 'astonished' by the library: 'they provided him with every book he wanted', the old communist said. Catchlove's book contains a photograph of the prison choir practising in the Thirties. It is impossible to tell if the choristers are chained by their feet, but their hands are free to hold the music sheets.

The King's secret police seemed to have made a major mistake in incarcerating all the country's communists there. They organised inside, enforcing a tough internal discipline with which they were able, over the years, to browbeat the guards and, in 1938, obtain the status of political prisoners. It became, then, less of a slaughterhouse and more like an austere, monkish seminary. (Grouping together a regime's politically motivated enemies in one prison is one of those acts that obey 'the law of unintended consequences'. For example, Robben Island, the prison home of South Africa's black leaders fighting apartheid, became known, not wholly tongue in cheek, as 'the university'.) Even so, the hardship that Ceausescu and his fellow prisoners underwent should not be denied.

The hagiographers say that Ceausescu was a wonderful cellmate. This is distinctly not the recollection of someone who did share a cell with Ceausescu, Gheorghe Apostol. Apostol went on to become a member of the RCP mafia, defined by Hannah Pakula, writing in *Vanity Fair*, as, 'the Communist old-boy network – as sure of itself as Skull and Bones, not so secretive, and a lot more dangerous'. More than that, he was after the death of Gheorghiu-Dej in 1965 one of the three *papabile*, along with Ion Maurer (of whom more later) and Ceausescu, for the post of first secretary of the Communist Party. Apostol lost and, so the Bucharest gossips say, never forgave Ceausescu. Certainly, his later posting overseas as ambassador to Brazil could hardly compare with the chalice of power that was taken from him by his old, unloved cellmate.

An old, brown, tortoise-faced man, deaf, and blind in one eye, Apostol started our interview by saying: 'I don't like to talk about Ceausescu because he was a despot, a paranoid and a madman. I and others had to suffer.' He then lapsed into a wordless torpor, broken only by the puff-puff of Kent cigarettes.

In the embarrassing silence Mrs Apostol, a former actress, clattered around with the tea trolley, a polite scream frozen on her face. Apostol's flat, in the shady, green zone of Bucharest near Aviator Square which the Party high-ups had made their own, was studded with books and kitschy knick-knacks the ambassador must have picked up on his travels. The most arresting was a tea towel bearing a map of London, hung up on the wall like an icon. The clock ticked. The teacups rattled gently in their saucers. No one spoke. Suddenly it dawned on me that money was required before Apostol was going to find his memory. But how much? Apostol had worked on the railways before he was jailed for his communism, then, after the war, successively a member of the Politburo, a general secretary of the party under Gheorghiu-Dej, a vice prime minister of the country, a candidate for the top job, a vice president of the Council of Ministers and an ambassador. He was a lifelong and high-ranking member of the communist aristocracy, the *nomenklatura*. So what was the going rate?

Twenty dollars? (Not a petty sum, but equivalent to a month's wages for the average Bucharest worker.) He curled his lip and fixed me with his one good eye. 'Twenty dollars is baksheesh. It's a tip for the waiters at the Inter-Continental.' Having registered his disgust at twenty dollars, he started to talk. 'Ceausescu didn't have many close friends in Doftana.' His accent and manner of speaking provoked derision, Apostol remembered: 'They laughed at him because he didn't pronounce words properly. For example, instead of saying Snagov, he would call it Sinagov. It was funny, but he didn't have much of a sense of humour. And he stuttered a lot. Even Gheorghiu-Dej used to mock him by mimicking the grimace he made to cover his stutter.'

Apostol explained that the prison was divided into two: 'light cells' and 'dark cells'; the latter had no natural light and were cold, damp and bleak in winter. According to Apostol, this 'light' and 'dark' division was an idea the prison governor, Savescu, had garnered from a tour of prisons in Hitler's Germany. Ceausescu had arrived at Doftana a few months after Apostol, who was then twenty-three years old. 'We were both in the dark cells together. Once in every twenty-four hours we were allowed out for half an hour in the open air. We were not allowed to have contacts with our families or to write letters.

'There was the punishment wing, section H. There was no bed. They threw water on the prisoner in winter, and this turned to ice. People who went into section H were not normal people when they went out. Many of the people in section H caught tuberculosis: some of these died in prison, others when they were let out.' Apostol did not volunteer any personal experience of section H. Rather, his description sounded like a recitation, part of the received martyrology of the RCP.

'We were very thin. The food was bad. Even the bread had a lot of grit in it, which hurt the kidneys. So when we went outside we used to get some water, put it into a mess tin and soak the bread, to get rid of the grit.' The detail here seemed more convincing, more personal.

Was Ceausescu popular? 'We were in G section together. Ceausescu was very impulsive. He used to provoke the guards, and because of that we would all get beaten up. The beatings angered the whole prison, so everyone shouted out, "Don't beat them, don't beat them!" So the guards stopped, but came back quietly, in the middle of the night, and beat us some more. They beat us with hammers, too. I was hit with the wooden handle of the hammer, but the unlucky ones were struck with the actual metal hammerhead. Some of us were sent to section H, but not Ceausescu or I. Because of Ceausescu's impulsiveness – it caused a lot of trouble – he was not very popular.'

Apostol went on: 'The guards dealt with us one by one. One night we heard them go into Ceausescu's cell and he started screaming, "Don't touch me, don't touch me!" The next day, during the exercise period, he said he had been beaten, so we asked "Where?" There were no marks on his body, his clothes were not ripped. Probably the state security had recruited him as an informer. But there was no evidence, so nothing could be proved.'

Ceausescu, terrified of going to section H, may have been an informer for the prison warders. On the other hand, it is possible that the warders could have been put off by the frenzied screams of the young Ceausescu. He may have survived unscathed simply because there was little sport in clubbing such an odd, youthful and small man. Even at maturity, he was a tiny five foot, two inches. And it should be remembered that the vendetta between the two men lasted their lifetime. Moreover, if one of Ceausescu's secret policemen can be believed, Ceausescu used compromising photographs of Mrs Apostol's chic parties – to which Apostol rarely came – to clear his old rival out of the magic circle at the top. Apostol and Ceausescu were bonded by a mutual, glowing hatred, so their judgements of one another must be weighed with that in mind.

At the end of the interview Apostol held out his hands. I gave him forty dollars, two months' average wages. His one eye looked at the money, then at me, the money, me. It was as if he had been given a thin slice of gritty Doftana bread. In the tiniest possible voice he whispered his thanks: *'Multsumesc.'* As an insight into the thinking and ethical quality of one of Romania's Communist overlords – once, almost, its leader – it was a performance worth every cent.

Ceausescu was released from Doftana in December 1938. His spell in prison had been invaluable. He had met and forged links with all the top men in the communist movement, including Gheorghu-Dej. Although, according to Apostol, they all mocked Ceausescu's accent, deformed speech and unsightly leer, they did not doubt the commitment of the young shoemaker. The Doftana 'graduates' would form the hub of the postwar nationalist clique of the Romanian Communist Party, the one which was eventually to succeed over the Romanian Marxists who had sat out the 'illegal' period in Moscow.

In August 1939 the police reported that 'the well-known Communist, Nicolae Ceausescu, member of the Central Committee of the Youth Group' was distributing leaflets at an open-air feast organised by the Leather Goods and Shoe Industry Workers' Guild. The police report – true, fabricated, who knows? – allegedly goes on to add that at the end of the feast:

Communist Lenutsa Petrescu, a worker at the Jacquard factory, identified as the leader of the youth section of the Fourth Green sector, addressed the workers, saying: 'We thank the conscientious proletariat for the efforts deployed in defence of freedom and the martyrs of the working class. We demand bread, justice and a legal status.'

Odd, really, for one of the King's secret policemen to exchange the usual police formulae for the no less wooden phrasing of communist rhetoric, and quote it so lovingly. There is more than a whiff of varnish here.

The great Romanian romance did not have long to flower. After climbing up one step of the ladder by being appointed general secretary of the Union of Young Communists in September 1939, Ceausescu slithered down a snake almost straight away. The authorities, hearing of his new appointment, put out a warrant for his arrest and tried him, in absentia, for contempt of court. He was sentenced to three years' imprisonment. There followed almost a year of being on the run again, as the 'phoney war' played out its spectral charades across Europe and, on the streets of Bucharest, the pro-Nazi Iron Guard intimidated everyone from the King down.

While he was on the run, Ceausescu met another young communist, who, shy of having his real name aired, will be called Vasile. Vasile, now a bespectacled pensioner, worked in the Central Committee building right up to the Christmas revolution; his lifetime's hobby has been to make a private study of the early history of the party from oral sources. Nowadays, in post-revolutionary

Bucharest, it is unfashionable to own up to a career as a lifelong communist. Certainly, Vasile wore an air of regret that things had turned out as they did, even though he realised towards the end that Ceausescu was 'a paranoiac'. The coffee shop where we met had no coffee, only ice cream and water. He made a gesture of quiet despair: 'You see what life's like after the revolution. . . .'

Vasile first met Ceausescu in August 1940. He spoke lovingly about the security precautions party members had to take in those days: 'Everyone was organised in small cells, following Lenin's principle, with each cell dedicated to revolutionary activity. The cadres had false documents and stayed in secret flats, only circulating at night. The party was very small, with only 726 members altogether, but this reflected the fact that party membership was an honour for specially selected individuals. In fact, there were another 13,000 people who followed the line of the party.

'We met in the house of a party sympathiser. Ceausescu was not in the first rank, but one of three secretaries of the Central Committee of the Union of Young Communists. He struck me as a clever worker. He simplified problems, which is typical of someone with a worker's mentality. Sometimes it was difficult for him to follow us when we were discussing the details of Lenin's theory of party organisation. But he was a worker and we respected him because of his simplicity. My impression of him then was a good one. He was not a great leader but his heart was clearly "in the right place", as you say. And he had a very sharp mind.'

A few days after that brief meeting, Vasile heard on the grapevine that Ceausescu had been arrested. He was sent to Jilava prison, a sprawling garrison south of Bucharest. Doftana had been destroyed in an earthquake, with the loss of ten wretched prisoners who had been trapped in their cells.

By September 1940 the creaking glacier of the old order outside the prison had broken up. The 'phoney war' had come and gone, the Allies had lost all of Europe, bar the British Isles, to the Nazis, and Hitler, in the Vienna diktat, flaunted his power to write his own terms. He rewarded the Germans' old friends, the Hungarians, with most of Transylvania, and the Bulgarians with southern Dobruja; the Russians had helped themselves to Bessarabia. The losses were a stunning blow to Romanian national pride, pushing the King off his trapeze wire as king-dictator. The British lecturer and Special Operations Executive agent Ivor Porter who lived in Bucharest before

the war in his book *Operation Autonomous* recalls the following
snappy little verse sung at the time, mocking the King:

> I've given the Russians a bit,
> I've left Mama at Balcic,
> The Hungarians are at Avrig,
> It's nothing.
> However small the throne may be
> I shall not abdicate.

(Mama, Queen Marie, was buried on the coast at Balcic, in what is
now northern Bulgaria. Avrig is a small town near Sibiu in
Transylvania.)

Stalin's great varnishman, Walter Duranty of the *New York Times*,
was in Bucharest for the expected abdication. Duranty had been
amusing himself in the brothels of Bucharest, where his wooden leg
had provoked howls of glee from the prostitutes. According to *Stalin's
Apologist* by S. J. Taylor (1990), Duranty told another reporter: 'I
spent the whole damn night doing nothing but putting on and taking
off my wooden leg for the amusement of – well, it seemed like
hundreds of lovely Romanian girls!' Ivor Porter recalls that on the
night of 5 September 1940, with abdication in the air, Duranty went
to bed earlier than the rest, giving instructions to be wakened at four
o'clock in the morning: 'He knew that abdications always take place in
the early hours.' He was one and a half hours too early; the King's
abdication was announced at 5.30.

The King made way for his son, Prince Michael, a shy eighteen-
year-old, but real power was vested in the hands of the pro-Nazi
general Ion Antonescu, who, though wary of the Iron Guard,
appointed a Guardist minister of the interior and chief of police. The
Iron Guard had been flexing its muscles for several months, and now
its time had come. That autumn the Guardists arrested Britons in what
was still theoretically a neutral country, picked up and killed Jews at
will, and started a terror campaign against the leaders of the old-
established political groups, the Liberal Party and the National
Peasant Party. The campaign culminated in the assassination of the
historian and politician Nicolae Iorga. For Romania, which had
enjoyed a prickly and unsatisfactory peace since the early Twenties,
the killing marked something of a watershed.

On 26 November the Iron Guard took over Jilava prison and,

armed with guns, clubs and iron bars, set about eliminating their captive political opponents. The first twenty cells they visited contained officers of the mainstream parties, ex-ministers and a police chief, many of whom had criticised the Guard. In all, sixty-five were slaughtered, many of them politicians waiting trial for alleged involvement in Codreanu's death, but not one communist.

According to Catchlove, the reason that no communists were killed was that Ceausescu had won over the soldiers and prison warders, so that they stopped the Guardists when they were poised to slaughter him and his friends. Catchlove quotes a fellow prisoner:

I often saw him speaking to the soldiers who stood guard outside the cells. He always appealed to their sense of dignity and national pride, and tried to convince them that the prisoners were fighting for a just cause. He spoke warmly, in a man-to-man way, and more than once his words hit their mark. Soon he had drawn quite a few soldiers to his side.

There are, however, more probable explanations. Firstly, an accidental one: the communists were grouped in cells farthest from the entrance where the Iron Guard stormed in. The Guardists would have started killing the first 'politicals' they came across. Secondly, after slaughtering sixty-four men, they may have become sickened at the butchery; the warders, too, were probably jolted into action at the realisation that so many prisoners had been killed. Thirdly, the communists, although they were the Guardists' greatest ideological foes, were much less of a target than the Jews, their chief emotional scapegoats, and the Guardists' principal political enemies, the leaders of the mainstream parties. In the bloody surge for power the Iron Guard staged that autumn, the minuscule, deeply unpopular Romanian Communist Party was an irrelevance.

The Guardists continued their butchery through the winter, while Antonescu and lawful authority looked the other way. The Jews, their population greatly increased by a torrent of refugees coming from Poland and occupied Europe, suffered the worst. Ivor Porter recalls:

There was a terrible Jewish pogrom on the night of January 22. Jews were taken in numbers to the Jilava and Baneasa woods and machine-gunned. Some were murdered at the abattoir with the machines normally used on animals. A large number were tortured and mutilated . . . at least 800 died.

The Romanian talent for cruelty was expressing itself once more. Antonescu, exasperated and embarrassed by the lawlessness, moved against the Iron Guard in the spring.

Night became day, bad, good, black, white when the Nazis invaded the Soviet Union in July 1941. Antonescu threw in his hand with the Germans, and to begin with things went well for the Axis powers. Romania won back the yo-yo province of Bessarabia; the great breadbasket of the Ukraine welcomed the invading Germans, and their Romanian allies, with roses and kisses. The invasion changed things dramatically inside Jilava. Suddenly, the communists became the number-one enemy of the Antonescu regime. With the Iron Guard extinguished as a force, the pro-Soviet communists became a potential fifth column. Antonescu's secret police started rounding up every communist they could find. Jilava swelled with prisoners, and one of the newcomers, arriving in October 1941, was Pavel Campeanu.

Campeanu, now a sociologist and an urbane contributor to the *New York Review of Books*, shared a cell with Ceausescu for two months. 'We took showers together. You see everything. I remember the shock when we went together to the shower. He was very ugly. Do you have the word *disgracieux*?' Deformed? Campeanu considered the word and shook his head. 'That is not quite right: he was very ugly. Not deformed, just unpleasant to look at,' and with that his nose wrinkled in a display of distaste. 'There were thirty of us in the cell. I had just been sentenced to twenty-five years for activity in the Union of Young Communists and we were waiting to be sent to another prison to carry out the bulk of the sentence. To pass the time we played chess. He was a nobody – no.' Here Campeanu corrected himself. 'That's not true. He was a somebody because he was especially unattractive. I'm not sure this feeling was a general one, but it certainly was not a personal one.'

Although Campeanu, like everyone else, suffered under Ceausescu, there seemed less animus between the two men than between Ceausescu and Apostol. But the recollections of both old cellmates, who lived with Ceausescu on fairly intimate terms, paint a distinctly similar picture: that of an unlikable, unpleasant man, quite different from the smiling child of Jebeleanu's soft-focus portrait. Campeanu recalled one event in Jilava that was to ricochet to his discomfort down the years:

'This is not an important incident, but it is a significant one. We were locked in this overcrowded cell and with no possibility of getting exercise. We spent day and night locked up inside. So to use up the time we made chess pieces out of bread and organised a kind of championship. I was not a bad chess player at the time, but in this company I was very good. One day I was watching him play another fellow, and I realised that Ceausescu was, compared to me, very weak. He looked up at me and proposed that we play together. I said, "Why? You're not at my level."

'We had a short, dramatic game. Everyone was watching. It was something of an event. I said: "You will lose in twelve moves." Everybody was laughing, some of them in tears. He was very offended, and just couldn't take the joke. In the end, he lost where and when I told him he would lose. I congratulated him, but he just stormed off. A few weeks later we shared the same cell but he refused to talk to me. It was he who broke relations. He was that' – here Campeanu searched for the right word – 'vindictive. But he was also dominated by the idea that he had to be the best in every field. If he was not the best in one field, then someone had to be guilty.' Campeanu's face clouded with puzzlement at the memory of that chess game long ago. 'The problem is that he never forgot it.'

Later, when he was dictator, people went out of their way to lose to Ceausescu at chess. According to Sergiu Celac, his official interpreter: 'He was not a bad chess player. I watched some of his games. But he was rather chaotic. He always tried to keep several options going, and normally played an offensive game. Almost always. He was out for the kill, not sport. That's why the people who played chess with him, when he was in power, were always careful not to win.' But in prison, when Ceausescu was just another near-skeleton in the grey, striped pyjamas the convicts wore, there was no reason for someone like Campeanu to let him win.

Campeanu went on: 'We didn't meet for probably five years. And then, in about 1950, I was working in the Central Committee's department of foreign relations, in charge of our efforts to help the communists fighting in the Greek civil war. After the defeat the Greek communist leadership wanted to give some military training to twenty or thirty Greek fighters. The Romanian leadership was under some pressure from the Cominform to help the Greeks out. Ceausescu, by this time, was a general in charge of the political department of the army. We met in his office. So we were old acquaintances from prison. I entered his office. He looked at me, did not ask how I was or anything like that, but behaved as if it was our very first meeting. He was still offended by the chess game.

'Ten years later, in 1960, he had risen to be secretary of the Central Committee in charge of party organisation, and I was the vice president of the Romanian Volleyball Federation. It was the first time volleyball was to be recognised as an Olympic sport, and at that time we had the best team in Europe. I was proposed by the federation to lead the team to Tokyo, something I was very keen to do. The practice was for the list to be sent to the Central Committee for approval, which was normally an automatic thing. But the list came back with my name crossed off.

'In 1961 I published a book of memories about life in the Union of Young Communists in the early years. Ceausescu secured a very, very harsh critique of this book by the most senior literary critic of the league's newspaper. One very special quality he had was that he was able to distance his own character from the attack, but it was always him behind these actions. There was a mutuality of dislike, but he had so much more power.'

Apostol, too, recalled from his time with Ceausescu in Doftana: 'He was a hard man who really wanted to win, all the time. He wanted to win at chess. It's well known that in chess when you touch a piece, you've got to move it. That's in the rules. But Ceausescu would touch a piece and then see that it was a bad move and say, "No, no, wait, wait. I haven't thought long enough." ' Cheating at any game he played was a lifelong Ceausescu vice. Ambassador Celac, his former interpreter, put aside his professional diplomatic ambiguities when explaining this side of Ceausescu's character: 'He had absolutely no notion of sporting ethics.'

Campeanu got to see more of Ceausescu when the two of them were moved to the Caransebes Special Penitentiary near Timisoara: 'We worked together in the same shop, painting toys and other objects. Forced to live so closely with him so long, I learnt much about this young peasant who was unaccustomed to life in the city and who, although he claimed to be a shoemaker, seemed incapable of learning a trade. He was both primitive in mentality and manner and endowed with remarkable intelligence.

'His most striking feature, though, was the deep hatred he showed his fellow inmates, even though they were fighting for the same cause at the risk of death. Not directed at any one person, this was a general and impersonal hatred, which seemed to consume him. It took the form of a free-floating anger and contempt for other people, particularly people his own age or in positions he considered inferior to his own. In his relations with the rest of us he seemed strangely empty of any normal human feelings.'

Life in Caransebes was made easier by the character of the prison governor, Dobrian, who, according to Catchlove, one day called Gheorgiu-Dej and Ceausescu to his office. Instead of administering the feared punishment, Dobrian allowed them to listen to news reports on his radio. Dobrian was, after the war, given the rank of general, and also given the honour of presiding over the court that passed the death sentence on Antonescu. As time went by it became increasingly clear that an Axis victory in Russia was not going to be automatic; the carnage at Stalingrad, when the Romanian troops fighting with the Wehrmacht suffered terrible losses, was the turning point in the war. From the collapse of the German Sixth Army on 31 January 1943, when Field-Marshal Friedrich von Paulus surrendered, the writing was on the wall. Conditions for communists, allied to the now conquering Soviets, improved day by day.

Ceausescu was due to be released from prison on 1 August 1943. Instead, he was taken to Vacaresti prison for a short while, then moved on to an internment camp at Tirgu Jiu, a town which nestles under the western slopes of the Carpathians. The prisoners were loosely supervised, grouped in huts of their own choice and allowed to work outside the camp. With the arrival in late 1943 of a new prison governor, Colonel Lioveanu, the regime became more easy-going than the previous one. The party historian Vasile, a committed communist, admitted: 'It was not so much a concentration camp, more like a sanatorium. They were able to come and go pretty freely. It was all very civilised. There was no question of brutality at all.'

In Caransebes and Tirgu Jiu Ceausescu became more friendly with Gheorghiu-Dej, to the annoyance of fellow prisoners like Campeanu: 'I remember how much time Gheorghiu-Dej invested in this young guy, who certainly had some natural gifts. Ceausescu delighted in reciting poetry, which showed off his memory, which was very good, as well as conquering his stutter. He loved to declaim poetry because it showed he could master his handicap. He did this only, I think, due to a tremendous effort of will. There was one poem he used to recite often called "We Want Land", written at the time of the Peasants' Revolt in 1907. When he declaimed this piece, he completely forgot his stutter – his fanaticism was that strong. Gheorghiu-Dej appreci-ated this combination of natural intelligence and real fanaticism, but

Ceausescu managed to hide from him the vicious side of his character that we young political prisoners knew so well.'

Mihnea Gheorghiu, a silver-haired seventy-year-old, first met Ceausescu in 1944. He was, for a time during the Ceausescu thaw in the late Sixties, relatively close to the dictator. He dabbled in what he self-mockingly called 'some cheap psychology' when discussing the relationship between Gheorghiu-Dej and Ceausescu: 'Prisons, like hospitals, are places where people use each other and hate each other and love each other. The circle of acquaintance is so small, relationships take place which might not otherwise prosper. Gheorghiu-Dej had two daughters but no sons. So it is possible that Ceausescu became his spiritual son.'

To pass the time the prisoners played chess – albeit warily with Ceausescu – discussed politics, what was happening in the war, studied foreign languages and foreign philosophers. The older generation of communists, a tiny elite of intellectuals, used the spare time to instruct the youngsters in Marxist theory. The prisoners were voracious, reading out loud Kant, Schopenhauer and Rimbaud. They also played word games. Apostol, who met up with Ceausescu again in 1943 at Tirgu Jiu, recalled: 'Ceausescu was not good at these games.' Of course, Apostol is not a Ceausescu enthusiast, but he did agree that the future dictator had a fine memory and could recite verses of great Romanian poets, like Eminescu, at will.

As 1943 turned into 1944, the Red Army grew closer to Romania's borders. Antonescu had now declared himself a marshal, but in every other respect power was draining from him. As well as playing word games, the communists occupied themselves with plotting various coup attempts. Apostol recalls that this revolutionary activity was made easier because prisoners were allowed to see their families and receive parcels from home. At the time Ceausescu was working outside the camp at a former monastery. They had planned to escape from the monastery and organise resistance to Antonescu with the help of the Yugoslav partisans. But then Antonescu decided to store some national treasures in the monastery as safekeeping against their possible destruction if fighting were to come to Bucharest. Faced with a stiff guard on the monastery, the communists scrapped that escape plan.

A second plan was to stage an insurrection against Antonescu in March 1944. The conspirators included Gheorghiu-Dej, veteran communist Emil Bodnaras, Apostol and Ceausescu. But the preparations were blown, according to Apostol, when it was discovered that there was a traitor in the highest level of the party. Suspicion, said Apostol, fell on the secretary to Stefan Foris, the party's general secretary, who was accused of being in the pay of the Gestapo. Within a month the charge had imperceptibly moved to cover both the secretary and Foris himself. The party was divided against itself in a bitter power struggle. The following month, April 1944, Gheorghiu-Dej held a meeting in the Tirgi Jiu prison infirmary, with Chivu Stoica and Emil Bodnaras. At that meeting the absent Foris was sacked and a new secretariat of Emil Bodnaras, Constantin Pirvulescu and Iosif Ranghet was appointed to replace him. Others were instructed to negotiate with the mainstream parties with the goal of unseating Antonescu.

There were two results to this jiggery-pokery. The first was that Antonescu was ultimately overthrown, not by a small clique of communist revolutionaries as the party would have wished, but by a coalition – made up of the politicians of the National Peasant, Liberal, Social Democratic and Communist parties – led by King Michael. Subsequently, there was a great deal of painstaking airbrushing of history to establish the communists as the leaders of the 23 August coup. Certainly there were a number of communists in the Palace at the time of the coup, led by Lucretia Patrascanu. But it was the King who carried the day. The King had Antonescu arrested in his own palace. He told the marshal: 'I must take measures to pull the country immediately out of the war and save it from disaster. To this end I have decided that you should this very day conclude an armistice and if you refuse I shall order your resignation right now.' When the officer of the palace guard told Antonescu that he was under arrest, he spat at him. The marshal told the palace guard: 'You'll live to regret this. Tomorrow you will all hang in Palace Square.' The King went on radio that night to tell Romania of his decision. For a Marxist-Leninist party reared on organising itself for the spark of revolution, allowing a monarch to steal its clothes can only be seen as a huge embarrassment.

The second consequence is that Gheorghiu-Dej won the power struggle inside the party. The more fortunate losers, like Ana Pauker, a co-founder of the RCP who had sat out the lean years under the monarchy in Moscow, were sidelined, and later purged from the party; the less lucky ones were shot. Those who had once been more eminent than Gheorghiu-Dej and had a fine record of political achievement were more likely to die. In the summer of 1946 Foris, accused of being an informer for Antonescu's secret police, was executed. In the spring of 1954 Patrascanu, the communist who had been inside the Palace at the time of the coup, was shot. His trial was a particularly rich farce. He was accused of being a spy and counter-revolutionary by some dodgy customers, most absurdly by Gheorghe Tatarescu, who had been one of King Carol II's favoured, weather-vane ministers before the war. Tatarescu had barely begun to speak, according to Ghita Ionescu's book *Communism in Romania* (1964), when Patrascanu rose furiously and shouted: 'Such scum of history are brought to this trial as witnesses against me, who am a Communist. If such an individual has to prove that I am not a Communist, it is only a proof of the low level of the Romanian Communist Party which needs such elements, as well as evidence of the total lack of proof in this odious trial, so that it has been necessary to resort to such a witness.' (As speeches made facing certain death go, this is to be compared with Danton's adrieu to the world imminently before his appointment with Madame Guillotine: 'Above all, don't forget to show my head to the people. It's well worth having a look at.')

There were going to be many, many more deaths of one-time comrades during the Romanian Terror. The lesson for Ceausescu, seated admiringly at the feet of his 'spiritual father' Gheorghiu-Dej, must have been clear even in the early days: to lose one's place in the Romanian Communist Party's idiosyncratic version of musical chairs was not good for one's constitution.

Ceausescu was too junior a figure to play any serious part in this first bout of jostling for power as the war in Romania drew to a close. The hagiographers say that Ceausescu's freedom 'coincided with the country's liberation from the fascists, on 23 August 1944'. By contrast Vasile, the party's painstaking and rigorous unofficial historian, identified a curious blank in the Ceausescu biography. 'He was liberated at the end of June 1944. He left the camp at Tirgu Jiu, but did nothing. He did not contact the Union of Young Communists, or anyone until 23 August' – the critical date of the coup against Antonescu. Vasile added: 'All the Communists were mobilised immediately after 23 August, but many were working before. Ceausescu and Elena did nothing before 23 August. This, compared to the activities of many other Communists, was a black mark. Why? No one knows. That fact is that he did not take part.'

The blank is doubly damaging to the Ceausescu legend because he did not take part in the successful escape attempt staged by

Gheorghiu-Dej from the internment camp shortly before the 23 August coup, with the help of Ion Maurer. 'I don't think he was a coward,' Vasile told me. 'But, even as a young man, he did have great hopes for the future. He was very aware of his importance. He admired himself very much. Someone with such high hopes would perhaps consider it stupid to lose everything just before one's dreams were about to come true. Such a cadre would not take risks.'

Vasile, spooning his ice cream, also suspected that Elena had a part in Ceausescu's strategic withdrawal from party activity that summer. 'She fell in love with him even though he was ugly and a stutterer. He was probably grateful for the rest of his life. Theirs was a long love. They both died in a very dignified manner. She was the closest person to him. He never had another girlfriend. There has never been the slightest gossip about him having sexual adventures. Elena was a kind of mirror. She really believed in him, even if they disagreed. She considered him the greatest man on earth.'

A man having spent a total of five years in prison was perhaps ripe for love. The details are not clear, but it seems likely the two of them got engaged towards the end of his lax time at Tirgu Jiu and married some time soon after his release.

The photographs of Elena taken just before the war show a dark-eyed, big-nosed but nevertheless catching brunette. As she grew older, she metamorphosed into a demigoddess of Venusian appeal, if the propaganda machine was to be believed. On 7 January 1984, the occasion of what probably was her sixty-fifth birthday – her true age was something of a state secret – the court poet Virgil Teodorescu wrote the following dithyramb:

> Her face is lit up by eyes that look far into the distance
> Being a beautiful gift of diligent nature,
> And the gentle energy radiating from her features,
> Is a perpetual model for the arts.

Vasile, something of a romantic himself, knew her slightly before the varnishmen touched her up. He said: 'She was a very pretty girl.' The recollections of some of the other old communists were less gentlemanly. Dumitrescu acted out her stomp-stomp peasant's walk for Hannah Pakula – head forward, bottom back – and said: 'She was very much a farm girl. Anything you put on her looked terrible. In Romania, there is a saying that when clothes look like that on you it's as if you put a saddle on a cow.'

She was the daughter of an unsuccessful ploughman in Petresti, not far from Scornicesti. On one subject all the observers are agreed: she was as thick as two short planks. It was the family trait. Her elder brother, who preceded her to Bucharest, enjoyed the nickname 'Blockhead' among his workmates. She was no different. For once, Bucharest gossip is backed up by documentary evidence. Her school report, long buried in her old school archives for fear of what revenges its dissemination might bring, was dug up shortly after the revolution. The true intellectual qualifications of the woman who liked to be known as 'Comrade Academician Doctor Engineer' ran to four years of dismal performance at primary school. In the school year 1929–30 Elena, who would have been about ten years old, flunked reading, writing and arithmetic, religion, history and geography with an average mark below the required five out of ten. She got five out of ten for hygiene. Only in physical education and singing did she pass muster. She did not take natural sciences at all. This must be a surprise to a number of scientific institutions around the world, including the New York Academy of Sciences, the Royal Institute of Chemistry in London and various universities, including Buenos Aires, Bahía Blanca, Manila, Yucatán and Tehran, who conferred a multitude of honours on her. At the bottom of Elena's last school report lies the succinct recommendation *'repetenda'* – requiring her to repeat the fourth year. Instead, her academic career ended there and then, leaving her barely literate.

Thanks to brother 'Blockhead', she managed to get a job in a weaving factory in Bucharest. She must have met Ceausescu when they were both living in a dreary sector of Bucharest known as the Park of Joy. With his stutter, balloon of hair, weak chin, short stature and lack of family connections, he was no catch. And yet he was warmth and light to her, and she to him. One story of their romance was picked up by the varnishmen. Officially, on May Day – that holy day in the Marxist calendar – Elena was anointed 'Miss Working Class 1939' at the Park of Joy ball in a workers' stadium by popular acclamation, being 'very young and beautiful'. The ball turned into a political rally which the fiery orator and communist agitator Nicolae Ceausescu addressed. . . . The workers' stadium was actually a rather seedy pub with a dance floor. It wasn't May Day but an ordinary Saturday night. The pub had staged a lovers' contest, the game being that whoever bought the most tickets for their fancied lady ensured her enthronement as 'queen of the pub'. 'The more you bought, the more you loved the girl', Dumitrescu explained to Hannah Pakula, still puzzled after half a century as to how Ceausescu got enough money to make Elena his queen.

Were they loyal to each other? Ceausescu was, almost certainly. He was a lifelong puritan, as faithful to Elena as he was loyal to communism. There are some tawdry stories about Elena's behaviour during the war when he was in prison. One of Nicolae's elderly sisters used to refer to Elena as 'the slut'; his look-alike brother Nicolae Andrutsa, after the revolution told a 'sociological investigator' for the newspaper *Adevarul* (it means the Truth, but often prints the converse): 'One day in 1943 I found her and her sister-in-law naked with two German officers.' Nicolae Andrutsa went on to claim that the other Ceausescus had persecuted him, a remark that prompted the interviewer to retort: 'Persecution, persecution. But you reached the rank of general.'

Apostol hated her as she hated him. The first time he met her, in 1944, she did not strike him as either impressive or significant: 'They were at a table in a restaurant. She was very mean, with a pinched face. She seemed then a simple and uncultured woman, but as time passed she became more powerful but no less stupid.' What about the claims made in the hagiographies that she was an important communist activist? Apostol's one eye flickered in disgust. 'She did no political work, but just looked after the children.' Vasile, the historian, confirmed that Elena in those days was not a party member and carried out no revolutionary activity that anyone can remember. These recollections square with the cultural attitudes towards women in Romania at the time: women were domestic creatures and did not play a part in politics.

Ion Maurer lacks the purity of Apostol's feelings towards the Ceausescu couple, though he, too, has reason to dislike them. In the Thirties he was a lawyer who defended many communist activists on trial. In the Fifties he became prime minister and was a loyal lieutenant to Gheorghiu-Dej until his death. In 1965 he was the third candidate for the top job, and was steadily eased out of power by Ceausescu. Next to his chair in the vast Valhalla of his living room, the empty space befitting his former high rank in the party, stood a picture of a much younger Maurer, his body rocking, his mouth as wide open as a hippopotamus's, caught in a rictus of laughter. Today, at eighty-eight, he is a wheezing, deaf, exhausted, lame and dying man. But one not without his wits. He tweaked his bulbous nose and recalled: 'She seemed to be a simple peasant woman who had almost nothing in her head. She was always very greedy for privileges. She treated other people in a vulgar fashion, calling them idiots, traitors, those kinds of insults.'

Shortly after the war she secured a job in the basement of the Foreign Ministry sorting out and clipping the foreign newspapers. Campeanu, who was working upstairs, recalled her performance: 'It was a big problem because she couldn't distinguish between them. She mixed the French with the English.' When she quietly went absent no one took any notice because 'she was not useful for anything'. A few years later, she enrolled in night-school classes at the Poly-technical Institute in Bucharest. During a test of Marxist theory, so the story goes, one of the invigilating teachers caught her copying out passages from a book. 'Comrade, that's not allowed,' he said, and after two warnings expelled her from the exam.

As the years ground by, Elena's standing in Bucharest society fell into an abyss of hate. As Ceausescu, towards the end, detached himself from reality, it was Elena who guided a 'sick-think' police state where paranoia was enthroned, it was she who presided over a disastrous campaign of social engineering which was to leave grotesque scars in wombs and hearts across the country. She spawned monstrous cruelties, and yet she was a mother, too. Her son Valentin, recalling those years in his flat, studied his whisky: 'He would say that he loved me, but I never felt it.' And your mother? The diffidence drained from his voice. 'Perhaps I think my mother loved me very much.'

Castle

Nicu Ceausescu lay on the hospital bed, smoking a cigarette. Officially he was dying of cirrhosis of the liver and a varicose oesophagus, penalties of abusing his body over a lifetime. His illnesses meant that he lay, in autumn 1990, in a curious medico-legal limbo. A Securitate guard, the holster of his handgun peeking out below the rim of his shabby, dog-eared suit, looked adoringly at his charge, like a dog at his master. Occasionally the Securitate man would perform little errands, such as passing round an ashtray or presenting a snack, wrapped in newspaper, a gift from one of Nicu's many admirers, on the table beside his bed.

At first Nicu claimed that he was too ill to see us, but shortly the door opened to reveal Ceausescu's youngest son. His eyes were closed, his voice weak, faltering, his face every now and then creased by a spasm of pain. But as he talked about his life as Romania's dauphin he became bored with lying down and soon sat up in bed to smoke, pass round chocolates and laugh at his own, rather good, jokes. His body had an almost simian wiriness, his hand movements were sharp and muscular, his eyes vital, sly, mocking and once or twice flashing a lordly contempt. He appeared, to the nonmedical eye, to be a lithe, handsome and vigorous thirty-nine-year-old man suffering from a severe dose of playing the invalid.

'Call me Nicu,' he said, and directed his roguish smile at my female interpreter. The conversation took place in Romanian, though every now and then Nicu paused to correct the interpreter's translation or crack a joke in English, which made me suspect that his ignorance of the Queen's English was, like his ill-health, something of a charade. There followed a long, rambling account of his part in Ceausescu's time, less analytical and dispassionate than Valentin's story, but also more intimate, personal and revelatory. Unlike Valentin and Zoia, the Ceausescus' middle child, Nicu played a substantial role in the running of the Romanian fear machine. He was the heir apparent who ran his own fiefdom in Sibiu. He knew the nuts and bolts of the Securitate: 'In all the histories of the communist countries, the most powerful person after the first secretary of the party was the chief of the secret police.' But this is to jump the gun on the narrative. What were his first memories of his father?

Nicu sighed at the effort of memory – he was born in 1951, so he was thinking back to 1953, 1954 – then burst into giggles: 'My first memory of him is linked to the Christmas tree. We were staying somewhere in the mountains. My parents came up from Bucharest. I can't remember what toys we had, but my father' – Nicu smiled at the recollection – 'my dad dressed up as Father Christmas.'

Nicu's memory of Santa Ceausescu is a dollop of sugar in a vat of acid. For a great number of Romanians the years between the end of the war and the mid-Fifties were irredeemably bleak. After the 23 August 1944 palace coup against Antonescu, there were many who hoped that the pre-emptive strike before the Russians invaded the country would ensure the return of the democratic parties to power under King Michael. These hopes were, in fact, scotched in a secret deal between Churchill and Stalin. At a meeting in the Kremlin that October, the two leaders carved up the Balkan cake. According to volume seven of Churchill's 'The Second World War', it was he who cut the first slice:

'Let us settle about our affairs in the Balkans . . . So far as Britain and Russia are concerned, how would it be for you to have ninety per cent predominance in Romania, for us to have ninety per cent of the say in Greece, and go fifty-fifty in Yugoslavia?' While this was being translated I wrote on a half-sheet of paper:

Romania
Russia 90%
The others 10%

Greece
Great Britain 90%
(in accord with USA)
Russia 10%

Yugoslavia 50–50%
Hungary 50–50%

Bulgaria
Russia 75%
The others 25%

I pushed this across to Stalin, who had by then heard the translation. There was a slight pause. Then he took his blue pencil and made a large tick upon it, and passed it back to us. It was all settled in no more time than it takes to set it down. . . .

After this there was a long silence. The pencilled paper lay in the centre of the table. At length I said: 'Might it not be thought rather cynical if it seemed we had disposed of these issues, so fateful to millions of people, in such an off-hand manner? Let us burn the paper.' 'No, you keep it,' said Stalin.

Although the switching of sides by the Romanians caught the Nazis off guard, and saved the Russians a lot of blood, Stalin would not easily forget whose side the Romanians had been on for most of the war. He kept to his 90 per cent. The Russians exacted a hard price in reparations from the Romanians: they appropriated the whole of the Romanian navy and the lion's share of its merchant fleet, amounting to some 700 ships. Half the country's rolling stock rolled eastwards, plus a great amount of the drilling equipment from the country's oil fields. Grain, timber, industrial machinery, food – the larder was stripped bare. The winter months in the late Forties were a harsh time as the Romanians experienced a famine far more severe than they had suffered during the lean war years.

But Stalin was not content with just reparations. The Red Army was on the streets of Bucharest, exercising, marching. It was a simple and unsubtle display of force, to back up the Romanian Communist Party's title to power. The leaders of the democratic parties – ignorant of Churchill's offer of 90 per cent – saw the knot tighten, but they did not give up without a fight.

Gheorghiu-Dej was later to claim that the old, 'bourgeois' parties had 'self-dissolved already during Carol II's dictatorship' in 1938. They had not. On 13 October 1944, a few days after Stalin and Churchill met in the Kremlin, a group of Liberals and National Peasant Party supporters staged a pro-democracy meeting in front of the Palace. They were attacked by armed communists, many from the Grivitsa locomotive factory which had been Gheorghiu-Dej's powerbase in the Thirties. The RCP's paramilitary group were the only civilians who were allowed to carry arms. The next morning the communist newspaper *Scanteia* (later on it was called *Scinteia*: both spellings are versions of 'spark') launched the propaganda campaign. The newspaper falsely accused the pro-democracy crowd of chanting 'Long live Horia Sima', the one-time leader of the pro-Nazi Iron Guard, and 'Long live Juliu Maniu', the revered leader of the National

Peasant Party. This was the first linking of the pro-British Maniu with a known fascist. The rewriting of history had begun.

Ivor Porter, an SOE agent, had been captured by the Romanians during the war. During his captivity he had been protected from Gestapo interrogation by the tacit support of Antonescu, who did not wish to inflame British sentiment by allowing the torture of their agents. He had been released from prison thanks to the King's coup and after August 1944, as a British diplomat based in Bucharest, he witnessed the slow throttling of Romanian democracy at first hand. As the months went by, all the omens for a democratic Romania were black. In March 1945, the communists became the 'de facto' government under the puppet regime of a fellow traveller called Dr Petru Groza, with all the key portfolios, the ministries of defence, interior, justice and national economy, being held by the communists; a few years later, they enjoyed power 'de jure' as well. Throughout this period any voice raised against communist hegemony was punched in the mouth. Opposition newspapers were smashed up, opposition lawyers picked up by the secret police and detained, opposition party members interrogated, beaten, abused.

Take, for example, the story of the Liberal Party journalist Adriana Georgescu Cosmovici, who managed to escape from Romania in 1949. He was arrested in July 1945 and pressurised to cry treachery against the leaders of the democratic parties:

Following my arrest in July 1945 the communist secret police investigators tried to extort from me an incriminating statement about Juliu Maniu and the other leaders of the national democratic opposition. Inasmuch as I refused to sign such a statement, the investigators beat me repeatedly with a sand-filled leather hose (called 'ranca'), struck my head against the wall and hit my face and chin until I was left with only six teeth in my lower jaw. Investigators Stroescu, Bulz and Nicolski threatened me with guns. The first also threatened me with deportation to the Soviet Union. All this took place at the Secret Service headquarters at 159 Calea Plevnei, Bucharest. It was there that I was forced to give up my clothing and cover myself with an overall which was so filthy that I became infected with scabies.

Even so, the resistance continued.

Porter's diplomatic despatch to London describing the circumstances of the November 1946 election is, with the benefit of hindsight, a signal document. Porter did not realise it at the time, but it represents virtually the last gasp of Romanian democracy until the Christmas revolution of 1989:

After this last effort on the part of the Government to prove the Opposition parties to be 'Fascist', the elections took place on 19th November. There were widespread cases of Government supporters voting several times and of ballot boxes being filled with Government voting slips either before the voting opened or during the count, at which Opposition representatives were not present. On the morning of 19 November, a number of Opposition representatives were arrested and physical intimidation during the voting was reported from many districts. Normally after an election in Romania, the results are announced by radio during the course of the night so that by about two o'clock in the morning, the public have a very fair idea as to who has been successful. On the night of 19 November, however, a few results were announced and then there was silence for three days. Telephone communication was cut with the provinces to prevent the Opposition obtaining district results and, it appears, these were so uniformly in the Opposition's favour that the Government soon realised that all their ingenious methods of falsification had failed. They were therefore ultimatedly compelled to falsify the official figures and publish what had been a crushing defeat for the Government as an overwhelming victory. As, however, the truth became known, it was clear that the Government had lost not only in the country as a whole, but even in the citadels of Communist activity. Many of their most ardent followers had clearly joined the Communist Party for personal gain only but, when the moment came to express their will, had voted for the Opposition. Even the railway workers, from whom Communist shock troops were chosen, and the employees of the Ministries of Finance and War had failed to support the Government.

Porter, now retired and living in London, feels passionately that the Romanian struggle against totalitarianism has been unfairly under-rated:

The Romanians fought for four years, from 1944 to 1948. I do not agree when people say that the Romanians are submissive to power and have no spirit of resistance. They struggled, with hardly any support from the west, for four years against the Communists, who had the Red Army behind them. They were running across roofs, chased by the secret police. They stood in the Palace Square shouting their support for the king and were clubbed down, and still they fought. Under the circumstances, the Romanians resisted a full-blown communist dictatorship longer than one might have expected.

The role of the secret police, the Securitate, was at the core of the Communist takeover. Far from being a grand ideal, which became corrupted over the years, the communist state in Romania was a creation of the cosh and the lie from the very start. The communists would never have won power in an open society; having won control, they had to keep Romania closed. That they succeeded in keeping rigid control for more than four decades is part of the explanation for the volcano of violence when Romania finally erupted.

This, then, was the dramatic backdrop against which Ceausescu, aged only 26 at the time of the 1944 coup, started his ascent of the Romanian Communist Party. He was made secretary general of the Communist Youth movement, a post fitting his years in prison and flowing from his close relationship with Gheorghiu-Dej. Vasile recalls: 'I got to know him a little better then. He was more mature, self-confident, but still prey to violent emotions. He was very impulsive, that was something new that I discovered in him.' That autumn a photograph was taken of him, giving a speech to the communist youth, standing in front of one of those old-fashioned microphones with the receiver sitting like a Communal host in a monstrance. He is wearing a black suit, with a Paisley tie, his face fuller and more handsome than earlier photographs reveal. His body is rigid, his teeth clenched in a grin, but it is his eyes which draw the observer. It is as if they are on fire. Although his looks are gripping, the content of his speeches are the stuff of Orwell's Doublespeak. On 29 September 1944, he called on the students of the law faculty at Bucharest University to form an armed, pro-communist unit within the university, Catchlove records approvingly '. . . to give an energetic rebuff to all those who are still in the service of the fascists, and who stand in the way of democracy in our country.' The reality behind Ceausescu's 'energetic rebuff' was less glowing: punches, blows, kicks to any student who opposed communist rule and, if they kept up their heresy, a discreet tip-off to the Securitate.

And, then, disaster happened. Ceausescu was fired from his job. He had fallen foul of the faction-fighting which had riven the party immediately after the coup. Worse, he had earned the displeasure of Ana Pauker, someone who, at that time, still enjoyed precedence over Gheorghiu-Dej, his protector, at the very top of the RCP. Loosely, this faction fighting has been described by academics as splitting the party into two camps, that of the 'home' communists grouped around Georghiu-Dej, including Ceausescu, and the 'Moscow' clique, who had spent the war years in Moscow, under the benign eye of Comrade Stalin, led by Ana Pauker. It is to some extent an artificial division which does not take enough account of the jarring personalities and chameleon loyalties that made up the higher echelons of the RCP. The most vivid of them all was Ana Pauker, to many who knew her the most brilliant communist of her generation. In Vasile's phrase: 'the cleverest woman in the world'. Pauker had been nominated as the new general secretary of the RCP in a secret session, but could not be seen publicly to lead the Party because, firstly, she was a woman, and secondly, she was a rabbi's daughter in a country where anti-Semitism had always been strong. So, for a time, the two rivals rubbed along in an edgy harness, Pauker the 'secret' general secretary, Gheorghiu-Dej the titular one, until he managed to squeeze her out altogether.

Pauker's record as a communist was more distinguished than virtually any of the old guard. She was first arrested for revolutionary agitation in 1918, and in 1921 was a founding member of the RCP with her husband, Marcel Pauker. She had been picked up and imprisoned by the King's secret police before she and her husband sought safety in the Soviet Union, where they formed an 'External Bureau' of the RCP. Her time in Moscow had not been an easy one. Her husband, Marcel, had been executed in Moscow in the Thirties during one of Stalin's purges. But come the coup against Antonescu, she and the rest of the 'Muscovites' poured back into Romania, to win over the hearts and minds of the people.

During the period when she was the most powerful figure in the RCP, before Gheorghiu-Dej wrenched control from her, Ceausescu was deposed as the standard-bearer of communist youth. Vasile went on: 'She didn't like him. She saw that his approach was very backward. She sent him to be first secretary of one of eight sectors of Bucharest. That happened in March 1945, clearly a demotion. Slowly, slowly, he came back.'

There is another possible explanation for Ceausescu's dismissal from his coveted post as the European war came to an end. The story is part of Bucharest folklore, which is not the most reliable source of information, but practically the only source when it comes to murder committed by a communist high-up. The story was told to me over sausages and a glass of the watered-down methylated spirits the communists turned into, or, at least, termed, wine. The source is a witty and gregarious academic who regrets that he spent not a few hours translating various tracts of 'Homage' into Shakespeare's tongue. He is now making amends by telling anti-Ceausescu stories with much more panache than he gave to his old, unloved labours.

'In March '45 Ceausescu, as ever a fiery and passionate communist, went to a landowner's house near Pitesti. The landowner was resisting the local communists who told him that he had to give up his land to the collective. The landowner called a man he knew, the prefect of the then governor of the county. When the prefect arrived at the house Ceausescu started arguing with him. The prefect stood up to Ceausescu and argued back, and Ceausescu became so angry that he took out his pistol and shot the prefect dead. The killing took place on 3 or 4 March, but the case never came to court. He was saved when the Groza government came just a few days later, on 6 March, with a communist as the new minister of justice. Immediately, the prosecution dropped the case. But you could still inspect the trial dossier in Pitesti until 1966, when it disappeared from the court archives.'

Is this story true? Who knows. It seems extraordinary that no documentary or unambiguous oral evidence exists to confirm the murder of a prefect, an important dignitary. No hard evidence leads one to the conclusion that the killing is part of the Ceausescu folklore. But he was, after all, a totalitarian ruler for almost a quarter of a century. If anyone was in a position to wipe clean all memories, to erase all the files, and if necessary all the people, who knew about this killing, then it was Ceausescu. The truth will never be known, a phrase which becomes something of a mantra to anyone studying Ceausescu's Romania. Perhaps the most concrete point to be drawn from this story is that it was, and is, believed. The myth is more vital than the man.

The cloud that hovered over his career in March 1945 soon passed. That October he was elected an alternative member of the Communist Party Central Committee; in 1946 he left Bucharest to become the secretary of the Dobrogea Regional Committee, switching not long afterwards to the same post at the Oltenia Regional Committee. In the elections of November 1946, the honesty of which Porter held in such low regard, Ceausescu was 'elected' a deputy of parliament.

Democracy, RCP-style, was a broken orchid. The repression

gathered pace. July 1947 saw the arrest of Juliu Maniu, charged with high treason. Both his National Peasant Party and their old rivals, the Liberals, were dissolved in July. The trials and imprisonment of the 'bourgeois' leaders took place that October.

Corneliu Coposu was Maniu's private secretary at the time. Today he is the chain-smoking president of the newly reconvened National Peasant Party. Although now aged seventy-five and a little deaf, he still has a mop of white hair, his lawyer's reverence for detail and an impressive presence. He started the conversation by a rehearsal of the statistics of terror. They may not be authoritative, but they contrast with official photographs of the citizens of Bucharest dancing the hora to rejoice in the victory of communism.

'The National Peasant Party had 2,150,000 members at the start of the ten-year period, 1945 to 1955. Out of these 2 million, 280,000 were arrested by the government. They were tried and jailed for a total of 900,000 years if you add up all the sentences. Out of the 280,000 members, 72 per cent died in jail.'

In addition to the arrests and the beatings, the propaganda streaming out of *Scinteia* was a further burden. According to Coposu, a contributor to *Scinteia* at the time was Silviu Brucan – today the darling of the Western media. Allegedly he attacked the National Peasant Party leadership at the time of Maniu's trial in October 1947. Coposu said: 'Silviu Brucan wrote that we were criminals, traitors and agents of British and American imperialism.'

Brucan is an important figure in the Ceausescu story. As a high-ranking member of the communist *nomenklatura* and a former ambassador to Washington, he knew Ceausescu well. He was a neighbour of the Ceausescu family in the Fifties, his daughter went out with Valentin Ceausescu for a time, and, in 1987, he was one of the very tiny number of Romanians who spoke out openly against the dictator, suffering house arrest as a result. This courageous stance has made Brucan lionised by the Western media, who tend to take at face value claims that he was involved in a plot that helped to make the Christmas revolution possible. Bald and rounded, his head is a pink billiard ball; he is as hard as a billiard ball, too. He has a showman's wit, with a laugh too demonic for comfort. Like Apostol, he has been known to charge for his time, but Brucan is a cannier operator – requesting more than $1,000, it is said, before he would tell all about his part in Ceausescu's downfall to a television network. His quotes are succulent and sexy (for example, on Ceausescu at the end, 'like

Captain Queeg in the *Caine Mutiny*'); his subtle hints that he was the *éminence grise* of the revolution are intoxicating to those Western journalists who despair, quite naturally, of ever making sense of the swirling, muddy waters of Romanian politics.

So it is not uninteresting – if what Coposu claims is true – that Brucan, the heroic dissident in 1987, was, forty years before, a Stalinist baying for the blood of Maniu and the others. Brucan's democratic sensibilities were not developed in the late Forties or early Fifties. The want of public outcry against false imprisonment, torture and killing is a charge that can be made against nearly all the communists, likable and unlikable, who were around at that time and have been quoted in this book.

The national newspaper library at Colindale, north London, part of the British Library, keeps *Scinteia*, all the way back to 1947. Silviu Brucan was clearly an important figure on the paper; for example, a long front page article on 19 October 1947, signed 'Silviu Brucan', invokes Romanian national sovereignty and deplores British and American imperialism. Next to that article on the same front page is another, signed 'S.B.', which covers the Maniu trial. 'S.B.' charges that Maniu delayed the anti-Antonescu putsch, whereas, in fact, he played a lead role in bringing it about. The Romanian armistice of 23 August 1944 became in the mind of 'S.B.' the date when 'the accursed plans of Maniu were overthrown'. On 10 November 1947, in a signed article Silviu Brucan demanded that 'the spies in the dock must be punished mercilessly, so that others will heed the warning.' An unsigned editorial in *Scinteia* called for the maximum penalty – death – 'in the name of justice' against Maniu and the others.

Scinteia did not get its way. On 11 November Maniu was sentenced to hard labour for life. He was seventy-five years old. Some years later one of Porter's old SOE agents, Olympia Zamfirescu, who also was mired in the Romanian gulag, met an unidentified prisoner who told her the following story:

One night they moved me to another cell where I found a very old sick man. It was Juliu Maniu, or what remained of him. He was half paralysed and could no longer leave his bed. They had not tortured him but systematically let him die for lack of medical attention and under-nourishment. I nursed him. I cleaned him. I fed him till he closed his eyes.

When he felt his death approaching he said: 'Absolution.' I knocked on the wall of the adjoining cell. I had reason to believe that there was a Roman Catholic bishop there. Those of us who had spent months and sometimes years in prison had learnt to use morse fluently as a means of communication. The good bishop spelt out to me the Latin words of the prayers, the Pater Noster and the Ave Maria, and it was I, an atheist and a sinner, who gave the dictated last rites to this saintly man, and closed his eyes.

By December 1947 King Michael was the only obstruction to 'socialist revolution'. On 30 December prime minister Groza and Gheorghiu-Dej, the nominal secretary general of the RCP, had an audience with the King and his mother. They were told that the King had to abdicate, since documents incriminating him had been discovered before the trial of 'Maniu and his band of fascist traitors'. The King left the room to discover that the Palace was surrounded by troops of the Moscow-trained Tudor Vladimirescu division and the phone lines had been cut. Groza showed the Queen Mother the revolver he had in his pocket, as hints go a rather heavy one. The King was told that if he didn't sign immediately thousands of people would be arrested the next day; there could well be civil war and a great deal of blood spilt. He abdicated that afternoon, at three o'clock.

The communists had open season on the opposition, on people linked to the British and the Americans, on anyone who stood in their way. What happened in 1948 was reported by the British Sunday newspaper, the *People*. In two successive issues, on 6 and 13 February 1949, the *People* carried the first-hand account of the ordeal of Alexander Evans, a British citizen and manager, for seventeen years, of the Steaua Romana oil company, who was arrested and imprisoned in June 1948.

While I was in jail I saw men who had been tortured to make them confess to activities in which they probably were in no way concerned. One man had been on crutches for eight months because of beatings on the soles of his feet. Another was in an advanced state of pleurisy after being in an underground cell for seven months without trial. At one time he was given only salt fish and bread to eat but no water. And all the time outside his cell a tap was dripping. Another had been beaten about the head so that the old war wounds were opened up again. These were some of the cases I saw myself. I heard of scores more. . . .

We lay in rows of 24 inches of space for each person. Tramps and pickpockets lay side by side with lawyers, doctors, owners of factories, and all sorts of people arrested for political offences. The floor and the walls were infested with vermin. At night every man had to clear his sleeping space of hundreds of them. Everywhere was stained with their blood. That made the jailers furious. 'You are spoiling our prison,' they told us, and we were given lessons in how to catch vermin and kill them without smearing the walls. Every morning I was hauled out of this hell and taken to court eight miles away. To get there 80 of us were forced into a closed van.

Evans left Romania realising that the regime's fear tactics were working:

I stood in the railway station in Bucharest, waiting for the Orient Express to take me from Rumania and the horrors of life behind the iron curtain. None of my Rumanian friends dared to see me off. But, just before, I had met an old friend. 'Tell them when you get back to Britain what things are like here now,' he whispered, after a careful glance around to make sure that no one could hear.

Another surviving witness to the terror was Annie Samuelli, seized in 1949 by the communists in a roundup of all those who had worked for the British and the American legations in Bucharest. Samuelli spent twelve years in jail before her release in 1961, writing up her prison experiences in *The Wall Between*. Perhaps the worst was the period of relentless interrogation at the beginning. In a letter written in October 1990, she gave the details sparsely:

Solitary confinement in special prisons, sitting on hard chair from 5 a.m. to 10 p.m.; interrogation carried out mainly at night. Led to interrogation room blindfolded with sightless goggles. Questioning by interrogator sitting behind spotlights, their glare directed on prisoner's face.
Ways and means of coercion: beating, being stripped, trussed like a fowl on pole thrust under knees, blows inflicted on buttocks and back. Minimum number of blows: 25. So-called 'manège': walking barefooted round empty cell, except for chamber-pot, under constant surveillance through peep-hole. This lasted for two or three days and nights. When warder considered exhaustion peak was reached, led back to original cell for three or four hours sleep, followed by interrogation. During 'manège' no hot food, only gruel and limited ration of water. After a three-day period, doctor was sometimes called in to approve continuation. He always did.

As soon as the communists had got their hands on power, in March 1945, the propaganda push for collectivisation of agriculture started. Many of the peasants bitterly contested losing their title to plots, however small, which they had only won in land reforms under the monarchy. Collectivisation was often carried out at gunpoint, against fiercely conservative peasants who would have had little truck with Marxist agronomics, had they ever heard of them. Gheorghiu-Dej himself admitted in 1962 that during the collectivisation period 'public trials' took place, affecting some 80,000 peasants. The peasants were accused of going over to the 'class enemy'.

Ceausescu was in 1948 appointed deputy minister of agriculture. In 1949 he became deputy minister of the army, with the rank of general. It meant that he held the top political commissar's job in the country. He was now within the magic circle, although it was a very dangerous time. Stalin was still alive, and the infighting between the 'home' communists and the Muscovites was very tense, until the latter lost the battle with the dismissal of Ana Pauker in 1952. There is a photograph of Ceausescu in general's uniform in *Nicolae Ceausescu: Builder of Modern Romania and International Statesman*. His uniform is too long for his short arms, his stomach bulges, and his trousers are buckled and crumpled.

But life was good for the guardians of the new order, men like Ceausescu, Apostol, Brucan and Maurer. To survive in those days required political finesse, smartness and a willingness to acquiesce in brutality; but to prosper as Ceausescu did required a manic desire to win – the other side of which was a savage, emotional reaction to defeat.

Life was less happy for those of 'putrid social origin', like Corneliu Coposu. He was in jail for most of this period, spending the months from 1951 to 1953 working on the infamous 'Canal of Death' at Capul Midia on the Black Sea. The canal was designed to take the huge kink out of the Danube as it neared the sea, saving shipping a journey by cutting straight from Cernavoda to the coast, south of Constantza. Every mile saved for shipping cost hundreds of lives. But the canal had a second, grimmer purpose. It would, in the words of Gheorghiu-Dej, be the 'graveyard of Romanian reaction'. In all, it is feared that 60,000 people perished working on the canal.

The slave labourers who worked on the 'Canal of Death' came from a broad sweep of Romanian society, encompassing anyone who opposed the 'socialist transformation' of the new regime. According to Vladimir Socor of US-financed Radio Free Europe:

Estimates of their numbers vary but it is generally accepted that well over 100,000 prisoners performed forced labour on the canal from 1949 to 1954; of this number the overwhelming majority consisted of acknowledged political prisoners and others who were in reality political prisoners and were so treated, although the authorities would not recognise them as such.

The regime invented a new vocabulary of hate to categorise all the social deviants in the camps that sprung up along the canal's length: 'saboteurs' meant artisans and merchants who had tried to avoid punitive taxation and peasant farmers who had resisted compulsory crop requisitions; 'gunners' were people caught possessing firearms; 'frontists' meant the luckless ones who were captured by the border guards as they tried to escape; and 'idlers' were people whose source of income had been taken away by the communists, such as the wealthier farmers and landowners, middle-class businessmen and the like, and anyone else who did not spout the new line.

The security at the camps was tight, according to Socor. The camps were bounded by triple barbed-wire fences watched over by sentries in towers and by foot patrols; prisoners who crossed into the forbidden perimeter zones were shot on sight. Permanent exposure to the harsh extremes of the baking Romanian summer and the icy continental winter, the rock-breaking work, starvation diet and diseases like tuberculosis, malaria, dysentery, hepatitis and furunculosis all took their toll. Socor writes:

The Securitate personnel and the other guards subjected the prisoners to constant beatings that left the majority of camp survivors permanently scarred or disabled. Virtually no one escaped without some physical infirmity. The prisoners were beaten for not working hard enough, for praying to God, for political remarks overheard by the guards, for complaining to each other or to the guards about camp conditions, for collapsing from exhaustion or becoming sick, and frequently for no other reason than for being – as their jailers would invariably shout while beating them – 'reactionary bandits': the designation applied to any person who ran foul of the regime for political or 'class' reasons. The beatings were usually public, and sometimes the victim was tied to a wooden post on the camp assembly grounds. Other forms of punishment consisted of withholding half or all of the food ration, cancelling the largely imaginary family correspondent rights, or solitary confinement for several days in 'cages' in which one could neither lie, sit nor stand.

In Coposu's two years at Capul Midia camp he saw 270 fellow political detainees die:

They died because of impossible working conditions, starvation, slave labour lasting 12 hours a day. The prisoners ate dogs, cats, grass, snakes, anything they could lay their hands on. We were 'supervised' with whips and clubs. We had to scoop out the earth by hand. Those who could not work as hard as the guards wanted were put overnight in a cage which was so small they could not lie down.

It was worse when the detainees got to the bare rock at the bottom of the canal. The tools they gave us were not up to the job. They kept on breaking, they couldn't attack the rock. So we didn't meet our work norm. That meant a night in the cage. The next day we still couldn't break the rock, so it was another night in the cage. After four or five nights in the cage we were so afraid of the cage that we broke the rock. It was so back-breaking that prisoners were paralysed down one side by the strain of the work and the terror of the cage. Not a few prisoners, but 70 I heard about. It was the first time in Romanian medical history that the doctors had seen cases like it.

On several occasions Coposu shared the cage with his friend Prince Serban Ghica, now seventy-one and living out his days in Bucharest. He belongs to one of the old ruling dynasties of Romania: the first prince to bear the Ghica name appears in 1500. His great-grandfather was the first Romanian ambassador in Britain in the nineteenth century. Ghica spent six months studying mining at Birmingham University in 1938, when Ceausescu was in Doftana prison. When Ceausescu was a general, Ghica was at Capul Midia. When I met him we spoke in French because, despite his time in Birmingham, his English was more rusty. He did not ask for dollars or explain his crucial part in bringing down Ceausescu during the Christmas revolution, but took off my coat with a touching courtesy, poured out two glasses of *tsuica* and cast his memory back to the black times:

'It was terrible. It was the worst. We were in a concentration camp, without news of family or contact with the outside world. The first time I saw my son' (who had been conceived shortly before his arrest) 'was when he was seven years old. The prison food was dire and not enough for a bird. When we saw a snake we used to leap for it and the first one to catch it would bite it like an animal.' He got up from his chair and acted out a sad pantomime of a starving prisoner marching like a zombie in file, then pouncing for the snake and ripping its neck with his teeth.

'It was hell for me. I was beaten by the militia every day. They jeered at my engineering qualifications. They spat at me and said: "You're not an engineer – you're a prince." Every day I was beaten till

I fell to the ground. Because we were political we were in a punishment battalion, a thousand of us, the worst off in the camp of 10,000 prisoners.'

He looked around at the dingy flat which was his home. It belongs to his wife. 'Today I have only a glass on the table. They took everything. I had the most beautiful house in Bucharest, where I was born, the Palace Ghica. Before the war it was perfect. They called Bucharest the "little Paris".' And the peasants? 'Before the war they had everything they wanted.'

Who was worse, Gheorghiu-Dej or Ceausescu? The old prince poured out some more *tsuica*, considering his answer as he did so: 'Gheorghiu-Dej put more people in prison, but he had a motive. Ceausescu had no motive to do what he did. Things were worse under the last ten years of Ceausescu. It was terrible what he did.'

We sat in silence for a long time. Ghica sighed deeply, then spoke again: 'I lost everything, everything, my house, my friends . . . they died in their hundreds . . . my friends. . . .' At the memory of his friends who were starved or beaten to death, the old prince could talk no more. I looked at his face. He was crying, and so was I.

King

Ion Maurer sat in the hangarlike gloom of his living room, his hands nursing the soft hillock of his paunch. Poor man: history will never forgive him for proposing Ceausescu as the new general secretary of the party on the death, in 1965, of Gheorghiu-Dej. But the system that enabled a man like Ceausescu to prosper was sick, and at the very top there were dangerous, sometimes lethal personality battles.

This elite world was described in a novel called *Incognito* by the writer Petru Dumitriu, written after he went into exile with his wife in February 1960 by way of East Berlin. The couple left their infant daughter behind with relatives in the hope that she would later be allowed to join them in the West. Instead, the child was removed and her whereabouts concealed from them by the Romanian authorities. *Incognito* is a cry of pain; more than that, it is Dumitriu's revenge on a system that stole his child. He writes of:

the far more mephitic air breathed at the meetings in a confined space of men more powerful than the people in the streets. The sense of danger, the potential threat which each man represents to his neighbour, the hatred, envy and malice, these create an atmosphere which is almost visible as a noisome mist hanging in the air. There is a spiritual intimacy at these meetings that is something like the physical intimacy of fat men wrestling in mud. It is not without a horrid fascination. . . .

Before the meeting that would settle the succession, Maurer went to see Gheorghiu-Dej, who was dying in agony. 'He could only speak in whispers.' He had throat cancer, which had invaded the rest of his body. Rumour had it that the cancer had been caused by the Russians secretly irradiating Dej while he was visiting the Kremlin for a Warsaw Pact meeting; this rumour is often given as an explanation for the peculiar lengths Ceausescu went to to protect himself from infection and poisoning.

Maurer said: 'Before dying, Dej asked me to take over. But I said no. My father was German and my mother French, so my blood was not Romanian. If I accepted this function, the fight for power would be open. And the one who wanted power would appeal to the Russians to come back.' One lasting achievement of Gheorghiu-Dej had been to secure the agreement of the Russians for the removal of Soviet troops from Romanian soil in 1958; keeping the Russians at bay became the single most important plank in Romanian foreign policy from then on. This, of course, begs the question whether the Russians were greatly bothered by a degree of Romanian independence. They had troops in Hungary and could have marched on Romania from two sides.

Maurer continued: 'After I had told him no, Gheorghiu-Dej told me to propose Apostol. So that was the plan. I called the meeting. It was clear that Dej had not long to live. The first to speak was Ceausescu. He proposed Maurer.' The old man seemed untroubled by referring to himself in the third person, after the fashion of de Gaulle. The third-person habit is a legacy of the communist idiom, which placed formal stress on 'objectivity' and devaluing the importance of personality, even as the mightiest egos clashed like cymbals. 'I said no. Then I proposed Apostol. There was a silence. Two people stood up: Draghici, the minister of the interior and Russia's man – he was against Apostol – and Ceausescu. Ceausescu said it was not the right time to elect Apostol because it would hasten Gheorghiu-Dej's death.'

But Maurer and Gheorghiu-Dej had been worried that a delayed or contested succession in Bucharest would enable the Russians to come back. Because of the party leadership's fear of such a power vacuum Maurer wanted to arrive at a decision. He waited in the silence for Apostol to make his move. 'But Apostol said nothing. If he had spoken it would have shown that he was willing to fight. Because he shut up and didn't say a word, I concluded that he was not willing to fight. We needed a ruler who knew how to fight, to maintain the relative independence of Romania and not to let the Russians decide who will be the new leader. That's why I decided to propose Ceausescu.'

Was Maurer telling the whole truth? In particular, was it true that he automatically discounted himself because he was not a true Romanian? Fear played a part in the succession passing to Ceausescu. As secretary to the Central Committee in charge of party organisation, a post Ceausescu moved to in 1954 from being number two in the army, he had ensured that the new blood in the Central Committee was faithful to him. All appointments to the Central Committee had to pass through his office, and he made sure, as Stalin had done during his subtle takeover of the Communist Party in the Soviet Union in the early Twenties, that only pro-Ceausescu men prospered. The other candidates, Maurer and Apostol, might have lost if the succession had gone to a vote of the Central Committee because of the number of Ceausescu's creatures in the *nomenklatura*. Both Maurer and Apostol were afraid of fighting for the top job and being seen to lose, a wholly natural fear which they would be unlikely to express to a foreign stranger, and a journalist at that.

Coping with the Russians was, and continued to be during Ceausescu's time, the single most important foreign policy question for the Romanians; it had been so since power seeped from the Ottoman Empire at the beginning of the nineteenth century. Romania was slowly edging away from the Soviet Union. The personal and political bonds the old communists had forged with Stalin, the conqueror of the Nazis, had severed with his death in March 1953; the ties with the new Soviet generation, led by the volatile Khrushchev, were weaker and more prey to the national interests of the two countries. Ideologically, the old RCP leadership under the ailing Gheorghiu-Dej had been more Stalinist than Stalin's heirs. But what really irritated the Romanians was the USSR 's strategic economic plan under its version of the Common Market, Comecon, for its satellite countries in Europe. This envisaged industrial growth for East Germany and Czechoslovakia, while Romania should concentrate on being a breadbasket. The natural consequence would be, in the Soviet view, for Romania to close its major heavy industrial factories.

This was anathema to the RCP. As good Marxist-Leninists, they believed that true communism could only be built in a heavily industrialised society; the proof of the pudding was the Soviet Union's victory over Nazi Germany. Because the RCP so admired the model of the Soviet economy, they wanted to copy its breakneck industrialisation, not be ordered to go in the opposite direction. Mary Ellen Fischer writes in her academic study of Ceausescu: 'The Comecon dispute should therefore be viewed not as a nationalist controversy between Soviets and Romanians but as a quarrel among Marxist-Leninists over the correct path of socialist development for Romania and who would define that path.' But to undervalue the emotional, maybe even subconscious role of nationalism in the debate would be to accept Marxist-Leninist ideology at face value.

The late Fifties and early Sixties were dominated by this confrontation, with Khrushchev frequently trying to intimidate the Romanians into giving up their plans for creating a bigger heavy-industry sector along the lines established by Stalin. And – if Maurer was telling the truth – the man who most notably stood up to the Soviet intimidation was Ceausescu. Many commentators have argued that Ceausescu's anti-Soviet stance, which became tougher and more visible over the years, was a mere blind, and that the Kremlin allowed Ceausescu's maverick foreign policy in later years because it was a double bluff. This analysis does not fit with the tale of the maize planting, which shows Ceausescu to be anything but Moscow's man.

Celac the interpreter recalled the story: 'I had just graduated from Bucharest University. In 1961 I got the job of being the second-string interpreter for Khrushchev's visit that year.' Everyone was in awe of Nikita Khrushchev, then Soviet leader, renowned for his angry outbursts, most infamously the moment when at the United Nations he took off his shoe and banged it on his desk – everyone but Ceausescu.

'I did not witness the actual incident myself, but I knew something had happened and found out the details of the story later. The visiting Russians, accompanied by Gheorghiu-Dej, some of the other ministers and Ceausescu took the train from Bucharest to Constantza. Gheorghiu-Dej left the train compartment, leaving Khrushchev, Moghioros, the secretary to the central committee for agriculture, and Ceausescu together. As the train went along they looked out of the window and at one point Khrushchev saw maize being planted. The peasants were planting the maize in rows. And Khrushchev, who was from peasant stock himself, said: "They're doing that all wrong. According to our experience in the Ukraine, you get much better results from planting maize in square plots, giving each more space. You should do that here."

'Moghioros then started to apologise for the backwardness of Romanian agricultural practice, and came up with a technical explanation that the rows were best suited for the tractors the Romanians used, when Ceausescu interrupted him: "People have been planting maize like that in this country for hundreds of years. We were one of the first countries in Europe to plant maize, so we know what we're doing and we're going to carry on doing it our way." '

Khrushchev was furious at Ceausescu's cheek. He complained to Gheorghiu-Dej; the upshot was that when the train arrived at Constantza, Ceausescu was not on it. Celac and the other interpreter assumed that he had, in disgrace, been turfed off the train at a small village station for his impudence.

Not long afterwards Khrushchev was deposed by the troika led by Leonid Brezhnev. Had he stayed in power, the Romanians might not have plumped for a man who had fallen out so badly with the Soviet leader.

For Celac, the incident shows Ceausescu's impulsiveness and that he 'was clearly willing to take risks with the Soviet Union, even with the omnipotent Soviet leader. He always viewed the Russians with disdain. He certainly was not a Russophile. He saw the Soviet Union as the direct heir to the tsarist empire.'

At eighty-eight, Maurer is an old, dying man. (I bet him five dollars that he would be alive when I returned to Romania.) His memory is far from fresh. Moreover, since he was a member of the *nomenklatura*, who took part in the communist terror of the Forties and Fifties, his word should not be relied upon as gospel. But he described Ceausescu as a reliable anti-Soviet comrade in a series of conversations he had with one of Valentin's colleagues and friends, Gabriel Costache, in 1975. After Maurer's fall from power, Costache had got to know the old prime minister well. Maurer told Costache what went through his mind in the years running up to the death of Gheorghiu-Dej. Costache, speaking in 1990, recalled Maurer saying in 1975:

'Khrushchev came here and asked to speak to the Politburo [formally the political bureau of the RCP and therefore the party's top decision-making body]. We were all assembled. Khrushchev looked at me and said: "Maurer is the most anti-Soviet communist in the bloc. My friend Maurer, whom I tried to protect in Stalin's time." He was shouting out accusations, very loud, in a real rage. No one had the courage to defend Maurer. Everyone there was stunned into silence. Then Ceausescu stood up and said: "This is a lie. Look, Mr Khrushchev, Maurer is one of the best communists we have in Romania and he is definitely not building an anti-Soviet policy." Ceausescu calmed things down. He had the guts to oppose Khrushchev, though he was aware of the fact that he was lying. Everyone in the Politburo knew that Maurer was anti-Soviet.'

Maurer recalled this incident a few years later, during the fateful succession meeting in 1965 when Apostol said not a word, even though his moment was ripe. Maurer wondered how Apostol would cope when he had to face Soviet pressure as the party's general secretary. He decided that Apostol was 'yellow'. By contrast Ceausescu, in backing him up against Khrushchev's rage, was not the slightest bit afraid of the Russians. So Maurer decided that Ceausescu should succeed Gheorghiu-Dej. The decision was not formally taken at the succession meeting, but rubber-stamped later at a plenary session of the Central Committee. At the end of Ceausescu's four-hour maiden speech, he proclaimed exultantly: 'The 9th Party Congress of the Romanian Communist Party will be written in letters of gold in Romania's history.' The RCP had a new pope.

The announcement was greeted with some warmth by many in the country and abroad, mainly because of Ceausescu's relative youth. At forty-seven, he was easily the youngest man to hold the highest office in any of the Warsaw Pact countries, where the system had an in-built creak towards gerontocracy. A young man, foreign observers assumed, would be better than an old one. But many of the old guard, who knew him well, were against Ceausescu from the start. They considered him arrogant and power-crazy. There were many people in the RCP who didn't like Ceausescu, but he was the candidate of the anti-Soviet hour. After 1965, it was too late. Maurer grew to regret the decision, as did the rest of the country.

At first things went well. Maurer told me that 'Ceausescu was very receptive to ideas and listened to discussions. He took action on what we agreed on. But then, later on, he went his own way.'

Ceausescu showed his peasant cunning from the start, building on the anti-Soviet feints and finesses played by Gheorghiu-Dej and Maurer. But his first real test was a dutiful visit by the RCP hierarchy – Ceausescu, Maurer and Apostol – to the Soviet Union in September 1965. Although Ceausescu made all the keynote speeches in Moscow and Leningrad, he went mum in Stalingrad, leaving the job of toasting the anti-fascist heroics of the Soviet citizens and army to Apostol. Mary Ellen Fischer notes that Ceausescu would have realised that the speech would have been relayed back to the folks back home, many of whom lost loved ones in the ferocious battle for Stalingrad when the Romanians were fighting on the wrong side.

Clearly Apostol found working under Ceausescu a strain. Playing was no easier. He had given up playing chess with Ceausescu, because of his unsporting behaviour. But it was more difficult to get out of playing volleyball at Snagov, the lakeside villa, not far from Bucharest, where Ceausescu made his home at weekends; Snagov is also the burial place of Vlad the Impaler. 'He always wanted to win. He played very aggressively. If he missed the ball or botched a serve, he would start over again, claiming that someone had moved. When he lost, he would stop playing and walk off in a sulk. He would throw the ball away and the game stopped.' Did anyone say 'stop being so childish'? Apostol's one seeing eye gazed with contempt: 'He was general secretary of the Central Committee.' It was obviously a stupid question. Apostol went on: 'He was full of vanity. No one had the courage to criticise him openly.'

Apostol and the other members of the Dejist old guard were picked off one by one. The old guard had never liked him; worse, they had long memories. They knew the rumours – that Ceausescu may have been a prison fink in Doftana, or had not played any part in the escape from Tirgu Jiu, or may have murdered the prefect in 1945 – which held the new general secretary in a less than perfect light. Many of them had more distinguished political records; nearly all of them were better educated and could pronounce long words without stuttering. To Ceausescu they were all enemies to be got rid of.

Apostol was rarely out of the public eye until mid-1966, when he vanished from the party newspapers, only appearing when the whole Praesidium was present as a group. He said: 'In 1965, 1966 and 1967 there started to be clicks on the phones. I began to be followed about by two Securitate officers. Everything became more paranoid.' Apostol's defeat at the RCP's version of musical chairs was clearly too painful for him to discuss in detail. There is a story of how Apostol lost his chair, but given in *Red Horizons* by Lieutenant General Ion Mihai Pacepa, which is a good contender for the title of the sleaziest book ever written.

Pacepa claims he was Ceausescu's Securitate foreign-espionage chief until he, tired with the intrigue and double-dealing, defected to the United States in 1978. In his book he says that Ceausescu 'had a special thing about microphones', which sounds all too credible. (An obsession with bugging is a dictatorial tic, like constant handwashing. According to the maids at Snagov, the film the Ceausescus had selected for their Christmas viewing in 1989 was *The Conversation*. The film is a thriller, starring Gene Hackman and written by Francis Ford Coppola, about a private bugging technician, Harry Caul, who after listening in to a conversation in a park becomes embroiled in a murder plot. The technician is mentally crucified by his own suspicions that he is being bugged. Hackman's portrayal of a mind disintegrating into paranoia forms an extraordinarily accurate psychological picture of Ceausescu in an eerie case of art mimicking life. Pacepa goes on:

Ceausescu's fascination with microphones was born in the early 1950s, when he was the military forces' political commissar responsible for replacing the Romanian capitalist army with a new, Communist one modelled after the Soviet Red Army. . . . In 1965, when Ceausescu became the supreme leader, population monitoring grew into a mass operation of unprecedented scope. Hundreds of thousands of new microphones were silently put to work. . . . As in the Soviet Union, corruption and prostitution reigned at the highest levels in Romania, and the microphones relentlessly recorded everything. Like Khrushchev, Ceausescu also ordered a monitoring room built behind his office, so he could personally check on the take from the microphones. They were his key to power.

Pacepa cites the case of Apostol, who was 'Ceausescu's main rival':

The microphones on him showed Apostol to be a devoted Marxist-Leninist with nothing to reproach him for except not having enough regard for Ceausescu. However, they also revealed that Apostol's wife, a young actress, was throwing frequent parties with her colleagues, very rarely attended by Apostol himself. His new minister of the interior presented Ceausescu with clandestine photographs of these parties. Ceausescu then personally dictated an 'anonymous' letter, written as if from a friend of Apostol's, in which Apostol was described as a bourgeois whose conduct was incompatible with his position as number two in the Party.

Pacepa goes on to explain that the fake letter was addressed to the general secretary of the party – Ceausescu – who, shocked by its contents, called a crash meeting of the Politburo during the 1967 party conference. He confronted Apostol with the letter. 'The Politburo, caught off guard by Ceausescu's aggressiveness and the unusual "evidence", agreed to remove Apostol temporarily from his position. . . .' Once that had happened, Apostol was finished.

Asked why he was pushed out of the magic circle, Apostol beamed his good eye in my general direction and delivered a long, rambling narrative which had the narrator as a heroic defender of the rights of the working class against the evil dictator. Pacepa's account has a certain ring of truth about it: the faked evidence of 'bourgeois' behaviour which half compromised the target, the Politburo uneasily taking away the condemned man's chair 'as a temporary measure', but it could be true of any senior figure in the RCP. As all too often in Pacepa's book, there is no supporting evidence or clinching detail.

Red Horizons is no better than Bucharest secret policemen's gossip: sordid, dully pornographic, intrusive, morally repugnant, incoherent yet endlessly fascinating. Ceausescu is seen as a power-mad, deeply dishonest paranoiac, as well as someone who cheats at chess. Elena comes off worse, if that is possible, as a sluttish, bad-tempered moron. There is a lot of cheap sex in the book, nearly all of it written around Elena: 'After Elena had emptied her second bottle of Cordon Rouge, she moved affectionately onto Ceausescu's lap. "I want you, Nick," she purred sweetly, rubbing one of his legs with hers. . . .' Pacepa writes that Stefan Andrei, one-time foreign minister, had a black book which contained all of Elena's many gaffes: '19 December, 1976. Andrei reported to Elena on preparations for a visit to Angola. Andrei suggested that Elena accompany the Comrade [Ceausescu]. Elena said: "Why not in the spring darling? It's too cold now." ' That too has the ring of truth about it.

The narrative is set down as Pacepa's recollections, delivered in the first person, in the last weeks of his service before defection. At the start the book carries a caveat about its worth as an item of record: 'The conversations in this book have been written from memory by Lieutenant General Ion Mihai Pacepa. They are as accurate as any non-recorded, remembered conversations can be.' Pacepa comes across as a sinister figure, even in the company of the medieval bestiary of creatures that crept and slithered around the top of the RCP. Celac recalls: 'He was short with a military bearing, straight-backed, exuding confidence and efficiency. He was a known and feared figure because he was one of the few people who were close advisers to Ceausescu and also held an official position in the Securitate.'

Nicu Ceausescu holds Pacepa in low esteem, so low that he winced at the very mention of Pacepa's name. Nicu said that Pacepa was never the number-one spy in the DIE, the foreign espionage branch of the Securitate, but held number-two position under General Nicolae Doicaru. Nicu went on: 'The main principle was that the spy chiefs never discussed with the junior man what was going on.' Nicu said he saw Pacepa once or twice in his life. 'He may have known a lot about me. That was their job. The book was clearly designed to be a bestseller.' And then he added a classic appeal to Romanian blood fascism: 'Don't forget that Pacepa was of Polish origin.'

And did Nicu place any value in *Red Horizons* as documentary evidence? 'It's a stupid book, full of gossip, rumours, lies.' This critical attack is unsurprising because he is roundly trashed in the book. The reader only has to struggle as far as Chapter Two before he can savour a description of Nicu, roaring drunk at a party in one of the *nomenklatura*'s private clubs:

A waiter came in with a silver platter full of oysters. Nicu said: 'They need seasoning, you idiot. This isn't a cat house, it's a VIP club.' He precariously climbed up onto the table and started urinating on them, careful to 'season' every oyster. . . . We left Nicu pushing a waitress towards the edge of the table while tearing off her blouse. 'I want to fuck you, here. Right here on this table, you slut.'

Perhaps *Red Horizons* is a scissors-and-paste job by an unsung, CIA-approved ghostwriter. The raw material reads like translated transcripts of Pacepa's debriefing conversations held in Romanian with his CIA case officers immediately after he defected. Pacepa often quotes chunks of Ceausescu's old speeches, freely available from Romanian embassies and in Western libraries, as 'remembered conversations'; occasionally he even quotes the text of Romanian decrees as spouting out of Ceausescu's mouth.

Red Horizons is confusing, unreliable and tawdry by turns. It seesaws from seedy titbits about Elena's obsession with the sexual peccadillos of the Politburo wives to amazing claims that the Romanians recruited top Western politicians as their agents of influence, so-called 'influ-Communists'. But the tone of the book seems faithful to the subject. The interpreter Celac, who rates four mentions in the index, is given a lowly, walk-on part, probably to his great relief. He does not dismiss *Red Horizons* out of hand: 'It certainly is a patchwork. There are exaggerations, probably due to the ghostwriter's imagination. But in essence it is accurate.'

It reeks all too unpleasantly of the smells of Ceausescu's time. More pungent than the thin perfume of self-excuse which Pacepa sprays from time to time to hide his own, not insubstantial role in the ruination of Romanian politics, civics and ethics is the stink of fear. A fear which began to tighten its grip round anyone who threatened Ceausescu's position, as early as his first year in office.

After Apostol went, Ceausescu turned his attention to Alexandru Draghici, under Gheorghiu-Dej Romania's minister of internal affairs and the country's most powerful secret policeman. Immediately after Ceausescu's accession in 1965, Draghici was moved from the ministry's Gothic, Addams Family house to the Central Committee building, to take over Ceausescu's old job of secretary for party affairs. Although still an important figure, Draghici had been split from his power base. Over the next two years Ceausescu allowed criticism of the communist terror under Gheorghiu-Dej to be aired; this was an implicit attack on Draghici, who had been closely connected with many of the old regime's barbarities. In mid-July 1967, Ceausescu moved his attack out into the open – or as open as any political strike could be in the cryptic gloom of the RCP. The Ministry of Internal Affairs had committed 'abuses' against socialist legality. Ceausescu proclaimed: 'There is no kind of secret or matter of a conspiratorial character that . . . can be a reason for an organ to avoid Party oversight.'

More criticism of the bad old days followed. In particular, the rehabilitation of old 'traitors' like former general secretary Foris and Patrascanu – executed for their 'espionage activity' – was bad news for Draghici. The rehabilitation process started rolling in November 1965, some months after Ceausescu achieved power, with the setting-up of a Commission on Party History. This commission presented its report to the 1968 party plenum, which decided that:

On 18 March 1954, based on the information presented by Alexandru Draghici, the Political Bureau of the Central Committee of the RCP decided to 'proceed to the trial of the group of spies headed by Patrascanu'. The trial took place in violation of the most elementary procedural guarantees . . . on the night of 16–17 April 1954 Lucretia Patrascanu was executed at Jilava prison.

And what of General Ceausescu's role? According to Mary Ellen Fischer, 'Ceausescu, not a candidate member of the Political Bureau or secretary of the Central Committee until two days later, could credibly claim not to have taken part in the decision to execute Patrascanu.' Far from having anything to do with Patrascanu's unhappy end, Ceausescu criticised 'the foul frame-up' and 'dastardly execution' in a speech to Bucharest party workers immediately after the plenum. Patrascanu's official executioner, Draghici, was again attacked. This, according to Ceausescu in 1968, was what he told a meeting of the Politburo in April 1956:

As far as the Ministry of Internal Affairs is concerned, Party spirit remains as thin as Party control . . . Comrade Draghici thinks that he can do anything. . . . Since Draghici has been there, the Ministry of Internal Affairs has not had a united executive. This is the result of Draghici's stand on the question of cadres. He likes to be surrounded by toadies. . . . He poorly guides the security work.

The dark hatred of the speech revealed to the party at large, perhaps for the first time, the inner workings of Ceausescu's mind as glimpsed by Campeanu and the others over the chessboard. The hint was broad enough. The plenum dismissed Draghici in disgrace. To outsiders, the moves to rehabilitate Patrascanu and Foris appeared to be evidence that Ceausescu was honestly keen to put the bad old days of Stalinism behind him. With the benefit of hindsight, a different interpretation can be made: that Ceausescu was using the liberal mood of the times as a brush to sweep his rivals from power. Into Draghici's place stepped a bright, ambitious young communist and Ceausescu protégé, Ion Iliescu. The new boy had done sterling work as a leading cadre in the Union of Young Communists, helping Ceausescu suppress those Romanian students, many of them ethnic Hungarians, who sympathised with the ill-fated Hungarian uprising in Bucharest. Iliescu's reward for the suppression of these 'reactionaries' was a still warm seat at the table.

Maurer was the next one to feel the heat. He realised that his phone was being bugged, something he had not endured during Gheorghiu-Dej's time. How? Maurer said: 'I knew a lot of people, even people in the Securitate. They told me.' The proof came after the revolution, when the Securitate came and took away the bugs: 'They even had them planted in the bathroom.' As a self-confident man, virtually untouchable because of his popularity in the country and abroad, Maurer was one of the very few people in the new leader's circle who were in a position to mock him. Ceausescu didn't like it. Maurer told the following story about a hunting expedition: 'This happened shortly after he gained power. He enjoyed hunting and thought of himself as a fine hunter. The truth is that he often bagged less game than anyone else in the party. To cover this up he used to get the gamekeepers to bring dead birds that they had killed and hang them outside his hunting lodge. On one occasion a fox appeared beside all these dead birds he'd have us believe he'd shot. So I said: "What a fine shot you are! Fancy bagging a fox, and a flying fox at that!" Well, everybody else burst into laughter, but Ceausescu said not a word and just stormed off.' Celac had heard a very similar story about this incident, but in his version, after Maurer had teased Ceausescu the dictator turned round and jumped into his helicopter, leaving the others to make their own, edgy way back to Bucharest.

By 1971, Maurer had had enough. He disliked the burgeoning personality cult, although it was a modest affair compared to later on. He realised that he was being continually sidelined, with Ceausescu hatching deals behind his back. And he could see that Ceausescu was surrounding himself with yes men. While he was thinking about retiring, he suffered a nasty car accident. He spent three months in hospital with a fractured pelvis, broken right leg and dislocated shoulder. Was it an accident? Maurer chewed this question in his mind and then replied: 'I think so.' After the accident, he determined to quit: 'When I had recovered I went to Ceausescu and we had a long talk. He pleaded with me to stay on for the good of the country, and told me that he would listen to my criticisms. But it was all nonsense. In 1974 things had got worse and he still did not listen to me, so I retired.'

Retirement was not an easy option, even for someone as powerful, prestigious and tough-minded as Maurer. Pacepa describes the following scene, part of the phone-tapping take from the Maurer household in 1978, when the old prime minister was allegedly reading his memoirs covering the 1965 succession meeting out loud:

Mrs Maurer's voice broke in, continued the transcript. 'Why are you reading me that now?' 'Because today is 20th March,' he explained. 'Today it's been thirteen years since Nic [Ceausescu] was appointed.' 'You would have been better off stinking for two days after eating a bucketful of shit thirteen years ago, instead of proposing the dictator. Now you'll stink for the rest of your life!'

Cunning at home was matched by cunning abroad. Ceausescu learnt quickly to make the right noises for the Western press. As early as June 1965, David Binder of the *New York Times* cheerily quoted Ceausescu's address to a meeting of artists and writers advocating 'a diversity of styles necessary in art. It is right and necessary for the artist to express in a work of art his entire personality and individuality.'

The address was cited as evidence of a new liberal mood, with Binder quoting an unnamed Romanian artist who called the Ceausescu speech 'a positive sign of relaxation in the arts'. The following year Binder wrote a longer appreciation in the *New York Times* magazine, the second sentence of which read: 'It may now be appropriate to say that Nicolae Ceausescu is the man who has taken charge of breaking up the Soviet Empire'. The West's lionising of Ceausescu – the better to chafe the Russian bear – had begun.

The article set the tone for the rest of the Anglo-Saxon world's scanty coverage of Ceausescu's Romania, touching on the old RCP martyrology of the Doftana hellhole, conceding that 'though he goes strictly by the book in most other matters' – meaning internal affairs – he was a good Moscow-basher. In support of the latter, Binder quoted a Ceausescu speech made in May 1966, on the eve of a visit to Bucharest by the new Soviet leader Leonid Brezhnev. Ceausescu denounced 'military blocs and the existence of military bases and troops [in foreign countries as] an anachronism incompatible with the independence and national sovereignty of the peoples and normal relations between states'. This, Binder decoded, was a dual-handed attack on NATO's forces in Western Europe but, much more significant, also on the Soviet Union's forces in Eastern Europe.

Ceausescu had found his foreign-policy tune and proceeded to play it on his tin whistle for the next two and a half decades. In the Sixties a reference to the 'Soviet liberators' was dropped from the national anthem, and in 1977 the regime scrapped the anthem altogether and replaced it with an old patriotic tune, reworked to merge nationalistic sentiment with communist jingoism. The regime's cuddling up to the Chinese communists, who by now were in the throes of the Cultural Revolution and screaming abuse at the Soviet deviationists, was a plain irritation to the Russians. But such moves were always tentative, veiled in a *faux-naïf* innocence. When the Chinese prime minister Chou En-Lai visited Romania in 1966 there was a genuine fear that he would be so rude about the Soviet Union that the delicate lacework of Ceausescu's foreign policy would be ripped apart; however, the Romanians successfully prevailed on Chou to speak cautiously. The novelty about the Romanian foreign policy was that no one else in the Soviet bloc was being so adventurous, even including the domestically far more liberal regime in Czechoslovakia under Alexander Dubček.

But the West's approval of Ceausescu's foreign policy, a

continuation of the line drawn by Gheorghiu-Dej and Maurer in the late Fifties, led diplomats, politicians and journalists like Binder astray. Much of the coverage of Ceausescu was written in the dark. As Binder despairingly wrote, the new president had refused all requests for interviews by the foreign press, with the sole exception of a journalist from the Italian Communist Party. In the absence of any hard evidence on his personality, the Western press lit up the chubby features of Nicolae Ceausescu in a soft-focus, rosy glow.

The Western media were not misreading all the signs. In the late Sixties there really was something of a thaw in the hideous cultural policing the Romanians had had to suffer under Gheorghiu-Dej. The writer Julian Hale in his book *Ceausescu's Romania* points out that in the late Sixties the three most popular television programmes in Romania were all English imports: *The Avengers*, *The Forsyte Saga* and *The Saint*. Later on, the broadcasting of such decadent programmes would have been anathema to the orchestrators of the Ceausescu cult. Writers found that there was a little more room for ideological manoeuvre. But head-on attacks on the system were not allowed. Editorial freedom had not changed very much from the time in 1960 when Petru Dumitriu fled, complaining that in exchange for their complicity writers enjoyed 'a sort of comfortable castrato's existence'. The opposition parties remained illegal, the opposition newspapers stayed dead, the dead stayed dishonoured. It wasn't much of a spring.

Rehabilitation of executed communists was interpreted as a good sign, but there was no whole-scale admission of the ghastly crimes of the communist terror, since that would have compromised all the system's creatures, from former General Ceausescu down. The tide of de-Stalinisation began to roll in, but it did not get very far before it started to lap at the feet of some very powerful comrades. It could go so far – washing away Ceausescu's old guard enemies on the way – but no further.

On social issues the new regime displayed fierce conservatism. On 8 October 1966 a new law was adopted which practically abolished divorce and abortion at a stroke. The idea behind the plan was a Gaullist fantasy of boosting Romania's birth rate; the social cost and human suffering that such a peremptory diktat would cause were discarded. Ceausescu made it plain that every Romanian woman should have at least four children – his wife had only three, but moral coherence was never a strong point of the dictator. The birth rate went up and divorces fell from 37,000 in 1965 to 4,000 in 1968: one reason was that, even if official permission could be gained, the fees for both abortion and divorce were extremely steep. The groundwork of Ceausescu's most abhorrent essay in social engineering had been laid.

The following autumn, in September 1967, the party announced hefty rent increases. A fanfare of publicity trumpeted the good news:

The new rent scheme will be conducive to a more efficient administering and a better preservation of the dwellings, to the increase of the dwelling stock and its higher comfort, all this contributing to the improvement of the working people's housing conditions – an important element of their living standard.

The state required more Romanians, but as to where to put them, the people had to shift for themselves.

Passports were still extremely difficult to obtain, refused or granted on a whim to individuals after months, sometimes years, of waiting. Hale reports: 'The bureaucracy is used to glossing over the truth, and to getting away with the excuse of "the Party said so".' He cites the case of Mihai R— who was 'typical of the majority'. He and three others were invited to a geologists' conference in Belgium, with all expenses paid by the organisers. The passport application was duly sent off to the foreign ministry. Nothing happened. Telephone calls were made. The reply was that the passport was being processed. Still nothing happened. Hale writes:

Finally the day of the conference came, and still no passports were forthcoming. It was no longer worth waiting. Mihai stopped telephoning and nothing further was heard about the matter. In despair, he went off to stay with his brother in the country, and got drunk. It would have been more tolerable if applications were given direct refusal. But prevarication and cowardice are among bureaucracy's least endearing characteristics.

Ceausescu substituted constructive action with frenzy. He went on a continuous rollercoaster, whistle-stop tour of the country. Once on this whirligig of official visits, speeches and congresses, he never got off it. The whirligig became faster and faster and more elaborate, with visits to foreign countries and a constant shuffling of ministers and ministries. It makes anyone who tries to follow it dizzy. It consumed his and everybody else's time; it wasted resources and achieved little. But inside Ceausescu's head frenzy equalled progress: it was an intellectual confusion to which, as time rolled on, the whole country was to succumb.

Celac observed the Frenzy as an interpreter: 'It was an exorcism: a replacement of real change by constant chaotic movement. For example, the Ministry of Machine Building was divided and re-established three or four times; the same applied to the ministries of Mining, Oil and Gas. It was all part of Ceausescu's ability to create novelty. The Frenzy became contagious. Some of the bureaucrats learnt the trick. They knew that they would not be staying in any one ministry for long, so they inaugurated changes. It was a great excuse for poor performance: you could always place the blame on the fact that you had not completed your reorganisation. The Frenzy all flowed from the top. In a pyramidal system, if you had frenzy at the top then it would spread throughout.'

The Frenzy started at the very beginning of his reign, in 1965. Mary Ellen Fischer went to the bother of counting up all the trips he made from July 1965 to January 1973. In that period 'he made 147 tours; most took two to three days and included several different places. . . . The staging of the visits was very dramatic, with motorcades in flower-draped cars, ovations, balcony appearances, and the traditional Romanian greeting of bread and salt upon arrival.' *Scinteia* described a typical visit on 19 February 1966 to the town of Oradea, near the Hungarian border:

The appearance on the balcony of the Party and state leaders was hailed with an ovation and prolonged cheers. Addressing the crowd, Nicolae Ceausescu conveyed . . . a warm salute on behalf of the RCP Central Committee. . . . Referring to the prospects for Crisana region, Nicolae Ceausescu said that further construction of industrial projects is planned under the new five year plan. . . . They will raise the region's economic strength and further increase the contribution made by the working people of the Oradea town and Crisana region to the blossoming of our socialist homeland.

The square resounded with cheers for the Party and its leadership. Leaving the regional Party committee the motorcade travelled the streets of Oradea, heading for the aluminium factory. The people lined up along the route applauded warmly, greeting the leaders. Large groups of Oradea workers waved red and tricoloured scarves and offered flowers.

As the years of Ceausescu's kingship went by, these displays of the working people's adoration became more ornate, but the main themes – a quasi-Oriental submission to Ceausescu, flatulent praise of the party and soulless displays of faked homage – did not change at all. They were all-singing, all-dancing productions of the hagiographies. How could people be willing members of the dictator's chorus? How could they, in the poet Mircea Dinescu's phrase, hurry out 'to praise his game'? Even during these early years of the so-called Bucharest spring of the late Sixties, the answer has to be fear. The 'conditioning' of the communist terror in the late Forties and early Fifties was so strong, so severe that it only required the lightest caress from the Securitate to have the average Romanian lying prone in a position of abject submission. Whatever liberal sentiments Ceausescu expressed in his speeches, the secret policemen were still present, waiting, listening, asking questions. There was no need for Ceausescu to clump heavy-handedly about, threatening people. It had all been done so effectively a generation before and people had not forgotten. The people barked to command, because they knew what happened to the disobedient. Once the dog is trained, there is little need for the whip.

And the dog always loves its master. This came true in 1968 in spectacular fashion when Brezhnev ordered the tanks in to crush the (genuine) Prague spring in Czechoslovakia. Under the benign leadership of Alexander Dubček, the Czech and Slovak newspapers really had started to kick up the dirt, people had been free to travel and to question the way things were. All the other countries of the Warsaw Pact – Poland, East Germany, Hungary, Bulgaria and, of course, the Soviet Union – supported the rape of Prague, but not, to his lasting credit, Ceausescu of Romania.

The summer of 1968 was a tense time for anyone living in Eastern Europe. The Czechs and Slovaks were upsetting Soviet hegemony; worse, they were dismantling the Soviet system in a way that Ceausescu, for all his foreign-policy adventurism, never attempted to do. The Russians let Ceausescu play host to President de Gaulle of France and even visit the first and greatest deviant of the Communist bloc, President Tito of Yugoslavia that May; such contacts were an irritant but did not pose a threat to the system. But what Dubček was doing in Czechoslovakia was beyond the pale.

As the Russians tightened the screws, Ceausescu became louder and louder in his protestations that socialist countries had the right to order their own internal affairs. In mid-July on a visit to an iron and steel factory he made the first of a series of unambiguous statements: 'The RCP does not share the view of those who are alarmed over what is happening in Czechoslovakia.' A month later he visited Prague, making great show of signing a 'Treaty of Friendship, Cooperation and Mutual Assistance'. At a press conference he was asked, cheekily, if he had noticed any anti-socialist behaviour in Czechoslovakia. He replied cannily: 'I think you [Czechs and Slovaks] know the situation better in Czechoslovakia than I do.'

Ceausescu kept up his support for Dubček virtually to the moment of invasion. Once the tanks rolled in, a huge meeting was called in the Palace Square in front of the Central Committee building, the same spot that was to see his downfall twenty-one years later. For once the Securitate cheerleaders were superfluous. The whole country was terrified of a repeat of 1944, of another 'fraternal' visit by the Red Army. Ceausescu was afraid, too – his speech for once was not delivered in a dull monotone but with intense passion – yet he had the courage to condemn the outrage. If Maurer had proposed Apostol, then Bucharest's response might well have been different.

Ceausescu declared that the 'penetration' of the Warsaw Pact troops into Czechoslovakia was 'a great mistake and a grave danger to peace in Europe, to the fate of socialism in the world' and 'a shameful moment in the history of the revolutionary movement'. In the light of Romanian history, this was tough talking. He continued to (genuine) cheers from the crowd: 'There is no justification whatsoever for military intervention in the affairs of a fraternal socialist state. . . . The problem of choosing the roads of socialist construction is a problem of the respective Party. . . .'

He finished off with a gut appeal to Romanian nationalism:

'It was said that in Czechoslovakia there was a danger of counter-revolution; maybe tomorrow there will be some who say that here, too, at this rally, counter-revolutionary tendencies were manifest. We answer all of them: the entire Romanian people will not allow anybody to violate the territory of our homeland. . . . We are communists and anti-fascists who faced prisons and death, but we have never betrayed the interests of the working class, of our people. Be sure, comrades, be sure, citizens of Romania, that we shall never betray our homeland, we shall never betray the interests of our people.'

Overnight the speech made Ceausescu a national hero. A fearful submission to the new party overlord was transformed into great popular support. It was said that if honest democratic elections had been held in Eastern Europe at the end of 1968 only Ceausescu would have won power; the rest would have been booted out of office. Foreign diplomats and politicians applauded him, intellectuals struggled to be next to him on the speaking platform, many burying their previous moral repugnance to join the RCP as a gesture of their support, but most of all he heard the joy of the people unconfined. They clamoured, 'Chow-chess-cu, Chow-chess-cu!' It was the sweetest of music, too sweet for his own or his country's good. Overcome by the emotion of the moment when he, the RCP and the ordinary people of Romania were united in their opposition to the threat from the east he came to believe that the brief shudder of unity was somehow permanent; applause his by right.

Immediately after the speech, Romania was fizzing with rumours that the Russians were poised to invade, or that they were plotting to kill Ceausescu. Shafir quotes an American visitor to Bucharest that summer: 'One of the more persistent rumours following the invasion of Czechoslovakia was that Hungarian tanks had "accidentally" strayed over the border and been welcomed with flowers by the Hungarian villagers on the Romanian side of the frontier.' Romanian people feared that their beloved leader might be snatched from their bosom. The cult of personality, which already was thriving before 1968, took off into the stratosphere.

The Ceausescu cult was fed by a job lot of Westerners keen to do business with the one Eastern European leader who could, it appeared, stand up to the Russians and survive. At first, there was a trickle, then a torrent of Western visitors all singing Ceausescu's tune, none of them too choosy about the reality of the man they met – the myth was too much to their liking. The first VIP was de Gaulle, but the second visitor, arriving at Bucharest's Otopeni airport in 1969, really set the tone for the West's subsequent adoration of the Genius of the Carpathians. His name? Richard Milhous Nixon, president of the United States of America. Catchlove and Newens give pride of place to the photograph of the two of them in cane chairs. Nixon is leaning forward in a purposeful pose; Ceausescu is sitting back in his chair, his pompadour flowing richly about his head. Poor old Celac is there to translate, perched on a stool like a gnome on a toadstool and grinning as if his life depended on it.

It was not Nixon's first visit to Romania; he had been fêted in Bucharest on an earlier trip in 1967 when he had been a mere former vice president and down on his political luck. Nor was it his first involvement with Romanian politics. Hannah Pakula in her biography of Queen Marie supplies a somewhat vinegary footnote about American support for a Romanian arms dealer, Nicolae Malaxa:

In 1946 Malaxa fled with a large fortune to the United States. Although he was a known Nazi collaborator, corporate partner of Hermann Goering, and supporter of the Iron Guard, he was helped to enter the United States, where he remained until his death in 1965, by high-ranking US officials. Among these was Richard Nixon, then the junior senator for California, who wrote a letter to the Defence Production Administration urging the approval of Malaxa's application for permanent residency. Nixon's efforts in Malaxa's behalf are documented in the Congressional Record of October 5, 1962.

The 1969 visit was the first by an American president to a Warsaw Pact country; part of its purpose was to gee up American public opinion for his later trips to communist China. The running thread was knocking Moscow by embracing the leaders of those countries who made public their disapproval of Soviet imperialism, but Nixon seemed to appreciate the lavish welcome given by cheering Romanians, perhaps not speculating too much on the secret police-men standing at the back, watching. And there does seem to have been some mysterious personal chemistry between the two leaders.

The most perceptive US commentator on American relations with Romania throughout the Ceausescu years was David Funderburk, an academic who served as ambassador to Bucharest from 1981 to 1985. His book *Pinstripes and Reds* is an indictment of America's appease-ment of a leader he rightly saw as a monstrous dictator for marginal foreign-policy gains; in the broad sweep of his argument Nixon comes in for a sharp smack in the chops:

Nixon has expressed the esteem in which he holds Ceausescu, in statements, books and in correspondence. For example, in January 1983, Nixon sent a congratulatory letter to Ceausescu on the occasion of his 65th birthday. In the letter, a copy of which was passed to me along with the original for delivery, Nixon referred to Ceausescu as one of the greatest leaders of the world who valiantly carries out an independent foreign policy. When I saw Nixon's letter to Ceausescu, I noted that anyone who could say such things: 1) does not know Ceausescu; 2) must be especially grateful for getting the welcome treatment in Bucharest which is not available to him everywhere; and 3) must share the conviction that the accumulation, misuse, and imposition of unchecked power equals greatness.

Funderburk's three points apply widely.

By the turn of the decade Ceausescu must have felt well pleased with himself: not only was the peasant boy from Scornicesti the most powerful man in Romania, but he was also greatly loved by his people and enjoyed the growing respect of the world's international statesmen, including the most powerful man on the globe, Richard Nixon. His son, Valentin, was less easily impressed.

Valentin Ceausescu returned to Romania in 1970, having spent three years out of the power game in London studying physics at Imperial College. 'When I came back things were different. I saw him all the time on TV. In just those three years, it was obvious that there had been a change.' The personality cult had grown, his father seemed more distant, more locked up in his own world than ever. Valentin sipped his scotch. 'When you asked me earlier what was he like, my first thought was "We never had a talk". And that's true. If you wanted to talk as a human being, he was very removed. I could never go and talk freely with him. Perhaps I never tried. This didn't just happen in the last year, but throughout the whole thing.'

No one describes the hollowness of the man better than Valentin. He was his eldest son and he didn't know him at all.

King Goes Mad

By common consent Ceausescu went mad during his and Elena's trip to China and North Korea in 1971. He went out an unstable paranoiac; he came back a madman. People close to him debate which had the more pernicious influence, China or North Korea. Terrible as Mao's China was as it emerged from the throes of the Cultural Revolution, North Korea was then and still is the more totalitarian society, and enjoys the distinction of being the most pyramidal society on earth.

North Korea is an abomination to man as a freethinking individual. Pyongyang, the capital, is a city turned into a shrine, an urban monument to Kim Il Sung, known as Our Great Leader. Every main road has a central lane solely for his use, vast photographs of father and son adorn every living room, public and private, and every adult has to wear a badge with Kim Il Sung's face on it. The badges are coded, with different backgrounds denoting the adult's status, high or low, in this rigidly stratified society. A sixty-foot statue of the Great Leader is visible on the city skyline from virtually any position. The Great Leader will be followed by his son, Kim Jong Il. A South Korean film director, Shin Sang Ok, who spent time in a North Korean prison, said: 'The only criticism of Kim Il Sung I heard in the North was the screams of those being led to execution.' Orwell, if he had been alive, would have been depressed that life had so crashingly outperformed his imagination.

And Ceausescu, seeing all this, was stunned. For when he glimpsed the grotesque, insane monolithism of North Korea, where homage to the Communist-cum-Confucianist 'thoughts' of Kim Il Sung was as automatic to its people as breathing, he wanted his own country to be like it. The long, horrible nightmare of the Romanian people was about to begin in earnest.

Celac the interpreter sees 1971 as a key date. 'Up to 1971, by Marxist standards, he was able to generate new ideas within the limits of the system. After his visit to China and North Korea in 1971, something of crucial importance must have happened in his mind. What he saw in North Korea was an image of real socialism – that is, total regimentation. Of course, everything was fundamentally wrong from the beginning. But the practical approaches until 1971 were mitigated by a degree of realism and independent thinking which had not yet become militant and destructive nationalism.

'I think that all his life he believed in what he considered to be the generous idea of socialism and Communism. But in 1971 he apparently discovered the uses of pyramidal organisation inherent in one-party rule. And he discovered the crucial importance of the top of the pyramid. He hated and despised Stalin who had enjoyed just such a position, but Ceausescu hated Stalin because he saw him as a leader of an Evil Empire. The evilness of it was its imperial character, not its ideology. Hence Ceausescu was blind to his own messianic bent. So 1971 was the moment of rupture for him and the date of the misfortunes he brought with him.'

Celac had clearly spent a great amount of time thinking through his ideas on Ceausescu. After he had been sacked in 1978, it took two years before he could think straight, he said. So he had a decade to marshal his thoughts. His analysis of his old master is compelling. He went on: 'The rupture inside his head in 1971 was also crucial because it led to a changed relationship between the two members of the Ceausescu couple. From that moment his wife acquired a definite influence on him. The explanation should be seen on two different levels: one is Freudian. It must have had something to do with their intimate life, perhaps with their sexuality.'

Pacepa's unreliable memoirs certainly speak of Elena as being the more sexually active of the two parties. As early as Chapter One of *Red Horizons* Elena appears in the doorway of Ceausescu's office, 'dressing gown entirely unbuttoned, hair in disarray, eyes red and swollen. . . . "That's why I love you so much." Slipping her hand under Ceausescu's sweater, she cooed, "I need you, Nick. Let's go to bed." ' And so on and so forth. Pacepa may, of course, have been amusing himself with erotic invention, but it seems odd that Elena would always be the main protagonist in a free-flowing sexual fantasy created by the secret policeman; perhaps there is some truth in the Freudian explanation of their changed relationship.

Celac continued: 'Until then she had been a submissive peasant wife. After 1971 she increasingly became the demanding, bossy, ill-tempered woman.' Here the evidence of Elena's behaviour, reported in Pacepa and by other sources, is far too strong to be dismissed. 'Another possible explanation of the changed relationship is a syndrome I have noted in families of peasant abstraction: after many years of otherwise normal family life, the starting point in terms of wealth – land – suddenly becomes important in their relationship, even though the property issue had not been relevant for decades. That is what precisely happened with Ceausescu and Elena. She came from a wealthier family. His father was a drunk and the laughing stock of the village. Elena could have married better, and decades after the wedding this old, long-buried power relationship returns.

'The other level of explanation is that she might have discovered, by instinct rather than wit, that Ceausescu's vulnerable point was his extreme, though well-hidden, egocentrism. He had a great sense of his own importance in history. It was precisely that weakness that was played on by her and the key figures in his entourage in subsequent years. On many occasions, I saw him confused and indecisive. That trait became more and more obvious as he advanced in age. He began to rely on her for strength and for constant confirmation of his importance and manhood or' – he paused to select the better word – 'manliness. This is, of course, a shrink's explanation, but I think there is something in it.'

After 1971, Ceausescu became a harder person to work for. 'He became considerably more brisk, even rude, and more intolerant of the people he was working with. And distrustful too.' Celac illustrates with a story, delighting in a harmless piece of *Schadenfreude* at the expense of Ceausescu's Spanish-language interpreter. In 1972, the year after the North Korea trip, Ceausescu went on a tour of Latin American countries. The region was still rocking from the CIA-backed coup in Chile when General Pinochet seized power from the democratically elected leftist government. 'During this tour there was, naturally, great mention of the word "agreement". Ceausescu agreed this, he agreed that. But whenever the interpreter could sense the word about to crop up in a conversation, he broke out into a cold sweat because he knew what was coming. The Spanish word for "agreement" is *compromisa*, which in both Romanian and English sounds like the word "compromise". Every time the Spanish interpreter said "*compromisa*" Ceausescu would stop in his tracks, cuff him, and say: "Listen, I didn't say compromise, I said agreement. Agreement. OK!" The interpreter had already explained countless times, but each time Ceausescu forgot. It was a clear sign of his mental deterioration. He just couldn't remember what was going on, and the word might crop up several times in the same speech.'

Elena did very little to combat these traits in her husband. Instead, she made it her life's work to bolster the huge, thin-shelled ostrich egg of his ego. 'A phrase she would often repeat to him, sometimes in the presence of witnesses – I was one – was "They don't deserve you. You are too great for them." ' The whole snivelling circle of sycophants, according to Celac, dedicated their time and energy to buoying up the Ceausescu ego. It was the only route to the top.

But Ceausescu was a tough-minded, shrewd man. How could he bear the sycophants? Celac mused on this: 'He certainly wasn't stupid. He had sharp peasant wit. I would not want to sound racialist, but a sudden fall in his creative thinking with all the psychological complexes that go with that may have been due to a genetic deficiency because he had no genetic record of intellectual work. So the year 1971 must have also marked the exhaustion of the creative part of his intellect.'

Although the dictator's mind was fizzling out, his physical strength was remarkable. Pacepa remarks on his ability to keep up with an exhausting schedule, hopping in and out of airports. Both his parents lived to a great age, a fact that caused mounting despair in Romania as the years rolled by and Ceausescu appeared as physically hale and hearty as ever.

The most obvious consequence of the trip to China and North Korea, to those Romanians not privy to Ceausescu's day-to-day behaviour, was that Elena's star began to shine so much that it became the second most dazzling in the firmament. The elevation of the party leader's wife was a scandalous break with revolutionary discipline in pure Marxist-Leninist terms, but Ceausescu had already shipped anchor on that in his nationalist speech in 1968 over the Soviet invasion of Czechoslovakia. Meeting Madame Mao, then in full song in Peking, was something of a mind-rupture for Elena, too. Here was a wife who was a leading political figure in her own right. Elena took the lesson to heart. In July 1971 she was elected a member of the Central Commission on Socio-Economic Forecasting and in July 1972 she became a full member of the Central Committee of the RCP. She was elected a member of the Executive Committee in June 1973. In November 1974, at the 11th Party Congress, she was made a member of the Political Executive Committee. (Ceausescu had renamed the Politburo thus in a classic exercise of the Frenzy.) In January 1977 she became a member of the party's highest body, the Permanent Bureau of the Political Executive Committee. This alphabetical soup was the only information the ordinary Romanian had to go on that Elena was getting fancy ideas about herself.

With Elena and the sycophants on the up and up, other, infinitely more capable people went down. 1971 was the year in which Maurer decided he had had enough, though he delayed his official departure until 1974. For Ion Iliescu, too, 1971 marked a turning point in what had been a fond relationship with the dictator. Before 1971 he was once photographed playing a garden game with the dictator and Elena: they make a happy threesome. The dictator and Iliescu were photographed again glad-handing in North Korea. But on the plane back Bucharest gossip says that Ceausescu and Iliescu had a furious row over what they had seen; whatever happened, Iliescu was shortly after demoted. Although, later, he climbed back into favour with the dictator, their relationship was – so the gossips say – never as close again. Iliescu accepted his demotion with a stoic, some would say cynical, grace. He never took public issue with the vilenesses of the Ceausescu regime, confining himself to one or two very rare coded remarks critical of this or that aspect.

A change that affected people's lives directly was the Mini-Cultural Revolution which started immediately on the couple's return from North Korea. What it meant in practical terms to people like Petru Clej, now an able and uncompromising journalist on the newspaper *Romania Libera*, then a young teenager, was 'a crackdown on western influences. The police would stop boys wearing long hair, women wearing short skirts, jeans. Western pop music was disapproved of: it just wasn't played on the radio stations. There were attacks on intellectuals who stepped out of line and against so-called decadent art. Writers were criticised for not supporting the RCP and educating the people.'

When people did not understand the new teaching, the Securitate stepped in. The misuse of psychiatry as a cosh to subdue dissent is well documented in the Soviet Union; but it was used extensively in Romania. Amnesty International painstakingly kept track of this abuse. Their reports make depressing, almost monotonous reading. Amnesty's record of gross human-rights abuses was available for everyone in the West to read at the time. If it was read by those who danced attendance on Ceausescu, they gave no sign.

Some of the wretches in Ceausescu's gulag had never been let out since Gheorghiu-Dej's time; only the names of the prison changed. Take, for example, the case of Ilona Luca, an ethnic Hungarian related to Vasile Luca, who was purged from the Central Committee in 1952. Ilona was first arrested in 1956 and charged with 'anti-state agitation' after demonstrating against the Soviet invasion of Hungary. She was sentenced to twenty years' imprisonment and served the sentence in various prisons throughout Romania. In 1972 she was transferred on a court order to a psychiatric clinic where she was reportedly treated for 'political paranoia'. A year later she was transferred to the Dr Petru Groza Psychiatric Hospital, named after the first pro-communist head of government, where she was still detained in the late Seventies. The Dr Petru Groza Hospital, situated in the Bucharest suburbs, makes Doftana prison seem like a sweetshop. According to Amnesty, the complex was surrounded by a two-metre metallic fence, topped with barbed wire. Around the fence were strong neon lights which altered each night. There were at least four watchtowers, each guarded twenty-four hours a day by armed militia men. Inspections with dogs – specially trained German shepherds – took place several times a day.

The death rate was high. For example, in January and February 1975 six people – one woman and five men – died from, variously, a heart attack, TB, syphilis, jaundice and other unspecified diseases. All were reportedly aged under thirty. Former prisoners told Amnesty that the deaths were due to drug overdoses injected against the prisoners' will, lack of sanitation and bad hygiene, which led to widespread skin diseases throughout the hospital. Coffins were made by the prisoners themselves. Relatives were not necessarily informed of a prisoner's death until months – in one case a year – after death.

One refinement of cruelty for the 150 or so politicals who were inside the hospital in 1975 was the presence of 250 or so genuinely psychiatrically ill people, many violently disturbed, some murderous. The stench of piss and shit was unbearable in the toilets, the threat of assault from a deranged patient ever-present. No wonder that at least one political volunteered to the authorities that he had become a 'convinced Marxist'; further, he said he now realised that the 'Romanian social order is better than any capitalist social order'. This 'convert' was soon released, presumably because the Securitate recognised that they had broken him.

Beatings were common; poor food a constant scourge, sometimes deliberately made extremely salty to drive the prisoner desperate with thirst. But the most feared ordeal was involuntary drug injections.

These caused apathy, lethargy, slowing down of the psychomotor reactions and, Amnesty writes, 'above all subjective fears of irreparable psychological damage'. Although the dissidents were sane when they went into the gulag, some were no longer so when they came out.

Virtually anybody could be diagnosed as mentally ill if he or she fell foul of the regime. Psychiatric ill-treatment was not the only tool used by the Securitate to screw down dissent. But, as a perversion of the medical ideal, it perhaps was the starkest example of the repression. The following cases are examples. Stefan Gavrila was a 33-year-old Orthodox priest when he wrote a letter in 1973 to the Patriarch of the Orthodox Church, complaining that church officials were corrupt and were cooperating with the Securitate. He received no reply, but was excommunicated and confined in a psychiatric hospital. Haralamb Ionescu was a 68-year-old lawyer and freelance journalist when he was arrested in 1975 for writing letters to the United Nations complaining about human-rights abuses in Romania. He was sent to Dr Petru Groza Hospital, where he was diagnosed as suffering from 'advanced stages of arterio sclerosis and senile dementia'. After spending eighteen months in the 'hospital', he was released to find his house and savings 'confiscated'. Vasile Paraschiv, an employee at a petrochemical works, suffered repeated arrests, detentions and forced psychiatric treatment from 1969 onwards. In December 1976 he was diagnosed as a paranoiac, suffering delusional psychosis. His medical background was described on his case report:

Persecution complex, neurotic behaviour, delusions, pathological hyperboulia, self-preservation drive disturbed (hunger strike).

The doctors found in their psychological examination that Paraschiv had:

discordant character structure; paranoiac; since 1969 depressive state has become much more apparent; overagitated by minor psycho traumas (claims his flat was taken away from him) [it had been, by the Securitate], facial expression rigid, depressive; querulous; angry monologues; systematic persecution complex manifested with his family, place of work and vis-à-vis his superiors and state authorities; writes numerous complaints to the authorities of the Socialist Republic of Romania and foreign officials.

Delete hunger strike, the missing flat and the complaints to the state authorities and Paraschiv's alleged behaviour becomes surreally like that observed by those close to Ceausescu on his return from North Korea. In Ceausescu's Romania madness was enthroned, sanity a disease.

In 1974 – the year Maurer walked away – Ceausescu made himself the first president of Romania. (Before there had either been kings or general secretaries.) What made his inauguration ceremony seem more like a monarch's investiture was the introduction of a sceptre, dating back to Vlad the Impaler's time when Wallachian princes used to carry a kind of truncheon. The presentation of the sceptre took place on 28 March 1974. A few days later, the surrealist painter Salvador Dali sent Ceausescu a congratulatory telegram. It appeared in *Scinteia* and read as follows: 'I deeply appreciate the historical act of your introducing the presidential sceptre.' Radio Free Europe reported that the editor, who had failed to spot the thinly veiled sarcasm, was rumoured to have been fired on the spot.

Later that year, to mark the 11th Party Congress, Dumitru Popescu set out a few modest thoughts on the personality of the dictator:

All people love and praise their heroes because [those heroes] quench their thirst for perfection. . . . Other peoples had in their history Julius Caesar, Alexander of Macedonia, Pericles, Cromwell, Napoleon, Peter the Great and Lincoln. We have Nicolae Ceausescu!

And there were always foreigners around willing to kiss the madman's cheeks. Step forward, Margaret Hilda Thatcher, the newly victorious leader of the Conservative Party. Her trip, in early September 1975, was billed as a success by the *Daily Telegraph*:

Mrs Thatcher, Leader of the Opposition, spent two hours discussing world affairs with President Ceausescu of Romania. It was a very 'open and candid exchange of views', she said. After meeting the president, she spent a further two hours discussing Romania's chemical industry with his wife, Dr Elena Ceausescu. . . . Romanian officials were much impressed by Mrs Thatcher's special knowledge of scientific matters and by the keen interest she took in the research institute run by the President's wife. Romania's 'first lady' is a scientist, a member of the academy and puts in a hard day's work at her institute.

Quite what Mrs Thatcher – who possesses a genuine chemistry

degree from Oxford University – really discussed with Comrade Doctor Engineer Academician Elena is unknown. The paper reserved a special coy tone for the Thatcher–Ceausescu talks. 'An experienced Romanian official said after the talks that President Ceausescu had obviously been captivated by a "beautiful and charming woman".' *Scinteia* and the rest of the Romanian propaganda machine also feverishly reported the meetings.

A fortnight later Harold Wilson arrived. Michael Davie of the *Observer* reported the visit with a wry bemusement as to its purpose: 'The Prime Minister's car got a puncture; the Union Jack became detached; on and on we went. . . .' Davie recorded that Wilson talked diplomacy with Ceausescu: 'The President of Romania is ready to be friends with anyone. The more visitors he gets, and the more visits he makes, the more countries (he hopes) will protect him against any Russian intervention. He engages therefore in a constant dance of visits and counter-visits,' as good a description of the Frenzy as any Western reporter ever made. The opaque rationale for the talks was made clearer to Davie when he met Lord Plurenden, the former Rudy Sternberg, who 'arrived in Bucharest on the same day as the Prime Minister and also left on the same day.' Lord Plurenden was working as a consultant to a firm that manufactured turkey-plucking equipment. Davie writes: 'Wilson, at Plurenden's urging, was attempting under the chandeliers in the Presidential Palace to push the turkey contract to a conclusion.'

After Wilson had gone, taking his chicken-pluckers with him, Ceausescu in the next few years almost disappears from view in a whirl of getting into and out of aeroplanes. He visited president Tito of Yugoslavia, president Félix Houphouët-Boigny of the Ivory Coast, president Todor Zhivkov of Bulgaria, János Kádár of Hungary, president Ernesto Geisel of Brazil, president Alfonso López of Colombia and José Figueres Ferrer of Costa Rica, and he hosted visits by Leonid Brezhnev of the Soviet Union, Edward Gierek of Poland, Erich Honecker of East Germany, Gustáv Husák of Czechoslovakia, president Agostinho Neto of Angola and president Mathieu Kerekou of the Popular Republic of Benin.

Bucharest was fast becoming a favourite stopover point for right-wing politicians like Nixon, who wanted to bash the Russians, as well as the predictable flow of fellow Marxists. Left and right knocked on Ceausescu's door: from Britain, as well as Wilson and Thatcher, he received Ron Hayward of the Labour Party, and Julian Amery and Edward Heath – the former prime minister – of the Conservative Party. Heath declined to divulge to the author his impressions of Ceausescu or explain why he sent 'congratulations and best wishes' on the occasion of the dictator's sixtieth birthday. Amery appears to have been a bosom pal. His garland in *Homage* was effusive: 'I am constantly reminded of the kindness with which you received me on the occasion of my visits to Bucharest, as much as when I was in Government [as a junior Foreign Office minister] as when I was in Opposition.'

It was not just readers of *Homage* who got the impression that Amery and Ceausescu were pally; so did Cecil Parkinson. At one time, Parkinson visited Romania but did not have an audience with the dictator. However, Parkinson in a letter to the author dated 14 May 1990 wrote: 'Although I went to Romania I did not in fact meet Ceausescu but the person who did meet him that week and on subsequent occasions was Julian Amery who knew him well.' When asked about this relationship, Amery volunteered a couple of Ceausescu's reflections on Mugabe and Nkomo – then rebel contenders for power in Rhodesia – and was otherwise unforthcoming.

The dictator certainly left indelible impressions on the Romanians who crossed his path. One such was Dr Theodor Ionescu, a bone surgeon at the city's great and long-lived emergency Brancovenesc Hospital. After the earthquake which flattened large sectors of Bucharest and killed an estimated 12,000 people in 1977, the Securitate told the doctors that Ceausescu wanted to visit the hospital and comfort the wounded. He said: 'The Securitate wanted a rehearsal with the sick, so we went through a visit with someone pretending to be the president. Everything was arranged with the Securitate beforehand: where he should go, who he was going to meet and so on. I noticed that he did not shake hands with anyone. He was dressed up in a doctor's white coat, which the Securitate had brought with them, but he did not touch anything in the hospital. As he left the hospital, I saw a little scene. The chief of the bodyguards took out this special bottle of alcohol he always carried with him and some sterilised handkerchiefs enclosed in envelopes. Then he and Elena washed their hands while the bodyguard poured the alcohol over them; then they wiped their hands on these special handkerchiefs. It was the first sign to us that he had a paranoid fear of illness.' A year later the dictator was to pull the same trick in Buckingham Palace.

The king was mad, but few dared to say so. There was one great exception. 'Romanian dissent,' Shafir wryly quotes a Western specialist in East European affairs, 'lives in Paris and his name is Paul Goma.' That remark is unfair – not just because the specialist was unable to wander around any of Bucharest's psychiatric institutes. There was an enormous amount of dissent in Romania, but it was passive, not active. There were far fewer workers and intellectuals who confronted brute power head on in Romania than in, say, Czechoslovakia or Poland. That has partly to be explained by the savagery of the Securitate compared to, for example, the Czech secret police, the StB, and partly by the Romanians' lack of a democratic tradition and the historic culture of submission that Valentin – another passive dissident – bemoaned. So the name of Paul Goma does stand out as one of the very few who gripped the live wire of active dissidence.

Goma was born in the province of Bessarabia in 1935, before his parents, village teachers, moved to Transylvania, where he was brought up. He was first arrested in 1951, at the age of sixteen, accused of intending to join the anti-communist partisans. Five years later he was in more serious trouble: for reading out loud parts of a novel where the young hero dreamt of organising a student movement similar to Hungary's, he was sentenced to two years in prison followed by five years' internal exile in some godforsaken part of Romania, away from friends and family. He wrote a novel about his experiences, *Ostinato*, seen through the eyes of a young dissident about to be released from prison. The novel was daring for what it didn't say: there was no fake optimism about the future, and, as Shafir notes, the 'crimes' were not attributed to deviation by relatively unimportant officials. Goma was indicting the system. The Securitate didn't like it. In *Dossier Paul Goma* (Paris, 1977) he recalled a Kafkaesque conversation with the censor who wanted him to demote the rank of the baddie in the Securitate from captain to something less important:

I was told: captain is not proper, make him an NCO. . . . Officers cannot abuse [power]. If they did, the reader might be led into believing the institution itself was wrong. . . . Also, you must carefully weigh the end of the book. . . . One must, at all costs, see the future shining brightly.

Goma stuck to his guns, the Securitate stuck to theirs. Publication of the book was not officially banned in Romania; instead, Shafir reports that 'the printers, allegedly, had refused to set up the type for such an obviously venomous script.' Goma kept up the ack-ack, sending Ceausescu a gloriously cheeky letter – addressed to him, care of the 'Royal Palace' – calling on him to support the Charter 77 activists in Czechoslovakia, like Vaclav Havel:

I turn to you in despair. . . . Only we Romanians keep silent. . . . The Romanians fear the security forces. . . . It consequently seems that only two persons in the country do not fear them: Your Excellency and myself. . . . An entirely different situation would be brought about, should Your Excellency send a similar letter, a declaration of support to Charter 77. I am deeply convinced that millions of Romanians would follow you.

Ceausescu, never noted for his sense of humour, did not see the joke. In a speech delivered in February 1977, the dictator attacked 'traitors of their country, slanderers who would not hesitate, from wherever they happened to be,' to betray it 'like Judas, for a few more pieces of silver'. Goma stung back that the true 'traitors, Romania's enemies are policemen of all ranks, uniforms and functions, I mean the police system'. He was arrested on 1 April 1977. Shafir neatly understates what the Securitate did to Goma: 'When I met him in Paris in the autumn, he still bore the marks of his detention'. Embarrassed by the international press caused by Goma's arrest, Ceausescu had let him go to France.

Of course, it can be said that it is to Ceausescu's credit that Goma's dissent led to exile, not death. But Ceausescu did try to have him killed. The Securitate despatched a hitman, Matei Pavel Haiducu, to Paris to 'take out' Goma. Instead, the hitman defected and told all in his book *J'ai refusé de tuer*. The hitman's book and the whole Goma episode had a profound effect on the French attitude towards Ceausescu, which became one of icy politeness. But the Anglo-Saxon world continued to sweetheart him.

A miners' strike in the Jiu Valley in 1977 was savagely repressed; the strike leaders were promised the world by Ceausescu, who appeared on the third day of the strike from the air. The strikers, they say, stoned the presidential helicopter. Ceausescu was brave to go in person. He was no coward. But nor was he a man of his word. The strike was squashed, its leaders both died in 'accidents' which were never properly investigated. The Securitate was sent in to organise the miners, which they did with consummate success. The fruits of their work were to be seen on the streets of Bucharest thirteen years later.

Six months after the miners' strike was brutally suppressed, Ceausescu was wining and dining in Washington, the guest of president Jimmy Carter. It is almost tragic that Ceausescu conned Carter so completely, because the Georgian peanut farmer was in many ways an honourable president who did succeed in placing human rights on the political agenda. Pacepa paints a portrait of Ceausescu and Elena in Washington, elated at being treated royally at the White House. There is one moment of terror – Pacepa reports that the dictator vomited – when a crowd of Romanian exiles shouted 'Dracula' at him as their limousine whisked by. But otherwise they were delighted. The couple knew the propaganda value of being received by the leader of the Western world: it was another turn of the screw for the down-pressed Romanians.

But American presidents come and go; some, like Nixon, are even fired. The Queen of England was (and is) somebody in a different league to the peasant boy. Ceausescu, Elena and the whole host of sycophants were really looking forward to their trip to London later that summer. Foreign minister Stefan Andrei – according to the unreliable Pacepa – could barely restrain himself at the thought of spending the night at Buckingham Palace: 'I can't wait to pee on its walls and on King George V's furniture.' And that, metaphorically speaking, is exactly what Ceausescu's entourage then proceeded to do.

King Takes Queen

In 1978 Sir Reggie Secondé, British ambassador to Romania, organised Ceausescu's state visit to Buckingham Palace. A well-placed source said that those who invited Ceausescu to the Palace were 'relaxed' about the decision. They knew very well about the reality of Ceausescu's rule. It would all have been in the embassy dispatch, which would have been read by all the key figures: the Queen herself, the prime minister, James Callaghan, and his foreign secretary, Dr David Owen. The Queen is said to have enjoyed the dispatch: 'Normally these things are eulogies,' the source said.

Let us imagine, then, a make-believe plenipotentiary who wrote a fairy tale about King Ceausescu of Ruritania: 'King Ceausescu is an admired and respected figure on the world stage. What can we expect of him when he comes to London? His power is total. Each time he makes a decision, his colleagues run to implement it. He is as authoritarian a tyrant as any found in the world today. His personality cult is ridiculous with crowds of press-ganged Romanians singing "Ceausescu-PCR" to the tune of "Sing a song of sixpence / a pocket full of rye". It's a sinister regime, all too reminiscent of 1938 and 1984. Madame Ceausescu is universally unpopular – a powerful and baleful influence on the King. He has kept himself in power by guile. A Stalinist at home, but he has been rude to the Russians in his foreign policy. At least he got a cheer from his people on that score. His country is standing up to the Russians. The scope and wiliness of his foreign policy is widely admired. As well as this, he is a theoretical exponent of Marxism' – an odd trait in a king, but this is an odd fairy story. 'He has a Cromwellian attitude to austerity and hard work. Judged by his achievements Ceausescu is not a man to be set aside.'

They knew. Her Majesty and the Labour government who told her to welcome Ceausescu as a house guest cannot plead ignorance of what sort of political creature Ceausescu was. They had been given chapter and verse. The explanations given by former prime minister Lord Callaghan and former foreign secretary Dr Owen are that much more curious.

Lord Callaghan wrote to the author on 6 September 1990:

We were in the middle of a vote of confidence in the Government and, as you may recall, the Labour Party did not have a majority. I was busy during the visit trying to ensure the continued life of the Government, so it is hardly surprising that the event took precedence over any such recollections as I have. I do, of course, recall that because of lack of orders at the time for the British aircraft industry we were very happy to be able to enter into an agreement with them to build the BAC 1/11 airliner.

More generally, the West at the time was ready to deal with Ceausescu because he was taking an independent line from that of the Soviet Union in the East West confrontation. You will no doubt remember that early in the war Churchill said something to the effect that he would be ready to sup with the devil if he was an enemy of our enemy. And although the Soviet Union did not fall into that category there was no doubt about the degree of strain in East West relations at the time, and it was very helpful to have one of the members of the Warsaw Pact taking a line that was opposed to the official line of the Soviet Union.

Callaghan's defence is based on two reasons: one, the realpolitik of the time; two, the £300-million-pound order the Romanians had placed in front of the British nose like a carrot in front of a particularly stupid donkey. In Bucharest I put Callaghan's 'realpolitik' argument – first used by Churchill in defence of his deal with Stalin – to Valentin Ceausescu. Valentin replied with a smile on his face: 'Ah, but sometimes the enemy of your enemy is also your enemy.' It's a shorthand rebuttal of the whole basis of his father's foreign policy, one which the Western politicians who fell so completely for the Ceausescu line should ponder. What was the value to the West of Ceausescu's dissent from Moscow's diktat? Was it of inestimable worth? Or was it, in fact, a marginal propaganda gain of little real substance? Ceausescu was an irritant to the Russians, but they never felt threatened by him. They did march their troops up and down near the Romanian border when Ceausescu was visiting China in 1971; but they invaded Czechoslovakia when the Prague spring got out of hand. The difference is clear. Dubček challenged the communist system. Ceausescu never did. He was not, then, a serious 'enemy of my enemy'. The West misread the cards.

The BAC 1/11 coproduction aeroplane project, known as 'Rombac', would seem to be of more concrete benefit to the British if – a rather bleak if – the then Labour government's foreign policy was to be dictated by Hobbesian self-interest. But the day after Ceausescu left the newspapers were carrying hints that all was not going to plan with the aircraft deal. Roland Gribben, business correspondent of the *Daily Telegraph*, wrote on 17 June 1978: 'Romania wants to pay for part of the £300 million aerospace deal with Britain with some of its own products rather than cash.' Such was Ceausescu's miserly reluctance to pay up in hard cash that the Romanians were to offer steel and textiles in exchange, and those of such poor quality that they could not be sold in the West for any price; when pushed for the money, the Romanians proposed part payment in ice cream, yoghourt and strawberries. The British Aerospace and Rolls-Royce accountants could not believe their ears when they were offered perishable fruit. 'We thought they were joking,' said one British Aerospace insider. It was all normal business practice, Ceausescu-style. He made deals the way he played chess, with a completely unscrupulous disregard for the rules.

The British were not the only suckers. Pacepa details the ruse, one of Ceausescu's favourites, in *Red Horizons*. When the two men discussed the terms of the contract between the Canadians and the Romanians over the sale of the CANDU reactor technology, Pacepa claims that Ceausescu ordered that:

Bucharest could make all kinds of non-binding promises to the Canadians, but under no circumstances should it agree to any limitation or precondition for the export of CANDU reactors, Bucharest should obtain a Canadian credit of $1 billion or more, as well as the right to pay not in cash, but in merchandise difficult to export to the West.

It was the same story for British Aerospace. The main revelation in the *Daily Telegraph* piece is that the precise terms of the deal had not been sorted out by the time Ceausescu had left Britain. Gribben writes: 'Details of the "barter" element have still to be settled, but British Aerospace confirmed yesterday that it was negotiating "return orders" for a proportion of the agreement.' Ceausescu had therefore savoured his sweetener – the stay at Buckingham Palace, a political gesture of staggering domestic worth to the dictator – without signing on the dotted line. He had run rings around her Majesty's government. In the end, the British had to send the foreign secretary, Sir Geoffrey Howe, off to Romania in 1985 to perform service as a glorified debt-collector.

Dr Owen wrote to the author on 3 September 1990. His letter is quoted in full:

My memory of the visit is not very good mainly because I think it was a pretty distasteful experience for everyone involved, from the Queen down. He basically manoeuvred for the visit in a way which made it very difficult to avoid. I think it was decided to have him before I became Foreign Secretary in February 1977 as these major visits are usually fixed up to two years in advance. But I say this not to avoid responsibility. I might well have felt as others had that refusing him was too damaging. Julian Amery had, some years before, in the early 1970s, promised a state visit and from memory he [Ceausescu] had fixed on this and refused to be fobbed off with a lower key government to government visit, wanting the full splendour of Buckingham Palace. He had already collected state visits in practically all the other major countries in the world.

I do not understand your statement that 'the visit came, if the newspapers are to be believed, at a difficult time for you because of tense negotiations between the Labour government and the Liberals'. The Lib-Lab pact was agreed in the spring of 1977. I think David Steel was pulling out of the agreement in the summer of 1978 but the private agreement with the Ulster Unionists was more important in underpinning the government. I do not think this had any relevance to the visit.

As to what was the thinking behind the visit, it is true that Ceausescu was the lone voice in the Soviet bloc who sang, in foreign policy, a dissonant tune, albeit an unattractive domestic tune. It was in relation to Israel that Romania was important. In terms of the Camp David Accord, Romania played a small but significant role. On June 15, for example, the Egyptians gave the USA a significant new proposal for the West Bank. There was a lot of toing and froing prior to Cyrus Vance's important meeting on July 18 and 19 at Leeds Castle with Moshe Dyan and the Egyptian Foreign Minister Kamel. I suspect you will find Romania had a little part in all of this. Certainly we were trying to win support from the Soviet Union.

As to memories I have of the visit. The formalities of the Ceausescu visit certainly were something of a waste of time. I am afraid I cannot remember any asides or comic vignettes, or even any telling apercus which will help you flesh out your book. It was reported soon after that the Queen found his 'taster' rather hard to take, whether or not as a slight on palace food or an insight into his paranoia I have no knowledge.

I do not think he was particularly forceful, clever or fatigued. Just a rather nasty dictator of which the world has far too many and which a Foreign

Secretary has to strain to be polite to. I was aware of his Securitate minders. Who could not be?

Who indeed? But Owen's justification for the visit was not the obvious one – to reward Ceausescu for his anti-Russian stance and sweeten him for the aircraft deal – but to ease the Middle East peace talks. It is true that the Frenzy whirled through the Middle East; Ceausescu did a rare balancing act between the PLO and the Israelis, recognising both parties. Ceausescu allowed Romania's Jews to emigrate, in return for which Israel paid the Romanians handsomely, in dollars or kind, for each successful emigrant. And the pro-Israeli lobby in the States also put pressure on the State Department to continue to grant Most Favoured Nation status to Romania, a plum Ceausescu had first been tempted with in 1975. Ceausescu had a close – some would say too close – relationship with Moses Rosen, Romania's chief rabbi. In Rosen's book *The Paper Bridge: Essays in Judaism* (Bucharest, 1973), he includes the following address he made to Ceausescu at a meeting on 29 February 1968: 'Permit me, respected Mr President, to add to this wonderful nosegay of homage the flower of the unanimous respect earned by Romania throughout the world thanks to its wise and large, humanistic foreign policy, which enjoys your direct and continuous guidance.' They were clearly good friends. Pacepa tells us in sickening detail about Ceausescu's links with Yasser Arafat, turned by the ghostwriter into a slavering homosexual monster. The question is, how important was Romania to the peace accord signed between Israel and Egypt? To accept that Romania was an important player in world affairs would be to take Bucharest at its own inflated valuation. There is little reason to suppose that the Israelis, the Egyptians or the PLO would – when it came to the nitty-gritty – place their faith in the Bucharest go-between.

The state visit, which started on 13 June 1978, went beautifully to plan. The source said: 'We do this sort of thing bloody well.' The nuts and bolts of the visit are to be found in the Court Circular page of the *Daily Telegraph*, as dreary in its own way as *Scinteia*: 'The Queen and the Duke of Edinburgh, with the Prince of Wales, Princess Anne, Mrs Mark Phillips and Capt. Mark Phillips and Princess Alice, Duchess of Gloucester, met the President and Madame Ceausescu at Victoria Railway Station. . . .'

The clockwork soldiers stamped around, the crowds cheered enthusiastically – including a phalanx of Securitate-whipped

Romanians, standing by the Admiralty Arch – the Queen wore her nicest smile as she and Ceausescu rode by in the landau, with Celac doing his incredible-shrinking-man act sitting opposite them. On the surface, it was a great success, with every last scene blasted across *Scinteia* and Romanian TV back home. The Queen gave Ceausescu a .270-bore hunting rifle fitted with a telescopic site, while Elena received a gold and diamond brooch. In return, the Ceausescus gave the Queen and Prince Philip two hand-made Romanian carpets.

Behind the scenes, things went not so sweetly. The Queen was said to be discomforted by the thuggishness of Ceausescu's minders, that is, the Securitate. Buckingham Palace prides itself on the excellence of its cuisine and the royal family on the quality of their hospitality, so the 'food-taster' Owen refers to was a sharp slap in the face. The Palace was (it is said) amazed to discover the Ceausescus' tic of washing their hands in alcohol after contact with anyone. According to Ceausescu's maids at his villa in Snagov, this tic was beginning to get out of hand by the late Seventies. 'There had to be a bottle of alcohol in each of the three toilets in the Ceausescu suite,' one maid explained. Pacepa too confirms the tic: 'The chief of his bodyguards was slowly pouring alcohol on their hands, a ritual repeated with religious fanaticism every time Ceausescu shakes hands, whether with people on the street or with foreign heads of state.' It did not take long, it is said, before the Queen realised she had a madman staying under her roof. Nor did the Duke of Edinburgh hit it off with Elena. She was not, it is said, his kind of lady.

The Romanians' antics became increasingly bizarre during the three-day visit. One day Ceausescu was spotted going for a walk in the Palace gardens, followed by his entourage, at six o'clock in the morning. Inside Ceausescu's paranoid head it was completely natural to expect that his hosts would be bugging every single word of his conversation – he would do the same – so the garden was the safest place for a talk. The Queen was not amused, and made it clear that there would never be a return state visit to Bucharest.

There were other unpleasantnesses during the state visit. This narrative has thrown up few heroes, so when a lone, questioning voice is raised it must be applauded. While the establishment – both left and right – kowtowed in front of the dictator, Bernard Levin cried 'boo, sirrah' from the pages of *The Times*. The Levin style is hectoring, obsessive, on a bad day like a battery-operated pub bore. But when wound up and aimed in a dictator's general direction he is rather

(*Left*) Nicolae Ceausescu aged 15.
(*Below*) Elena Petrescu Ceausescu in 1939.

(*Above*) Nicolae Ceausescu aged 37, now a member of the Romanian Communist Party Politburo. (*Right*) The Communist-King Ceausescu depicted by an unsung painter. His sceptre was satirised by Salvador Dali in a letter to the Romanian press. The irony was lost on them and the letter published, leading to the dismissal and disgrace of the editor responsible.

Happy families: (*Top to bottom*)
Nicolae and Elena at blossom time;
daughter Zoia perches on her father's
knee; Zoia, Nicolae, Elena and son
Valentin at home; son Nicu plays
chess with his father (Ceausescu
often cheated).

(*Below*) Ceausescu goes hunting in Snagov, 1975. He was a showy but poor shot, often 'bagging' game that had actually been killed by Securitate snipers.

(*Above*) Elena, Nicolae and Ion Iliescu enjoy a garden game back in 1976.

(*Below*) The swimming-pool in the Ceausescus' villa Neptun, by the Black Sea: to Western eyes a study in kitsch, to the Romanian people an unheard of luxury.

Britain welcomes the Dictator: (*Top*) the Queen, Ceausescu and (facing them in the coach) Sergiu Celac, the interpreter, trot by the crowds on their way to Buckingham Palace in 1978. (*Above*) the Dictator enjoys the attentions of James Callaghan (left foreground) and Harold Wilson (right foreground) after breakfast at Chequers, while Roy Hattersley looks on (2nd from left, back row).

(*Left*) Ion Maurer was one of the contenders for power in 1965 until he ruled himself out of the race, allowing Ceausescu to go forward – a decision he would live to regret.

(*Below*) Power slips from the Great Dictator on 21 December 1989 as he addresses a jeering crowd. This picture is taken from a live broadcast on Romanian television which made the people suddenly aware that Ceausescu was vulnerable, and helped to trigger the revolution.

Tanks in Bucharest's main square on Christmas Day 1989.

The death mask of the Dictator, looking astonishingly youthful, after his execution on 25 December 1989.

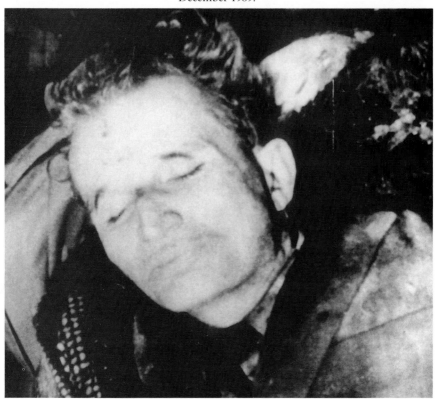

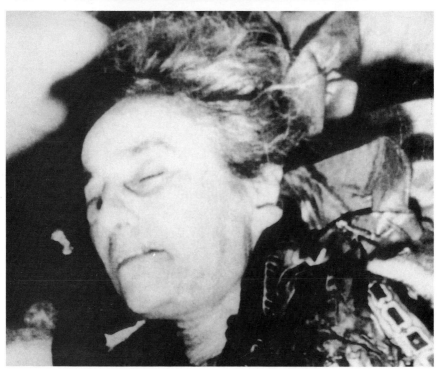

Elena, his lifelong mate, stayed with him until the end.

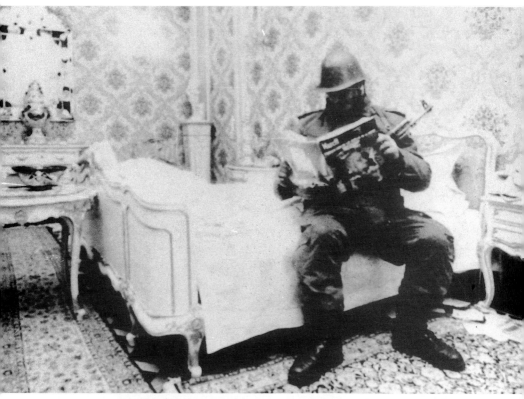

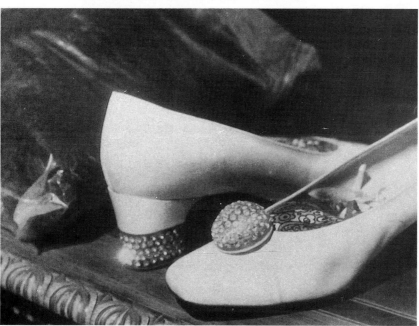

Despite long-lived rumours, the Romanian people were stunned by the Ceausescus'
luxurious lifestyle. (*Top*) A soldier reads a banned French magazine in the Ceausescus'
bedroom in the Primavera Palace, 29 December 1989. (*Above*) Elena's
diamond-studded shoes are displayed on 5 January 1990.

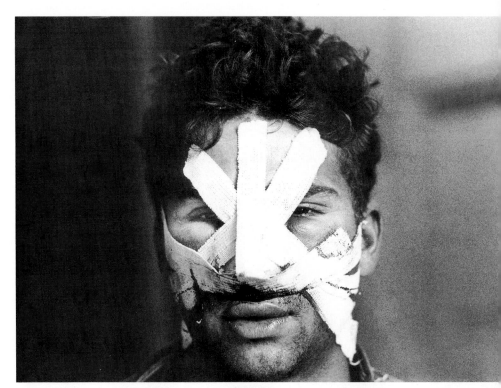

Aftermath: in June 1990 fighting broke out in Bucharest, sparked off by President Ion Iliescu's order to clear a protest group of tramps from the streets. (*Top*) A casulty of street violence. (*Above*) a group of miners who 'spontaneously' turned up and ruthlessly quelled the fighting.

wonderful. His first article, timed for day one of the visit, Tuesday 13 June, was entitled 'And how is your family, Mr Ceausescu?' The text was extremely rude. To pick out some of the choicer cuts:

Beside the political corruption and nepotism Ceausescu practises, Castro and Tito are modest men, Brezhnev is a political ascetic, and Stalin himself was a humble servant . . . racketeer. . . . Romania has one of the harshest and most complete of communist dictatorships when it comes to the internal liberties of the Romanian people. The Securitate are ubiquitous and the country's rulers (Ceausescu and his relations, that is) are above the law, while thought control and censorship rival anything to be found in the Soviet Empire.

Levin understood the value of the visit to the dictator:

A state visit, mind, not a head-of-government one; the distinction may seem unimportant, but it is crucial in defining the status of the visitor and of his visit, and the fact that he is being officially received by the Queen on behalf of Britain, rather than by the Prime Minister on behalf of the Government, will certainly be used in Romania (and indeed here) to suggest that Ceausescu and his policies commend themselves to the British people.

Over three days, Levin cited political and religious oppression, as the great and the good scraped and bowed before the dictator. Levin did succeed in souring the atmosphere, according to the source – not his selection of words, but the tone with which he articulated 'Bernard Levin'. Ceausescu or his minders were sufficiently embarrassed to grant exit visas to one suffering family Levin's articles highlighted, perhaps the only good consequence of the visit. The source mentioned this bonus too, with a quiet nod of approval.

Another hero is Ion Ratiu, then a Romanian exile in London, who staged a protest against the visit outside Claridge's, when the dictator was holding a return banquet for the Queen. For his lonely blow for Romanian democracy, he was arrested by the Metropolitan Police. Ceausescu was made an honorary Knight Grand Cross of the Order of the Bath, the highest award that can be given to a foreign citizen. The Queen was given a Star of the Socialist Republic of Romania medal, First Class.

The *State Visit of President Nicolae Ceausescu to the United Kingdom, June 1979* – printed in Timisoara as part of the propaganda machine – is the book of the tour. It quotes various politicians in keen anticipation of the visit. Mrs Thatcher was generous in her praise: 'I have been to

Romania, one of the first visits I paid after I became Leader of my Party and my conversation with President Ceausescu made a deep impression on me. I greatly admire . . .' et cetera. The Labour government gave Ceausescu lunch at Number Ten. The book gives lengthy coverage to an article by the journalist 'Melvin' Stockwood in *The Times*: 'Whether or not we favour a Communist economy there has been a marked improvement in the standard of living since Mr Ceausescu came into office. . . .' The journalist 'Melvin' was in fact Mervyn Stockwood, then bishop of Southwark, who got it into his head that Romania was nice as pie. When contacted by the author he said: 'Don't bother about me.'

A 'Reception in honour of President Nicolae Ceausescu and Madame Elena Ceausescu [was] Given by the Speaker of the House of Commons at the Palace of Westminster':

During the Reception, which took place in an atmosphere of warm friendship, President Nicolae Ceausescu and Madame Elena Ceausescu had cordial conversations with Members of Parliament from the Labour, Conservative and Liberal Parties, with the Rt. Hon. Michael Foot, Lord President of the Council and Leader of the House of Commons, the Rt. Hon. The Lord Frederick Peart, Lord Privy Seal and Leader of The House of Lords, the Rt. Hon. The Lord Elwyn Jones, CH, Lord High Chancellor of Great Britain, the Rt. Hon. Margaret Thatcher MP, Leader of the Opposition in the House of Commons, ex-Prime Minister Edward Heath, the Rt. Hon. The Lord Goronwy-Roberts, Minister of State for Foreign and Commonwealth Affairs, with chairmen of various Parliament commissions and members of the Parliament Group of Anglo-Romanian friendship in the House of Commons, the Rt. Hon. James Johnson, MP, Labour Party, Chairman of the Group, the Rt. Hon. Barnaby Dreysen, MP, Conservative Party, Vice-Chairman, the Rt. Hon. Richard Crawshaw, MP, Labour Party, Secretary, the Rt. Hon. Ray Mawby, Conservative Party, MP, Treasurer.

Further establishment names were published in *Homage* later that year. Under the 'Outstanding Personality in Contemporary History' section, the following names are listed as having sent congratulatory telegrams to the dictator: Stan Newens, British Labour MP; James Callaghan, prime minister; John Parkinson and David Wise of the British Co-operative Party; Professors A. Cameron and P. Owen of Imperial College, London; David Rockefeller; Sir Kenneth Keith, chairman of Rolls-Royce; Allen Greenwood, vice chairman of British Aerospace; A. Bernard of Shell International Petroleum; Maurice

Hodgson, chairman of ICI; Lord Mais, of the Chamber of Commerce and Industry; B. R. Long of Stuncroft Ltd; Everett Long, director general of General Electric; A. C. R. Cunliffe-Mitchard, chairman of Casroyle Ltd.

Ceausescu's joy meant the people's despair. Mariana Celac, the interpreter's sister, recalled her depression at seeing Ceausescu fêted by the Queen of England and all the Queen's men: 'The coverage on TV ran for one week, for several hours a day. Everything was shown, the carriages, the costumes, the jewellery, the breakfasts, the lunches, the dinners, the banquets. . . .' What was so distressing for Mariana was that she and others had unsuccessfully lobbied sources close to British diplomatic circles, beseeching them not to allow Ceausescu to go to the Palace.

The Romanians doing the begging were not unknown to Her Majesty's government. One such petitioner was, according to Mariana, Dan Hurmuzescu, a 'delightful old gentleman, who was very pro-British, I loved him'. He had, she understood, worked undercover for the British secret service during the war, and spent the years from 1947 to 1964 in Gheorghiu-Dej's prison network. (Ivor Porter did not know him, but then he worked for the sabotage arm, the SOE, and would not necessarily have known about Hurmuzescu's work.) Certainly, Mariana recalled, when he died in 1985 the British military attaché appeared at his burial in full uniform. 'He was very close to the British embassy. He specifically told me that he had protested to the British embassy that the trip would prove to be a "disaster". The Hurmuzescu argument was: "Because the prestige of the British royal family was so high, it would contribute to the consolidation of Ceausescu's authority. People would be enormously impressed that the head of such a small country would meet the Queen of England. The President of the United States is a commoner, but the Queen . . . that was different. Ceausescu did not deserve such backing and support."'

The visit really upset Hurmuzescu, Mariana Celac said. He was an economist, after all, having studied for his doctorate at Lord Keynes's feet at Cambridge before the war. He told the embassy that 'even in economic terms it was a very bad deal. He could not see any economic value behind this deal for Britain.' The old man's complaints were swept aside. At least, thanks to the military attaché, we gave him a good funeral. The visit sapped the morale of those who sought to oppose Ceausescu, more powerfully than a million issues of *Scinteia* or a thousand extra Securitate men on the streets. Prince Ghica was another who was depressed to see the Queen play host to Ceausescu: 'I was very angry'; he sounded fiercer in the original French: '*J'étais très fâché.*'

And the source's summing-up of the whole jamboree? 'He was given a knighthood. It's a thing that goes with state visits. Has done since Elizabeth I's day. It's meaningless.'

King Takes Pawns

One morning the civil engineer woke up to find his hole had gone missing. It wasn't just a small hole, but a huge one, measuring 12,000 cubic metres, the vast access for an underground station he was building for the new Bucharest metro. The civil engineer, let's call him Petre, drew a sketch of it in my notebook: five metres deep by six metres wide by 30 metres long. Petre had that morning got on the tram to take him to the hole as he had done the day before. He went all the way to the end of the tramline. No hole. He got on the tram and retraced his route. Still, no hole. He got out where the hole should have been and found, instead of the hole, no hole. There were trees and grass and park benches and flowers peeping out of the soil. Petre could not believe his eyes. What had happened to his hole?

The night before – after the engineer had gone home at seven o'clock in the evening – the dictator had decided to make a welcome speech to the new students at the Polytechnic Institute in Bucharest, as he had done from time to time in the past, the following day. The park opposite the Polytechnic where Ceausescu normally made the speech was in mid-air, because of the engineer's hole. So, throughout the night, hundreds of labourers, army soldiers and specially requisitioned trucks and mechanical diggers worked flat out to fill in the hole. Then they planted uprooted trees, turf, park benches and flowers to make everything look exactly like it always did. They finished the work at six o'clock in the morning, half an hour before Petre started work. And all because no one dared tell the dictator that he couldn't make the speech because there was a hole.

One morning the maids at Snagov woke up to find the parrot had gone missing. As had its cage. Maria 'Mia' Popescu, a red-haired maid who lived in the nearby village of Snagov, where the church bells, dogs and radios were silenced lest they upset the Ceausescus, told me the story. 'There was a talking parrot in the villa which counted to ten.

It was really clever. It got to know our names and would call them out. It used to say to me "Eh, Mia, eh, Mia". There was a gardener at the villa, who used to act the fool a lot. His name was Nicu. So we used to call after him, "Ah, Nicu, don't be so stupid." The parrot heard this and started repeating it: "Stupid Nicu, stupid Nicu, stupid Nicu." One day Ceausescu and the ministers arrived for a conference. And one of them said in a quiet voice, when Ceausescu wasn't around, "Stupid Nicu", because they were often angry about the son's bad behaviour. The parrot heard this and started saying, "Stupid Nicu, stupid Nicu, stupid Nicu." All the ministers went silent. Then one said: "What's the matter with the parrot?" But the parrot would not shut up. It kept on saying: "Stupid Nicu, stupid Nicu, stupid Nicu." The ministers moved away from the parrot so they could not be blamed for what it was saying. And then the Securitate came around and started interrogating us all. "Who has taught the parrot to say bad things about the Comrade's son?" Well, they were told about the gardener but they didn't believe it. The next morning when we started work, one of my first jobs was to clean the parrot's cage. But it had gone, vanished, and the cage too. The Securitate had taken it away.'

And then one morning Ceausescu woke up to find that Pacepa had gone missing.

The defection of the number-two man in the Securitate's external espionage system to the CIA in July 1978 was a numbing blow to the dictator, coming just after his great triumph in London. Nicu recalled: 'Being the number-two man he knew a lot of important information about Romanian intelligence and all the networks abroad. That's why they were forced to change all the networks. At the same time they created a new unit to look at the Pacepa problem.' This team of witch-hunters interrogated everyone who seemed close to Pacepa. If someone knew Pacepa, they were in trouble. Many were fired or knocked down the Securitate or party pecking order. Suspicion raged in Bucharest after all Ceausescu's paranoid insecurity was proved true. There really had been a viper in the nest.

Pacepa, or, more correctly, the ghostwriter, says in *Red Horizons*:

A few days after General Pacepa's disappearance, the United States embassy and other Western diplomats in Romania described Bucharest as a city under siege. The headquarters of the RCP's Central Committee and the residence of its leader were under heavy guard, while security troops patrolled Bucharest night and day. Nicolae Ceausescu, reportedly ill and confined to his residence, cancelled all activities and disappeared from public view. In September 1978, Western press and diplomatic sources in Bucharest reported that General Pacepa's disappearance was followed by the greatest political purge in post-war Romania. A third of the ruling Council of Ministers were demoted. Twenty-two ambassadors were replaced, and more than a dozen high-ranking security officers were arrested, while several dozen more simply vanished from sight in the turmoil.

As is often the case, the ghostwriter is overegging the pudding. It may have been the greatest purge in Ceausescu's time, but it was not the worst purge in the era of postwar Romania. Nevertheless, there was an awful lot of vanishing going on.

The effect of Pacepa's defection on Ceausescu's mental state was to destabilise him even more. He became quite crazy for a time and suffered a further, permanent loss of proportion. What talent there remained in his circle was removed in the witch-hunt that followed the defection. Among many others, Sergiu Celac was fired. His subversive chat and contacts with known dissidents was discovered in the witch-hunt, though the explicit reason for his dismissal was a lack of reference to Ceausescu's thoughts in Celac's published writing. He was now no longer interpreter to Ceausescu, but was, as ever, listening to the drums: 'The gossip in the months that followed said it was a traumatic shock. Ceausescu and his family liked and trusted Pacepa. That is why his defection came as such a shock. Stefan Andrei, Ceausescu's foreign minister, told me that he would never refer to Pacepa by name, only as "the traitor".'

Faced with the loss of Pacepa, Ceausescu turned even more for support to Elena. Nicu, who by the late Seventies was beginning to emerge from his playboy grub-stage into the full-blown butterfly of the anointed heir, watched the power relationship between his father and mother more closely than anyone else: 'Until the end of the Seventies, my mother's personality was not visible but overshadowed by my father. At the end of the Seventies – after Pacepa left – she started to take control of the political situation. She was the one who had most influence over my father. She spent more time with him than anyone else, and that matters too. The political and economic situation became worse and worse, but with Elena always there it became more and more difficult to talk to him. She didn't have the political training. After Pacepa, the circle of people around him became smaller and smaller. They reached a situation where all the decisions they took only reflected this small circle.'

Ability became even more of a hindrance in Ceausescu's Romania. The only test was blind obedience to the dictator. Both Nicu and Valentin are openly scathing about the people their father chose to have around him. Nicu said: 'They blocked ideas. The old men in the party were not adaptable. Worse, they kept new people with new ideas from coming in. Nothing of the beautiful principles of communism remained. It is difficult to draw a line between stupidity and unwillingness to change. In general, they were extremely conservative.' Part of Nicu's irritation with the old men who surrounded his father can be explained by his frustrated attempts to win more power for himself, but he undoubtedly had a point. Nicu reserved a special contempt for Tudor Postelnicu, an interior minister and effective head of the Securitate for the whole of this period, leading right up to the revolution. After Elena, Postelnicu was the most powerful person in the regime. One character in *Red Horizons* describes him in not exactly glowing terms as: 'That freak? That dwarf? That lush?' Nicu was equally polite: 'He was little, fat and stupid. And deceitful.

'Postelnicu just wanted to have power. He was in a position to find out anything about anybody and to blackmail everyone, just in case. Perhaps, when Pacepa defected, this helped Postelnicu because they had to clear out some people in the Securitate. He may have used Pacepa to clear out his enemies.' Nicu paused, to let the accusation that Postelnicu too might have been in the pay of the CIA hang in the air. He made no further comment and supplied no evidence. Almost certainly there is nothing in this unspoken hint – otherwise Postelnicu would have got out before the revolution – but it reveals the web of suspicion and personal hatreds which entrapped all the creatures at the top of the Socialist Republic of Romania.

Valentin was less involved in the power play, but equally contemptuous. He said: 'The quality of the people was obvious. They were incompetent. They were hollow men. They spent most of the time playing cards. Some of them I got to know in prison.' He made a shrug, eloquently suggesting worthlessness. Valentin and his friend Gabriel Costache then discussed what was known as the 'complex of indications'. These were orders, but 'indications' was the word that was used. No one in a position of authority in Romania could arrive at an important decision, but waited for 'indications'. Valentin said: 'Certain people would appeal to higher judgements for their own interests. No one could challenge a wrong decision because the higher-ups could invoke "the complex of indications". No verification was possible, because who would go and seek it? At the top there was no challenge. No one would contradict him. No one would say "nonsense".'

The 'complex of indications' eased corruption; otherwise, it worsened the paralysis of the system. In a pyramidal system there is a huge weight of decision-making on the top. And as the Eighties grew older, those feeding the apex with information became a smaller and smaller clique of self-serving sycophants, led by a secret policeman derided as a 'freak, dwarf and lush', the whole circus being whipped by Elena, the ring-mistress, a woman of stunted intellect but forbidding hatreds. And right at the apex stood an ailing madman. The mystery is not that there was a bloody revolution, but that it took so long in coming.

How did the sycophants come to be chosen? Celac dryly refers to 'a form of natural selection. The holes in the sieve were of variable size. They varied over time, with his personality changes. In Russia one of the criteria for political survival was to be able to hold one's drink – that was Brezhnev's trick. In Romania, it was sycophancy. The champion for playing the game, as long as he could hold his own, was Stefan Andrei, long-time member of the government, who certainly had an intellectual grasp of the situation. He had a very acute sense of timing and mood. He could wait weeks before putting through a proposal, waiting for Ceausescu's mood to be right. That was the only real basis for the competition for favour in the ruling hierarchy: how to please the boss.' Shortness, too, was an asset, Celac said. Postelnicu and Emil Bobu, vice president and also 'little, fat and stupid' in Nicu's generous appraisal, were both near pygmies. Celac himself, though of ordinary height, is certainly not a tall man. 'The pictures of Ceausescu at airports with foreign dignitaries were always taken from a foreshortened angle to make sure that he looked as big or bigger than the other person. This is often very difficult to do, so they had to touch up the photographs quite a lot.' The stock *Scinteia* pictures of Ceausescu in the Eighties show a man about twenty years younger, with all the wrinkles and lines smoothed out. Occasionally, the retouching work was so poor that the dictator appeared to sprout extra limbs. Celac referred to a famous photograph of Ceausescu and Zhivkov, the more easy-going Bulgarian dictator, in 1989: 'For some reason Zhivkov had a hat and Ceausescu did not in the original, so they painted in a hat for Ceausescu. And that meant they had to paint in a hand to hold the hat, which they did. But they didn't think to paint out one of his real hands, so Ceausescu appeared in *Scinteia* with three hands.'

But in Ceausescu's mind the sycophants' three-handed reality became the truth. Celac cited one of the most interesting examples of how Ceausescu's mind worked: 'He always took his own inventions as external outputs. They became trumped supports for his actions. Long before I was sacked there was some Warsaw Pact meeting in Moscow when a new, tighter structure was discussed, with Romania arguing for a looser structure. In order to give that position popular support, he asked the propaganda chief for "spontaneous" meetings of the working people to cheer him on his return. So the sycophants filled pages and pages of the press, in almost identical language. That was done on his orders, after an important event. On the next trip, he did not give any orders for "spontaneous" demonstrations and was amazed and even angry that such "support" was not forthcoming. The sycophants drew the obvious lesson and the propaganda machinery worked automatically from then on.'

The sycophants had a more difficult time of it as Ceausescu grew older. The reality of a doddering, elderly man, suffering from a variety of debilitating ailments, not the least of which was madness, was far removed from the wonder-working, lion-hearted 'Genius of the Carpathians' of the legend. Their ingenuity was especially taxed when it came to hunting. Ceausescu was enormously proud of his prowess with the gun, a prowess which had no basis whatsoever in reality. Celac said: 'The sycophants even invented a special device, a portable fence, which they would arrange like a funnel, with the opening exactly in front of his stand. The animals would be trapped by this funnel and all come towards him.' Even so, he often missed, with the game being picked off by Securitate snipers and then credited to the dictator. There is a photograph of Ceausescu hunting taken towards the end. It shows an old man, his body jerking spastically at the gun's recoil, with the barrel flailing in the air.

David Steel, then leader of the British Liberal Party, went hunting in Romania in the late Seventies. Steel had been invited to Romania when he met Ceausescu on the state visit in 1978. The fact that he took up the offer is something he probably regrets today, but he agreed to talk to the author about it. Steel recalled: 'I first met him at Buckingham Palace in 1978. Mrs Thatcher went out of the room as I came in. It wasn't much of a conversation. There was hardly any banter, but Ceausescu knew his stuff. My abiding impression of him was that he was very wooden. He invited me to come to Romania and I accepted. I went fairly soon after Edward Heath had visited the country. The drill was that you stayed in a guest house. These dachas are very isolated with high walls and servants. You were taken backwards and forwards in a car with a police escort visiting ministries. It was all rather secluded. We asked to see something of the countryside, and flew up north. For the journey back Ceausescu sent a coach from the presidential train up to Suceava [in northern Moldavia]. We trundled back in this carriage which was attached to a humdrum train. The presidential carriage was rather like the Orient Express, with lots of carved woodwork.

'On the day we went hunting it was something of an expedition, lasting the whole day in a great forest with the trees planted in blocks. We had Ceausescu's own gamekeeper with us. He wore a sort of Swiss mountaineer's uniform, dark green, and a hat with a feather on it. We were pulled along by two beautiful black horses with red feather plumes. It was really quite medieval. There were at least four of us in the party: the gamekeeper; myself; Andrew Gifford, my research assistant, who was much more keen on hunting than I; and a man called Dalea, who I think was vice president at the time. At the end of the day, Gifford had done very well, I had shot twelve birds and the vice president had hardly bagged one. Then the gamekeeper announced the score: the vice president had the highest total; I, the honoured guest, came second; and Gifford, the unimportant functionary, came last. It was all done according to protocol.'

At the end of the day Steel realised that the Romanians had no hunting dogs. 'We had children who ran after and retrieved the game for us.' To thank the president for his hospitality, Steel arranged for one of the puppies of his black labrador, Jill, to be given to Ceausescu. 'We called it Gladstone, after the Balkan connection,' said Steel. The dog, renamed Corbu, meaning 'Raven', was an instant success with the dictator. The puppy was to grow up into a companion that would never betray him. Steel met Ceausescu one last time at the funeral of President Tito of Yugoslavia in 1980. Ceausescu clearly had no recollection of meeting Steel and stared blankly at him until the Liberal leader said in French: *'Ça va, le chien?'* Steel said: 'At this he became very effervescent and embraced me.'

Ceausescu did not make Corbu a senator, as Nero made his horse, but the Bucharest wits called the animal 'Comrade' Corbu. It became a regular sight in the capital, being whisked up and down the highways, sometimes in its own private motorcade. Irene Holmer, the wife of the next British ambassador after Sir Reggie Secondé, spotted Corbu one day: 'I saw this black dog sitting all on its own in the back of a Dacia, looking rather pompous with its nose in the air, as black labradors often do.' Corbu was joined by Sherona, a gift from Valentin, a black labrador bitch. The two dogs ate royally. The maid at Snagov, Mia Popescu, said: 'The Securitate told us never to feed the dogs. There was a special doctor who checked the food – it was the best sort of meat. Only when this doctor had tasted the food could they be fed. Corbu always slept with the Comrade at night. During the day the dogs slept in villa 12a, complete with bed, luxury furnishings, television and a telephone. Between 2 p.m. and 4 p.m. every day, the two dogs covered themselves with blankets.' Mia mimed a dog pulling a blanket over itself with its teeth. She said that the dogs were washed daily with a special shampoo and they had their paws wiped clean with a cloth and brush dedicated to the task. The shampoo was called Fa, a West German make, and afterwards the maids had to spray deodorant on the dog. Did the dogs always eat meat? 'Sometimes it was spaghetti bolognaise or sausages. If Ceausescu had a piece of steak, he would always throw some to the dogs.' The dogs' dinner was prepared in the villa kitchens, often cooked with spices. She would pick it up from there, where it was wrapped in cellophane, because they were afraid the dogs would be poisoned.

David Steel added: 'The Romanian ambassador in London, I was told, had to go to Sainsbury's every week and buy British dog biscuits and Winnalot and send them to Bucharest in the diplomatic bag.'

The dogs were a rare touch of normal life in the Ceausescus' cavernous, echoing, unhomely homes. They had a villa or palace in every one of the forty counties in Romania, but there were three main ones they used: Primavera in Bucharest; Snagov, a short ride from the capital, where they had a villa on one side of the lake and a palace on the other; and Neptun, by the Black Sea, which the dictator and Elena visited each summer for a month. All four sites were decked out in the worst possible tyrant-kitsch. There is something international about despotic bad taste, and wandering around their homes after the revolution it was possible to imagine that this was how Ferdinand and Imelda Marcos or Idi Amin's entourage would have lived, if they had been Romanian. But more striking than the tackiness was the lack of individual personality in any of the homes. Valentin provides a good explanation: 'The homes were all decorated by architects – not very good ones in my opinion. Except for their personal belongings, nothing was their own.' The ornateness of the gold toilet-flush handles, the ludicrous bigness of the living rooms and the acreage of the beds conspire against any sort of cosy domesticity. From the uneasy soullessness of their party-decorated homes it becomes almost possible to believe that Ceausescu and Elena were also prisoners. The jail was gold-plated, but, like the rest of the Romanians, the presidential couple could not escape.

Quite the cattiest, and therefore most enjoyable, description of Primavera is drawn by Hannah Pakula, writing in *Vanity Fair* in 1990:

Like most Romanian villas, this one combines elements from three cultures – Turkish, French and German – a cross-fertilisation which often produces charming architectural specimens. Not here. A bastard conglomeration of Germanic lumpishness, Turkish claustrophobia, and dimestore French frou-frou, the Ceausescu home is an all-too-apt metaphor for the lady herself. The furniture is pure party issue – cheap and clumsy. The fabric in the boiseris panels is rayon, heightened by Lurex thread. Everything else is pure kitsch, comrade kitsch – porcelain ballerinas in tutus, synthetic anti-macassars, with gold fringe, little china deer frisking on tables.

The most arresting feature at Neptun, beneath a Securitate watch-tower, was its enormous indoor swimming pool. The circular pool had a coloured mosaic on the bottom, depicting dolphins, starfish, bearded Neptunes with tridents and sea horses. The pool's roof was made up of an extraordinary blue and white tubular cluster which hung down in an effect drunkenly lurching between chandelier, stalactite and central-heating boiler. Light streamed from the cluster's centre, and this could be controlled by a gadget on a wall, which reduced or widened the cluster's aperture. Built in the Sixties, Neptun gave off a strong sense of that period. It was like walking through the set of *Goldfinger*.

The 007 theme was heightened by the datedness of the technology inside the house: an elderly Philips TV with no remote-control switch and a Grundig tape-recorder with spools, not cassettes, at least twenty years behind the times. The Ceausescus slept together in one bedroom, with comrades Corbu and Sherona nestling down on a chaise longue at the foot of the bed. Only Valentin's room at Neptun had some character to it. A bookcase held a good number of thumbed paperbacks, including Samuel Pepys, C. P. Snow, William Faulkner, Maxim Gorki and *The Wounded Toe*, a novel by the Romanian writer Ana Blandiana. Blandiana was, for most of the Eighties, in disgrace; her book was banned because it was considered covertly critical of the regime. The Snagov rules of silence applied in Neptun too, so the music in all the discos and hotel bars of the nearby holiday resort were switched off by police at 10 p.m., to the astonishment of foreign holiday-makers.

The revolution has made it necessary for everyone close to Ceausescu to disparage the old days. But talking to many of the maids, it became clear that their revolutionary ardour was often cosmetic. In a country peopled with food and petrol queues, anyone on Ceausescu's personal staff, no matter how lowly, did a little bit better than the others. The maids at Neptun, for example, enjoyed access to a special Communist Party shop, where fine cuts of meat, fresh vegetables and other goodies were available. They only had to work for the couple one month in the year. So the huge majority were ready to accept the peculiar working conditions the Ceausescus set, in return for their favours. The maids had to work from three to seven in the morning, communicating in whispers, lest they wake up the sleeping couple. Before they started work, they had to pass a medical inspection every single day. The doctor saw that they had no cuts or colds that might infect the presidential couple. Anyone who had the slightest illness was barred from working that day.

One of the maids recalled: 'He once asked us whether there was any food in the shops.' Of course, none of them dared to tell him the truth. But there was less food in the shops from 1980 onwards. That year was the start of the food crisis. The Romanian foreign debt stood at roughly $12 billion. At this juncture Ceausescu decided to repay all the country's foreign debts in the shortest time possible. Why? Only Albania and North Korea had no foreign debts. For the economic purity of autarchy they had paid dearly in terms of reduced living standards and all the horrors of a closed society. But Romania had logged up a substantial foreign debt in the Sixties and Seventies and now – at the click of Ceausescu's fingers – it was going to pay it all off. The rationale was Ceausescu's fanatical nationalism: Romania had to be free of foreign moneylenders – only that way could the country be truly independent. But there was no pressure from the world's banks so long as Romania kept up with the interest payments. And at the time a large portion of Latin America was bouncing its cheques on the interest, with many of the world's banks realising to their dismay that there was little they could do to force any country to keep paying.

Exports were boosted, imports cut. One of the few Romanian commodities of good enough quality to export was food. The bulk of this went to the Soviet Union. According to Radio Free Europe research based on Soviet figures – not phantasmagorically unreliable Romanian ones – Romanian meat deliveries to the Soviet Union more than tripled from 1983 to 1985, more than doubling in 1985 alone. In 1985 meat accounted for 52 per cent of the value of Romanian food exports to the Soviet Union. The meat delivered by Romania amounted to 24 per cent of the Soviet Union's total meat imports in 1985, with Romania becoming the Soviet Union's biggest supplier of meat to Comecon. It was the same story for maize, vegetables, fruit and wine. From the end of 1983, food rationing became part of ordinary life. Queues for staples like bread and potatoes stretched around the blocks of Bucharest. Queues for petrol were counted in days. A special employment subculture was created, with the elderly and the underemployed being paid, often in kind, to queue while the better-off went to their underheated, underlit offices.

As well as paying off the capital of the foreign debt, these food exports helped to subsidise the chronically inefficient industrial white elephants Ceausescu so loved to conceive. For example, the Romanian steel industry consumed mammoth quantities of energy, so much that Ceausescu introduced a light-bulb law, restricting the country to the use of only 40-watt bulbs. But the end product of the steel industry was such dross no one would buy it. The Danube–Black Sea canal – the Canal of Death where Prince Ghica watched his friends die – was finally completed at great expense. Work had stopped in the mid-Fifties, perhaps in mute recognition of the appalling loss of life, so Ceausescu was supremely delighted formally to open a project which had seemed too big for Gheorghiu-Dej. But to what end? The canal by 1987 was running at only a tenth of its potential traffic. The big plan may have looked attractive, but no one at the top of the decision-making pyramid ever bothered to study the glum details. Frenzy ruled: do this, do that, came the commands. And no one answered back.

These monstrous economic deformities would not have been possible in an open society. But Romania was anything but open. Overarching every activity was the Securitate, watching, listening, waiting. Criticism was clubbed, cramped, confined. The novelist Saul Bellow, who visited Romania in the early Eighties, described the atmosphere beautifully in *The Dean's December* with just one phrase about the listening bugs with which the Securitate monitored foreigners staying at the Inter-Continental Hotel: 'devices behind the draperies, tapes spinning in insulated gloom'. The clicks on the telephone line were pregnant with menace; the most casual conversation with a stranger was guarded as if one's life depended on it. Throughout the country, every conversation was conducted as if a third party was listening in.

And still the West's leaders came to pay homage. America's vice president George Bush arrived in Bucharest in September 1983 for four hours of 'vigorous, real and frank' talks with the dictator, whom he called 'one of the good communists'. The usual propaganda blitz took place around this visit. It could be argued that it was very difficult for the Americans to understand what was going on because of the Securitate's grip on life – but in 1983 Pacepa had been informing the CIA for five years as the highest-ranking defector from the Warsaw Pact.

Ceausescu's weapons of oppression were put down on paper too. In March 1983 – six months before Bush wafted through the capital – the Great Romanian Typewriter Decree was enacted. It is a stunning document of totalitarian control, published openly for all the world to read:

The renting or lending of a typewriter is forbidden. Every owner of a typewriter must have for it an authorisation from the militia, which can be issued only after a request has been made. All private persons who have a typewriter must, in the next few days, seek to be issued with such an authorisation.

Such a request, in writing, must be sent to the municipal militia, or the town or community militia, wherever the applicant happens to reside, and the following details must be supplied: first and second names of the applicant; names of his parents; place and date of birth; address; profession; place of work; type and design number of the typewriter; how it was obtained (purchase, gift, inheritance); and for what purpose it is being used.

If the application is granted, the applicant will receive an authorisation for the typwriter within 60 days. On a specified date, the owner of the typwriter must report with the machine at the militia office in order to provide an example of his typing. A similar example has to be provided every year, specifically during the first two months of the year, as well as after every repair to the typewriter. If the application is refused, the applicant can lodge an appeal, within 60 days, with his local militia. If the appeal is dismissed, the typewriter must be sold within 10 days (with a bill of sale) or given as a gift, to any person possessing the necessary authorisation.

Anyone wishing to buy a typewriter must first of all apply for an authorisation. Anyone who inherits a typewriter or receives one as a gift must apply for an authorisation at once.

Defective typewriters which can no longer be repaired must be sent to a collecting point for such material, but only after the typewriter's keys, numbers and signs have been surrendered to the militia.

If the owner of a typewriter should change his address, he must report to the militia within five days.

The penalties for those few who dared challenge this or any other of the system's diktats were severe, the more so because, as there was so little dissent, it was easy to pick off the few mutinous voices.

One such brave soul was Ioan Guseila. Immediately after the revolution he told his story. He was a taut knot of a man, and spoke with a quiet intensity which was not quite normal. One could see straight away that he had endured a lot for his dissidence and was still suffering mentally. He had been the chief of the energy commission in the Department of Food Industry. He was, then, one of very small number of people in Romania who knew the real statistics of starvation. Under Ceausescu there were two sets of figures – the 'official' lies and the real ones, for the eyes only of the top tier of the RCP. Guseila compiled the real figures. He knew that the regime was enforcing massive cuts in the country's energy demand. And he knew the consequences of those cuts for the country's food supply. 'Bread, meat, milk, beer: the recipes for the constituents were being faked. They were using animal feed instead of flour for bread.' The information revolted him.

He set out to disseminate the facts that passed over his desk. He suffered from the illusion that if more people in the top tier knew the facts, they would act to reverse the policy. So Guseila wrote, anonymously, to a number of important names in the *nomenklatura*. One letter was written to Ioan Ceausescu, the president's brother, who – like everybody else with the magic surname – was a powerful figure and worked in the same ministry. At great personal risk Guseila left his unsigned letter on Ioan Ceausescu's desk. In the letter he explained his fears about the worsening food crisis, he gave the figures to back up his points and pleaded with Ioan to ask his brother, the president, to do something. At night Guseila went round the ministries in Bucharest, phone boxes and a few other places and put posters up on the walls and window panes, highlighting the food crisis and giving the true statistics.

He knew something was wrong when his boss, the minister of food industry, Marin Capisiscu, asked him for the notes he had taken during a meeting. It was odd to ask for the handwritten notes, instead of waiting for them to be typed up.

They came for him on the morning of 6 November 1985. He had just left his modest home for work and had crossed the first street when the Securitate got out of a yellow Dacia and pulled him inside. There were two Securitate colonels in the car; one of them was called Duma Mihai. Guseila was taken to the Securitate wing inside Rahova prison. There he was stripped naked and searched roughly. They looked inside his mouth and prised open his toes to ensure he was not carrying anything subversive. There the two colonels were joined by a third, Colonel Popa. Guseila recalled: 'They shouted at me so much I was intimidated. I felt very afraid. They said they were going to accuse me of armed insurrection – the penalty for that would have been very severe. They had everything. Copies of all the letters I had written, including the one I had placed on Ioan Ceausescu's desk, all the letters to the different ministers and the flyposters I had stuck up.' And they had the window panes from the public phone boxes and the ministries, on which Guseila had pasted his posters. The Securitate had taken out the panes whole lest they damage the evidence of his wrongdoing.

The questioning continued after his first, terrifying night in prison. Colonels Popa and Duma kept on asking him 'Where's the gun?' Guseila had no gun but they would not believe him. They asked him where the explosives were, believing that he was planning to blow up a congress in Bucharest. Guseila said, without altering his low monotone: 'They questioned me for sixty-one days.' He didn't know this at the time, but they went round to his house and searched it, from top to bottom, and asked his wife, Margareta, 'Where are the guns?' They dug up the garden too. And they asked him where the others were.

They found no guns. So one day they went round to his house while his wife was not looking and broke into the electricity meter. They told him they had evidence that he had been stealing electricity. If he did not admit his guilt he would be charged with armed insurrection

–the sentence for that would be between twelve and seventeen years. He was very happy to plead guilty to stealing electricity because the sentence for that was only one to four years. He had thought they were going to shoot him. He was fined 32,851 Lei and sentenced to the maximum, four years in jail. It is ironic that the man who tried to let the people know that the regime was stealing energy from them was himself charged with stealing electricity.

Guseila stayed in Rahova, locked up in the fifth section for political prisoners. He had been recalling his story in a state not far from a trance, but he suddenly looked up: 'They tried to exterminate me in there.' His time in prison was made hellish by three common criminals. He said they were Gypsies. One of them was inside for rape, the others for assorted nasty crimes. But they received comforts and benefits from the warders, and in return they made Guseila suffer. He said: 'I know these three were in cahoots with the Securitate. They had all the privileges, packages from home, more food. They were even allowed to watch TV. They pushed me around, wouldn't let me go to the toilet. At wintertime when I was on the toilet they threw water on me.' At the height of the Romanian winter temperatures can plumb 20 degrees Centigrade below freezing. 'They were allowed to sleep during the day, but I was not. They slept like pigs, but at night they wouldn't let me sleep. They stole my food. Sometimes they knocked my food on to the floor. There was one time when I didn't eat for four days. They taunted me so much there was no escape.' He looked up again: 'the bullying got so bad I tried to commit suicide.'

The misery continued when he was finally released from prison to get a labourer's job in a bakery. His family had suffered too, his son was abused at school and Guseila had lost the right of residency in Bucharest. In all we spent two hours in his company. He never smiled once.

Suicide was the one form of self-expression the regime was powerless to stop. It became increasingly popular when Ceausescu decided to knock down old Bucharest, the better to make his monument. Petre the engineer was one of the 15,000 termites who helped to build the House of the People, the Stalinist monstrosity which in so many ways embodies the madness inside Ceausescu's head. Vast as the house is, it was only the centrepiece of an enormous destructive sweep – like a giant's hand brushing down a toy town – across the city. Anything that stood in the way of the House and the Boulevard of Socialist Victory that led up to it had to come down. The people knew the sign. When Ceausescu got out of his limousine and made a gesture like shooing away an angry wasp, they knew they would soon be homeless.

Petre recalled: 'It started in 1982 with a complete block on any construction or renewal of the old buildings. You had to ask for permission to make any improvements to your home and that became impossible. By the end of that year the demolition started. They said they had to demolish homes for the metro, but that was only some of the houses. After a while we realised it was for the new civic centre. But to begin with there was only rubble.' Petre, a transparently decent man, said that he didn't do any demolition work. Perhaps he did, but was too ashamed to talk about it.

The human cost of the demolition programme was not something that disturbed Ceausescu. He may not even have had the faintest inkling of the everyday tragedies that he caused. But today a few enquiries lead immediately to a sea of bleakness. One Romanian friend had three neighbours who lost their homes. Her own was saved by being nine feet outside the swathe. The first neighbour, Emilian, was sixty-eight when his house came crashing down. It was directly on the site of the Big House. He could not take it, and jumped from a nearby block of flats. He was not killed outright but ended up completely paralysed from the neck down, incontinent and brain-damaged. The second neighbour was called Ion, and was a composer. He had a lovely house with a large living room where his grand piano stood and a garden full of cherry trees. His wife loved the cherry trees, the way the stones of the fruit used to crunch underneath her wooden clogs come autumn. They knocked house and garden, cherry trees and all, flat in a matter of days. Afterwards his wife used to look at the soles of her clogs and ask, 'Where are my cherry trees?' They sent her off to a psychiatric clinic. The third neighbour, Petre, was seventy-nine when his home was demolished. He couldn't stop crying and went around Bucharest with a placard around his neck saying: 'They have demolished my house.' Everyone knew who 'they' meant. The Securitate picked up the old man and interrogated him: 'What are you playing at, Granddad? Aren't you afraid?' The old man shook his head. 'No. You've destroyed the house where I was born. What more can you do to me?' They let him go.

A fine bureaucratic twist to the destruction was that the property-owners were required to sign paperwork requesting demolition of their own homes; many victims even had to pay for the cost of demolition. Compensation was always derisory, with people getting a hundred times less than the sum they had paid yearly in rates on their old home.

The Romanians told a joke about Ceausescu's fearful wasp-shoo flick. 'What happens when a wasp gets inside the dictator's car? The whole city comes down.' The joke was truer than what was in the newspapers or on television. Everything went in the swathe: parks, homes, flats, hospitals. Dr Theodor Ionescu was the bone surgeon at the Brancovenesc Hospital in Bucharest – as steeped in traditions and as much a part of the city as Bart's in London – who met Ceausescu when he came to see the earthquake victims in 1977. The hospital treated 30,000 patients a year, handling 50,000 emergency outpatients a year, 200 to 300 emergency patients a day.

But it lay in the path of the Boulevard of Socialist Victory. The doctors in the hospital saw with mounting dismay the demolition of the homes around them, till in 1985 only the hospital stood like an isolated stump in the wasteland.

Dr Ionescu told me: 'One morning, it was a Sunday, without any announcement, he entered the hospital gate. With him was the mayor for this district of Bucharest and his dog, Corbu.' The doctor had heard that Corbu by that time enjoyed the rank of Colonel. 'Of course, there were many Securitate bodyguards around. Inside, there was a discussion about the future of the hospital. While this was going on, Colonel Corbu saw a cat.' The hospital, like many public buildings in Bucharest at the time, was infested with rats, partly because the regime was economising on rat poison. The doctors' response was to resort to nature: the hospital thronged with cats.

'The dog left its master for the cat. The cat skittered off with the dog barking after it. Eventually the dog caught the cat on a doorstep. There was a terrific fight. The dog caught the cat by the neck, but the cat scratched the dog's nose and made it bleed. Ceausescu's reaction was very violent. He first shouted "Corbu" when it ran away after the cat. Then he started screaming at the bodyguards: "What are you doing standing there? Move!" Three of them ran to split up the dog and cat fighting. Of course, all three of them ended up being scratched to pieces. Corbu came back with blood on its nose. Ceausescu hit the dog with his fist. It was a moment of despair, because his closest companion had left him for a cat.

'Ceausescu was very furious. He turned around and left. The bodyguard who looked after the dog picked up Corbu and took him to Elias Hospital.' (This was the one of the best hospitals in Bucharest, the preserve of the party's sick.) 'That afternoon a Securitate car came around, with three bodyguards, to look for the cat. The three Securitate men were very desperate to find the cat because they were afraid they would lose their jobs. So the whole hospital started to look for the cat. All the administration, all the nurses and the porters looked up and down, searched high and low. They caught lots of cats and brought them in front of the three Securitate men and the director of the hospital. But there were so many cats in the hospital. They couldn't find the right one. Cat after cat after cat was caught and shown to them – but it wasn't the right one. At 10.30 that night, having searched all afternoon and most of the evening, they found the right cat. They knew it was the right one because it had a tear on its skin where Corbu had bitten it. The carpenter of the hospital made a special cage. While he was doing so the cat was put in an emergency room and looked after by a special bodyguard. The cat was guarded all night and in the morning she was fed and watered. Usually,' the doctor said, 'we didn't feed the cats. Then the cat went in the special cage to the Institute of Veterinary Medicine. After two weeks we received a note from the Institute of Veterinary Medicine saying the cat had been checked for disease but was all right. In those two weeks Corbu was not allowed to go anywhere near Ceausescu. But even though the cat was all right, we knew that this fight between the dog and the cat meant the end of the hospital.'

The bulldozers came when Ceausescu was on a trip to North Korea. In three days they demolished the hospital, its wards, its gardens, its traditions and memories and an exquisite marble staircase. The staircase had been built by the hospital's founder, a nineteenth-century Romanian aristocrat called Grigore Constantin Brancoveanu, who had promoted something of a cultural renaissance in the country in the 1840s. The hospital had an inscription, set in marble, bearing the legend: 'Who endangers this hospital will be cast out from the love of God.'

When Ceausescu came back from North Korea he asked the district mayor: 'There used to be a hospital here. Where is the hospital?' The mayor was fired. Dr Ionescu said: 'Ceausescu always made sure that someone else took the blame for the decision. That's why, although he always made the decision, he had the party to rubber-stamp it. There was no official document to confirm the demolition of the hospital. There was a report from the mayor's office demanding that the hospital should send a letter asking for its own demolition. But we never complied.'

The doctors were as vulnerable as the rest of the country when it came to destruction. Dr Ionescu himself suffered a heart tremor shortly after the hospital was turned into rubble; the director sustained a massive heart attack on the way back from watching the demolition of the century-old marble staircase and died.

Those people who were fortunate enough to keep their homes had no heat, little light and less food. The winters of 1984 and 1985 were particularly cruel, with the cold cutting a swathe of mortality across the old and very young as wide and unforgiving as the bulldozers. People died from the cold, from pneumonia for standing in the food queues for too long, from starvation because it was too cold to stand in the open. Queues are not invisible; the West knew what was happening from their diplomats' stories of the everyday struggles of ordinary people. And much could be deduced from the regime's decrees. As early as October 1981 the Council of State of the Socialist Republic of Romania decreed:

It shall constitute illegal trading activities and, in accordance with the terms set down in the Penal Code, shall be punishable by six months to five years in prison, to purchase from any state commerical centre or cooperative store, either with a view to hoarding or in any quantity that exceeds the requirements of a family for a period of a month, oil, sugar, wheat or corn flour, rice, coffee and all other foodstuffs the hoarding of which might affect the interests of other consumers and proper provisioning of the population.

People cut down trees in Bucharest's parks for firewood and slept close to their lit gas ovens in their kitchens in the endless hunt for warmth. They died this way, too. An anonymous writer in the *New York Review of Books* recounted in October 1986 the deaths of Grigore Hagiu, a prominent poet, and his wife, Gabriela Cressin, a statistician:

They were at home in the unbearable January days in the winter of 1985 when the temperature sank to minus thirty degrees Centigrade by the window thermometers and minus twenty degrees Centigrade by the radio. After midnight a thin stream of gas appeared in the kitchen. The couple sat down by the stove and tried to get warm. They fell asleep. Some time in the night as they slept the gas went off and came back on again. The couple went on sleeping. They never woke up.

Of course, there were pools of warmth and light. The dictator enjoyed heat in his office and his homes, as did the various tentacles of the Ceausescu octopus. And there was heat aplenty in the crematoria. Saul Bellow in *The Dean's December* described the only warm place the main, quasi-autobiographical character Corde encountered in Romania: the oven where the body of his mother-in-law, Valeria, was burnt.

Here was the heat he had felt underfoot in the hall. It was like a stokehold. It went into the tissues, drove all your moisture to the surface. Corde, who had come down shivering, now felt the hot weight of the fedora, his sweatband soaking. He tried by shallow breathing to keep out the corpse smoke, protect his lungs. . . . There were other bodies preceding Valeria's. Corde could only think of her as the dead, waiting to be burned. As between frost and flames, weren't flames better?

But dying was easy compared to being born. The electricity cuts were blind: bringing instant gloom to ministries, catching old people trapped in lifts in blocks of flats and withdrawing heat and light from hospital incubators for newborn babies.

The horror started back in 1966 when Ceausescu launched his campaign to boost the number of births. The statistics – which were still published then – show that the number of infants born rose from 273,687 in 1966 to 527,764 in 1967. But the comparative figures for Romania, Hungary and East Germany show that this campaign was not needed: in those years Romania had more than double the birth rate of Hungary and twice that of East Germany. The figures, studied closely, pass a quietly devastating indictment on the regime's social engineering. The anonymous writer in the *New York Review* points out that though it took nine months to double the number of newborn babies by banning contraception and abortion, it took more than six years to double the number of gynaecologists, obstetricians, pediatricians and wet-nurses to care for them; never mind the greater number of hospitals, houses, schools and baby milk and baby clothes required. The real tragedy lies in the infant-mortality figures for 1967. The number of births went up by 92.8 per cent; the infant-mortality figures by 145.6 per cent. The state could force women to have unwanted babies. Monthly gynaecological checks were made to ensure that women were not using any banned contraceptive devices; the penalties for doctors helping in illegal abortions were severe. But the state could not force the babies to survive. Hence the bureaucratic change in the way the figures were drawn up. As the writer says: 'By not issuing the birth certificate for a month, the state avoids recognising any deaths that have occurred that month. The infant who has never been born in the sight of the law cannot die.' The origin of the rumour that Ceausescu drank the blood of newborn babies must have come around this time; but the truth is more horrific than the fiction.

As in Britain during the First World War, the agony of what was taking place in Romania was most honestly recorded in poetry. Virtually every other medium of cultural expression – the novel, film, drama, television, journalism – collapsed under the pressure from the Securitate. But some poets found their voice. One such was Ana Blandiana, whose poem 'The Children's Crusade' was circulated widely in samizdat form:

> An entire people not yet on earth
> Condemned to march along from birth
> Foetuses from left to right
> Devoid of hearing and of sight,
> Foetuses on every hand
> Who cannot even understand.
> All march towards the tomb
> Torn from suffering mother's womb
> Condemned to bear, condemned to die,
> And not allowed to question why.

The results of Ceausescu's exercise in social engineering could be seen immediately after the revolution throughout the country in orphanages and hospital wards where the unwanted children lay. The unwanted included the babies suffering from AIDS – though the regime did not recognise that Romania had an AIDS problem. This official blindness made the problem worse, disastrously so. An old medical habit – abandoned in the West long before the Second World War – had lingered in Romania. It was to inject newborn babies with blood to give them greater strength. One batch of blood contaminated with AIDS, probably in a rare aid package from the United States, was the root cause. The lack of fresh, clean needles for the injections led, through cross-infection, to an AIDS epidemic among the young. But as this too officially did not happen, nothing was done about it.

There were other unwanted infants too: mentally handicapped, crippled, or just plain unwanted. They were left to rot in out-of-the-way hospitals and clinics. The Romanians called them the 'irrecuper-ables': literally, unrecoverables. The official policy was that they were so sick no resources should be wasted on them. I only visited one such hospital for 'irrecuperables', Plataresti, about twenty miles from Bucharest. It was enough.

Grey walls, white ceiling, cement floor, no toys, no pictures. Far worse than their sick bodies – unnaturally white, with limbs like sticks, frail trunks topped by huge, domed heads – was the noise the children made. It was a click-click-click sound, dry, not loud, like something a big insect might make. It took a while before we realised they were grinding their teeth. They lay, some of them four to a cot, dotted with flies like currants on dough. The nurses looking after them impressed me as doing the best they could; but they seemed utterly without the benefit of medical training, lacking proper drugs, medical equipment, drips, nappies and good food for the children. There were, in all, three nurses and two cleaners looking after 107 children. There were no doctors on duty that day.

One little click-click-click boy lay on his cot shaking his head and rolling to and fro, to and fro. His name was Emil Teodorescu, aged four. He was half the size of my son, not yet two. His mother, the nurse said, had tried to have an abortion but she didn't succeed. He was suffering from 'Hepatitis B'. The nurse looked around the ward and said most of them came from Bucharest. Before the revolution they had 1.9 Lei a day for each child for medicines; that's a little over a penny.

The next ward was better, with two children to a cot. There were flies again feeding at one child's mouth, and the teeth-grinding noise. One child was foaming at the mouth; his opposite number in the cot was staring dully at him. Infections were a danger. The next ward was the hepatitis isolation unit. One child had sores on its leg; the stench of urine stung the nostrils. Another child had sores on its head. The fourth ward stank like a farmyard. It was full of older children, screaming, wafting flies away, rocking to and fro, to and fro. Before the revolution, the nurse said, they had no one to complain to.

On the way out of the hospital a red-framed noticeboard hung in a place of honour where, before the revolution, they had pinned up a photograph of Nicolae Ceausescu, president of Romania.

Zugzwang

No respite, that autumn of 1985, for the milky-skinned 'irrecuper-
ables' who continued to grind their teeth, unheard, in the wards of the
Plataresti asylum; no respite, either, for wretches like Ioan Guseila
about to enter Rahova prison for his timid dissent; nothing for the
families of the suicides, driven mad by the destruction of their homes
to make way for the Boulevard of Socialist Victory. But buck's fizz for
the members of the 'Guinle Rindalbourne British Parliamentary
Business Delegation Visit to the Socialist Republic of Romania', led
by the former Labour prime minister Harold Wilson, more correctly
titled Lord Wilson of Rievaulx, as their executive Vickers Viscount
aircraft, G-BNAA, specially touched up in Rindalbourne livery, lifted
off from Gatwick airport.

They had been picked up early that morning – Thursday, 17
October – from their homes by uniformed chauffeurs in a fleet of blue
and black Daimler limousines. According to one delegate: 'It was the
sort of freebie which left you agog at the cost of it all.' They were
driven straight on to the airport tarmac before going through the
passport and customs formalities at the VIP north suite at Gatwick,
where the first group photo was taken. The second photo has Lord
Wilson standing at the aircraft door with the rest of the party lined up
on the steps, the gentle grin and heavy, black pouches under his eyes
giving him the appearance of a bewildered panda. There were
seventeen delegates in all, a rum cocktail of MPs, peers, an academic, a
businessman, with a few journalists thrown in, a woman senior pilot
–an *avis rara* in the male-dominated business of flying – and a purple-
robed bishop of the Church of England who, adding yet more lustre
to the delegation, was also the Clerk to the Closet of the Queen.

The trip was organised and financed by Rindalbourne, a rag-trade
import-export business risen to riches partly thanks to Ceausescu's
Romania. The firm operates from a chic, quietly expensive street not
far from Buckingham Palace, hidden behind dwarf orange trees and

miniature firs in a windowbox. A security camera monitors all those who knock on its door, but Rindalbourne does not court publicity. Nigel Edgar Bertrand John Guinle, known as Nigel, and Hilton Ralph Leopold Guinle, known as Tony, are the two brothers behind the firm. They declined to talk to the author. According to the firm's accounts filed at Companies House in 1989, Nigel Guinle's other directorships include Cahoots Clothing Ltd, Man-go Leisure Ltd, Pappa-Ya Ltd, Kee-Wee Company Ltd, the Fruity Fashion Group Ltd and Fruity Girl Ltd.

The accounts list 'importation and sale of ready-made children's, men's and ladies' clothing' as Rindalbourne's business. Much of this was with Romania. Nigel Guinle, the firm's chairman, had visited the country on dozens of occasions, suggesting that he enjoyed Bucharest's confidence. Rindalbourne acted as a middleman, selling Romanian-made textiles to the West. Judging from the sleekness of its head office, it was not an unprofitable trade. The firm's turnover for the year to 30 September 1988 was £11,806,210; its highest-paid director received £160,000. From this comfortable, if not hugely resourced base, Rindalbourne had signed deals with Romania worth £200 million – clearly its directors were self-confident and ambitious entrepreneurs.

The purpose of the visit was to give a high-powered VIP gloss to Rindalbourne's attempts to break out of its rag-trade base into the coal business. Romania was heading for another bitter winter, with its energy supplies dangerously low. Britain had just come to the end of a ruinous coal strike, and now the victorious Conservative government was closing pits and making miners redundant wholesale. The scheme Rindalbourne was working towards was for Romania to buy British coal – perhaps even a recently shut British pit – to ameliorate its own energy crisis; given Romania's shortage of hard currency and Ceausescu's manic drive to cut the country's foreign debt, no hard cash would change hands. But the British coal could be paid for in kind, such as Romanian-made textiles, marketed, of course, by Rindalbourne. This sort of deal is known as countertrade.

The October visit was, in fact, a follow-up to a smaller delegation made in March that year, attended by Lord Wilson and some of the others, when two separate £100-million trade protocols, one for general trade and another for coal, were signed between Romania and Rindalbourne. The numbers, though big, are somewhat illusory. A protocol sounds grander than it actually is, meaning only a draft deal.

Moreover, part of the outline coal deal had envisaged that the National Coal Board, as it was then known, would supply the Romanians with high-quality Rank 301 coking coal. The NCB had since told Rindalbourne that it did not have the supplies of Rank 301 available. Worse, the NCB made it clear that it did not like countertrade arrangements, particularly with Romania. Its stern views had been influenced by an earlier deal between an NCB subsidiary, National Smokeless Fuels, and Romania through another intermediary countertrade company. There had been, typically for Romania, mysterious delays in paying up.

The spring trip had been uncomfortable for the parliamentary delegation, made in a small, noisy aircraft which took an age. This time Rindalbourne was determined to get everything right. The Guinles hoped that the Romanians, impressed by the British dignitaries, would make an unshakeable commitment to the coal-for-clothes deal by signing the first coal-import contract under the terms of the trade protocol already set out. There was talk in the coal business of a contract involving a 50,000-tonne shipment, known in the trade as a 'Panamax' after the maximum tonnage that can be shipped through the Panama canal.

There was not much pretence that the trip was anything other than to further trade between Britain – especially, Rindalbourne – and Romania. Lord Wilson is a director of Rindalbourne. As such, he was in the habit of sending Ceausescu congratulatory telegrams on his birthday until his very last one, in January 1989. In 1988 readers of *Scinteia* were treated to the following:

Only those who have had the responsibility of leading a government can appreciate what this entails. You have raised the Romanian nation to a unique role in the world. Let the wise deliberations of your leadership continue. I'm very glad that in the last three years our relations were able to continue and I have had the opportunity to contribute to the development of economic and cultural relations between our countries.

The style is so different from the Harold Wilson who used to make po-faced, perfectly timed mockery of Edward Heath at the dispatch box in the 1960s that one wonders whether another hand wrote his lines for him. The effect of reading these telegrams, signed 'Lord Wilson of Rievaulx, former Prime Minister of Great Britain' on those few nerve-racked souls inside Romania who sought to oppose

Ceausescu can only be guessed at. The deduction many Romanians might have made is the obvious one that Ceausescu was well supported in the West by eminent people.

Though physically he is remarkably resilient for his age, even in 1985 Lord Wilson's intellectual grip seemed to have lessened somewhat. The former premier's grip on the world was further weakened by alcohol, his favourite tipple the markedly unproletarian one of cognac, which quickly followed the champagne as the Vickers Viscount flew east. One of the group who watched Wilson closely said: 'It was like watching a once great batsman, long past his prime. Wilson stumbled about, not quite with us, and then there would be a little aside, a witty remark, a little flash of genius which reminded you of his old, masterful form.'

The delegation was in practice guided by Lord Wilson's friend and Rindalbourne codirector, Lord Whaddon, the former Labour MP Derek Page. (The fifth director of Rindalbourne, according to Companies House, is Bernard Leigh Krabbendam, who was not on the trip.) Although Lord Whaddon has a gammy leg and uses a walking stick, his mind is perfectly sharp. He was accompanied by his wife, Angela.

There were three Labour MPs, all with mining connections, who seemed genuinely anxious to promote a deal that would give work to British miners. The much-respected deputy Speaker of the House of Commons, Harold Walker, who represents Doncaster in the heart of the South Yorkshire coalfield, with his wife, Mary, was making a return trip to Romania, having been on the earlier, March delegation. The second was Frank Haynes, a former miner who sits for Ashfield, in the Nottingham coalfield, and is something of a House of Commons character. He has been described by *The Times* as 'Albert Steptoe playing the Godfather'. The third socialist was another coalminer, Ron Lewis, the member for Carlisle, who died in 1990. He brought his son, John, along with him. Lewis stood out in the party by being teetotal.

Two Conservative MPs, Andrew Hunter, the member for Basingstoke, and his friend, Richard Alexander, who sits for Newark, also in the Nottinghamshire coalfield, came, turning the trip, with Lord Whaddon, who left Labour to become a Social and Liberal Democrat, into an all-party parliamentary delegation. Given Ceausescu's constant hunger for propaganda accolades, the inclusion of the two Tories was a godsend.

Alexander, described in Roth's *Parliamentary Profiles* as 'aquiline, saturnine, overly serious', once had a package blown up by the Bomb Squad which turned out to be his own alarm clock. In early 1990 Alexander drew some criticism when he advertised his wares in the *House of Commons Magazine*: 'Hardworking backbench Tory MP of 10 years' standing seeks consultancy in order to widen his range of activities'. Such naked honesty is rare in the Mother of Parliaments. He was a paid consultant to Rindalbourne from 1985 to 1990, and once asked a parliamentary question about 'the importation of articles of apparel and clothing accessories' from Romania.

Hunter, a roly-poly former army officer and school teacher, was another enthusiast for Anglo-Romanian trade, having also been on the spring visit. In 1985 and 1986 he asked a total of three parliamentary questions on UK trade with Romania. Neither Conservative MP at this time asked parliamentary questions about human rights in Romania.

Hunter asked these questions, he told the author, 'out of academic curiosity'. He expounded this explanation in a long fax about his interest in Romania. The MP's paternal grandfather, Frederick Ebeneezer Hunter, had worked in the oil business in Romania in the Twenties, under the monarchy: 'My grandfather loved Bucharest, then flourishing as "the Paris of the east". My family folklore duly sanctified the city and from my childhood I had heard stories of its magic. For many years I had therefore longed to see what Bucharest had become.' (Hunter is a man of fine discrimination when it comes to his interest in foreign regimes. He is a vehement supporter of the black quisling homeland state of Bophuthatswana, an ink-blot created by the white South African government, which otherwise enjoys international derision.)

The Right Reverend John Bickersteth, then bishop of Bath and Wells, provided an antidote to Mammon. He brought his assistant, or dresser, along as well, Tim Gregson. The numbers were made up by a businessman, Michael Lanning of Glaxo; Dr David Husain, a chemist of Pembroke College, Cambridge; and three journalists, Lord 'Jock' Bruce-Gardyne of the *Sunday Telegraph*, who died in 1990, Alan Spence of the *Financial Times* and Eve-Ann Prentice of the *Guardian* (who is the daughter of Lord Whaddon). Ms Prentice wrote two articles for the *Guardian* about the Rindalbourne Romanian trade visits. No mention was made in either article that one director of the company was the journalist's father.

Nigel Guinle and his secretary, Sheila Pringle, were the

Rindalbourne presence. An American congressman, Harold Rogers of Kentucky, and the Romanian ambassador to Britain and his wife, Vasile and Venturia Gliga, pulled out at the last moment. For connoisseurs of the tragicomedy that was Ceausescu's Romania, the absence of Mrs Gliga was a loss. Less than a year later, in September 1986, she was apprehended by a store detective in Boots the chemists in Kensington High Street after she had shoplifted a pair of scissors worth four pounds. She and her husband were recalled to Bucharest shortly afterwards.

To mark the company's thanks in anticipation of their hard work, the delegates were each given a document wallet, silver paper knife and an Asprey's silver medallion, the latter valued by the shop at roughly £50 each. The medallion bore the legend 'Anglo-Romanian Peace and Goodwill', with the two flags on one side; on the obverse was the Asprey's punch and silver hallmark, and above: 'The Guinle Rindalbourne British Parliamentary Delegation to Romania led by the Rt Hon Lord Wilson of Rievaulx.' The medallion came in a purple box embossed with a silver decoration, with velvet innards.

There was only one minor irritation to mar the group's outward journey. *The Times* that day carried a long article by – yes – Bernard Levin, entitled 'Repression in single spacing'. Levin wrote:

In addition to his fear of samizdat documents that might make Romanians think about freedom and how they might acquire some, Ceausescu has the no less worrying problem of some bold spirit drawing attention in writing – it is common among his people, of course, by word of mouth – to the almost incredible thieving and looting from the public purse that he and his wife and their enormous families – there are dozens of Ceausescu relations on the padded payroll – have been doing for years.

Now the terror that stalks all tyrants has tugged Ceausescu by the sleeve again. It is no longer enough, in Romania, to limit the ownership of copying machinery to institutions sufficiently reliable not to permit misuse of them: the Romanian dictator has turned his attention to typewriters.

The control of typewriters is much more difficult. For one thing, there are far more of them than of copying machines. For another, there must be thousands of typewriters which only the owners know to exist. And yet a typewriter, given sufficient patience and assiduity on the part of some miscreant, can speak heretical thoughts almost as loudly as the most up-to-date Xerox machine. Whence the Decree of the State Council . . . .

He then proceeded to quote the typewriter decree in full.

Romania has had, in Britain particularly, a much better press than she deserves. Because Ceausescu has, with great skill, gained a limited but genuine independence for his country within the Soviet empire . . . he has come to be thought of as some kind of benign and gentle autocrat rather than the brutal thug that he actually is; the suppression of dissent in Romania has probably been more widespread and more cruel than anywhere in eastern Europe other than the Soviet Union. . . .

One or two of my readers who share my pleasure in poisoning the atmosphere at gatherings of *bien-pensants* sympathetic to the 'socialist' countries of the East may find that their ability to engage in this agreeable sport is enhanced by a recitation, at any inappropriate moment, of the Romanian Typewriter Decree . . . .

Such a hostile piece naturally attracted comment from the group as they read that morning's newspapers. Nigel Guinle's secretary was seen gathering together the copies of *The Times* and stowing them on the aircraft, lest they cause offence in Romania.

It was all smiles, however, on arrival at Bucharest's Otopeni airport. The party was met by Vasile Pungan, Ceausescu's foreign-trade minister and a former ambassador to the Court of St James's, a big, coarse-featured fellow with something of a resemblance to the late fez-toting comedian Tommy Cooper. The current British ambassador to Romania, Philip McKearney, was at the airport, too. A shrewd, tweedy 'old soldier' with a straightforward dislike of the Ceausescu regime, McKearney was uneasy at the opulence of the visit and fearful of what propaganda coups the Romanians would make out of the delegation. He said afterwards: 'The first I heard about the trip was a telegram from the Department of Trade. On meeting them at the airport I thought that some were a bit naive.' A few members of the party, including Alexander and Hunter, went to the British embassy for a chat with McKearney. One of the talking points was whether the embassy was bugged; McKearney agreed with the suggestion that it, like virtually everywhere else in Romania, was. The flight crew in turn were warned by Nigel Guinle not to say anything disparaging about Romania in the hotel rooms, for fear of bugging devices. They were assigned a minder who, they later realised, must have been a highly placed officer in the Securitate.

Andrew Hunter later told the author: 'We were warned that our hotels were going to be bugged. And so with a great deal of tongue in cheek one night as I went to bed I said "I'd like to have a blonde".

Needless to say, one didn't appear. But when we departed a caricature of a baddie from a James Bond film came up to me and said in a Romanian accent: "Mr Hunter, I am sorry that we couldn't provide you with all your requirements."'

At nine o'clock that evening, the party clattered off in a flotilla of ageing Dacia taxis, cannibalised Renault 12s which are omnipresent throughout Romania, to a reception and dinner at the Restaurant Parcul Trandafirilor. (The restaurant was formerly an exclusive dining club for members of the Romanian Academy; it was thrown open to a wider public in a spasm of pique by Elena Ceausescu after the Academicians failed to elect her their president.) The streets seemed dim and empty as they crossed Bucharest. Lord Whaddon told the author later: 'It didn't take much IQ to tell that it was a grim place – the standard of the lighting. It was always one of the things that hit you in Eastern Europe.'

That night at a dinner thrown by the Romanians Lord Wilson rose to his feet, albeit a trifle unsteadily, and delivered an amiable speech of thanks which hobbled to a close when he lifted up his glass and proclaimed: 'To our toasts'. He meant, of course, 'hosts'. He then proceeded to sing 'On Ilkla Moor Baht 'At', a Yorkshire drinking song, in his flat, northern accent. Mouths dropped, gasps were exhaled, the British ambassador, who was also sitting on the top table, blushed puce with embarrassment. Long, low groans were to be heard coming from his direction. The flight engineer, Brian Mees, recalled: 'Someone looked at me and said "I don't believe it". Harold certainly wasn't Pavarotti, but he knew the song all right.' Some of the other delegates, after they had recovered from the initial shock, joined in.

> Wheear has tha' bin sin' ah saw thee?
> On Ilkla Moor baht'at
> Wheear has tha' bin sin' ah saw thee?
> Wheear has tha' bin sin' ah saw thee?
> On Ilkla Moor baht'at
> On Ilkla Moor baht'at
> On Ilkla Moor baht'at.

Lord Wilson sat down to applause. Lord Whaddon got up. He sang Paddy McGinty's goat:

> Now McGinty's goat had a wondrous appetite
> And one day for breakfast he ate some dynamite
> A big box of matches he swallowed all serene

And then he went and swallowed down a pint of paraffin
He sat by the fireside, he didn't give a hang
He swallowed down a spark and exploded with a bang!
So if you get to heaven you can bet a dollar note
That the angel with the whiskers is Paddy McGinty's goat.

Lord Whaddon flourished his stick in the air to beat out the rhythm, adding to the poignancy of the lament.

The following morning one delegate took an early morning dip in the inter-Continental's penthouse swimming pool. He was stunned to find the water, like much else in Romania, unheated.

All day there was a relentless series of meetings with various Romanian officials, beginning with a visit to the chairman of the Romanian Grand National Assembly, Nicolae Giosan, who had been the host of Bernard Weatherill, the Speaker of the House of Commons, on his trip to Romania that year. The party was politely chaperoned around Bucharest, always under the eye of the watchful Securitate. After the Grand National Assembly there was a session with the minister of chemistry at 10.30 a.m., followed by the minister of metallurgy at 11.45 and then a three-hour buffet lunch at the Tei Palace restaurant in Bucharest. And so it went on throughout the visit.

The rolling meetings ensured that it was difficult for any member of the party to mix with 'real' people and kept the delegates from realising what was actually happening. The talks were meaningless because the Romanian officials would not dream of speaking frankly. It was their job, pretty much their sole function, to maintain appearances while genuine power was wielded by a tightly controlled circle centring on Ceausescu, his intimates and the Securitate. The officials were part of the Ceausescu con trick, staging for the Wilson delegation an act well honed for the Romanian public.

Tight as the schedule was, a few of the delegates had been able to do a little shopping. Michael Lanning, the Glaxo man, noted how 'run-down and tatty' the shops were, with very little stocks. Harold Walker, the deputy Speaker of the House of Commons, did manage to buy a tin of fish, which he told the others he would present as a gift to the lobby correspondents of the House of Commons. The fish tin bore the simple, homely legend: *Crap*.

And then there was a change in the programme. Ceausescu had cleared time to meet the most important members of the delegation himself; the journalists, Michael Lanning, Dr Husain and the crew

were not invited. The rest of the party buzzed with anticipation. The
meeting took place, as usual, in Ceausescu's first-floor office in the
Central Committee building, watched over by the painting of
Michael the Brave on his white charger. The Labour MP Frank Haynes
remembered: 'There were no people about, only lots of guards. It was
certainly a big place.'

The colourlessness of Haynes's description chimes with that of his
political opponent Sir Geoffrey Howe, then foreign secretary, who
met Ceausescu in February 1985. Sir Geoffrey was in Bucharest, a city
shivering in the cold apart from the hothouse temperatures within the
dictator's office, to play debt-collector. British Aerospace and Rolls-
Royce were seeking £5 million in payments arrears on the ill-fated
BAC 1/11 deal signed on the 1978 state visit. Sir Geoffrey at first
replied to a letter sent by the author saying that he had no particular
recollections of his meeting; to a second letter, he replied: 'Enough
pestering! Ed.' before going on to write:

Curiously I have no recollection of the building itself, in which my meeting
with Ceausescu took place. But the room felt rather like a modest, gilded,
ballroom with Ceausescu perched none too grandly in the middle of the space
and few, if any, attendants apart from an interpreter and a secretary.

That autumn, according to Haynes, the Wilson delegation 'sat
around the table, but he kept us waiting for about half an hour. When
he came in, the cameras started whirring, and then he did most of the
talking.' This time Ceausescu had some of his lapdogs with him:
Gheorghe Oprea, first vice prime minister, Nicolae Giosan, president
of the Grand National Assembly, and Vasile Pungan.

For some of the party the principal interest was Ceausescu's health.
He had just returned from a gruelling trip to China, where he had
conferred his country's highest honour, the gold-and-silver star of the
First Order of the Socialist Republic of Romania, on the elderly
Chinese leader Deng Xiaoping. A week before the Wilson delegation
met him, *The Times* reported that in China Ceausescu 'delivered his
speech in a weak and somewhat halting voice'. The report quoted a
Romanian journalist who said that Ceausescu was 'very tired' and that
he had been suffering from diabetes for more than a year, but added
that Romanian officials denied that he was suffering from prostate
cancer or another serious illness. The officials were not telling the
whole truth. Ceausescu had been diagnosed as a diabetic in 1976 and it

seems likely that he did undergo surgery on a nonmalignant tumour in his prostate gland that summer.

But the following week there were few signs of ill-health. The British ambassador, Philip McKearney, said: 'Then, as always, really close up he didn't look half bad for his age at all.' Richard Alexander agreed: 'He seemed to be in complete control, willing to talk about local and international politics. He was small, not a timid man, quite well dressed and stood upright.'

Hunter was taken aback with how quietly sinister Ceausescu was: 'My abiding impression of Ceausescu was his eyes. Blue eyes, very, very deep; they were utterly without emotion, sense or sensitivity. They were cold and feelingless; they were utterly ruthless. I shuddered as I found myself, half mesmerised, shaking hands with a mass murderer.'

The conversation between Lord Wilson and Ceausescu was constrained. Maureen MacGlashan, the counsellor at the British embassy in Bucharest and number two to Philip McKearney, said: 'It would have been a very formal meeting in the Central Committee building. The exchanges were always very formalised and stilted, passing through the interpreter, which again would slow things down. But you can't expect to have a serious exchange with a demagogue.' Sir Geoffrey Howe came away with the same impression after his visit earlier in the year: his conversation with Ceausescu 'was almost entirely set-piece and predictable'.

The meeting closed with general expressions of good will on both sides but no firm commitments and no deal. A gift from the Rindalbourne delegation, a large ornamental table centre from a well-known firm of London jewellers, was ceremoniously presented. McKearney said: 'It was something quite big from Asprey's. It was a large piece, a globe surmounted on something. I remember my eyes goggling a bit at the lavishness of it all.'

The Wilson delegation – 'rather naive' in the judgement of Ms MacGlashan – may not have realised, but the real audience for the meeting was the Romanian public, who were treated to a lengthy item on the television news that night and a numbingly dull article in *Scinteia* the following day. For British readers, an unofficial account of the meeting was made later that month in the pages of the *Sunday Telegraph* by the journalist Jock Bruce-Gardyne. He wrote:

Last week I was seated at the feet of President Nicolae Ceausescu of Rumania, the first of Europe's rulers since Napoleon to lend a new dimension to the concept of the Family Man.

He has some little local difficulties. The day we paid our call he'd put the troops into the power stations. Householders in Bucharest get hot water just three hours a day, and the acquisition of a lamp bulb of more than 40 watts can send you to the salt mines. What life is going to be like for your grassroots Rumanian when winter comes does not bear contemplation.

It would have been difficult for the party to find out more about the troops going in to the power stations – even so, it would have been a clue that all was not as rosy as their hosts made out.

Ambassador McKearney was no more inclined to be generous about the visit: 'It seemed that the idea behind the trip was to build up Rindalbourne's position vis-à-vis the authorities. Any back-up they could receive from British politicians would have been very helpful. They hadn't examined the motives of the firm and the use that the Romanians would make of the visit. The whole thing was not a good idea from the point of view of Her Majesty's government. It was not helpful, desirable or useful.'

Rumours in the coal business, a not necessarily reliable source, suggested that Anglo-Romanian coal trade did not flourish as a result of the visit. Even Lord Wilson in a somewhat incoherent interview with the author, which started, 'Ah yes, Ceausescu – he's dead now, isn't he?' did not wax positive about the trip.

Endgame

As reality grew gloomier and gloomier – despite such morale boosters for the regime as the Rindalbourne trip – the sycophants became louder in their claims on behalf of the dictator. The tone was shrill, the content blasphemous to both Christians and Marxist-Leninists (a rare achievement to upset those two ideological camps) and just plain ludicrous to any uncommitted observer.

No Marxist could take Ceausescu seriously after he was seen wandering around on state occasions carrying his sceptre in 1974, the one which so delighted Salvador Dali. The sceptre was the physical embodiment of Ceausescu's drift from the anti-statist, anti-personality bedrock of Marxist thought and practice. Of course, these principles had more often been breached than obeyed in the various communist states since the October revolution, but to play king so blatantly was thought somewhat indecent even among the unblushing despots of the Soviet empire. The 'Bourbonification' of the Ceausescu dynasty can be traced back to the early Seventies, but in the late Eighties it became more and more crass.

'I feel bound to praise you and kiss your temple' wrote the court poet Dumitriu Brandescu on the occasion of the dictator's sixty-eighth birthday in January 1986. Such praise was quite common. Ceausescu's cult of personality became the prescribed opium of the people. The cultists wrenched traditional Christian imagery and metaphor and applied it to their master in rather sickening fashion. Dan Ionescu analysed the religious elements in the glorification of Ceausescu for Radio Free Europe. He noted that some cultist poets had Ceausescu at the head of the 'Romanian Trinity' with Elena and the RCP or Elena and the homeland making up the other two elements. In Ceausescu 'this earth [ravaged by] wars has [found] its saviour'. The dictator was also 'the sacred word', the 'Chosen One', 'a miracle', a 'unifying nimbus' and 'our creed told in Romanian'. The court poet Pavel Peres praises Ceausescu's 'saintly modesty'. Ionescu identified immortality as the divine attribute Ceausescu liked the best. One of the frequent wishes addressed to him in the late Eighties was that he should 'live for ever for the homeland's sake', or, in another poet's words: 'His immortality is our ardent wish / And he will live as long as Our Earth.' One cultist even paraphrased the Nicene Creed:

> Humanity will return to Eden.
> And the Ceausescu Epoch
> Will have no end.

Hardly a cheering thought, Ionescu noted, for the Romanians.

Others, in private conversations with trusted friends, were less enthusiastic. Abuse was rich, varied and imaginative, ranging across the sweep of Romanian society. Sophisticated friends of Dr Dennis Deletant, of London University's School of Slavonic and East European Studies, described the dictator not as the 'Genius of the Carpathians' – as the personality cult claimed – but the near homonym the 'Genitals of the Carpathians'. In the winter of 1988 Celac saw an old man in the street carrying a 'perhaps' bag. (It's a Russian phrase meaning a bag that perhaps may be filled with longed-for foodstuffs if its owner has some luck. Perhaps there will be fruit, perhaps there will be bread, and so on.) Celac carried on: 'He had obviously been queuing for many hours. As I was standing there watching him, he tripped and almost fell. He recovered his balance and said: "Curse them both." It was so deep in people's minds.' Even the highest echelons of the Securitate had their inner, secret, treacherous thoughts they shared from time to time. General Marinescu, who was from 1977 to 1980 the Securitate chief in charge of the dictator's bodyguard, told a Romanian friend of the author that the dictator's plans for agriculture were absurd, and confirmed that the statistics reporting good harvests were inventions. The general, who later became Ceausescu's ambassador to North Korea, saw deep, unsettling similarities between the dictator and Kim Il Sung. 'Nonsense there, nonsense here,' he told my friend.

But still people sang his praises in public. The big rallies in Bucharest and provincial towns continued. They were the result of a mass synchronisation of people, orchestrated by the Securitate, all the more impressive given that there was not a soul among the cheering thousands who did not hate him. The Romanian journalist Petru Clej, who before the revolution was a computer analyst, recalled how the rallies were organised:

'Bucharest was divided into six districts. Each district had a mayor who was also the first secretary of the party in the district. Each mayor had to come up with between 30,000 and 40,000 people, depending on the size and importance of the event. He gave orders to all the party secretaries and institutions beneath him.' By all, Clej meant all: he was working at Fundeni Hospital for some of this period, and knew that hospital technicians and other important workers were not exempt from the ritual.

'Each secretary had to come up with the number of people the mayor required from him. The day before the event the local factory secretary would ask the comrades in charge of each party cell in the factory – perhaps there would be ten cells in a medium-sized factory – to come up with three, five or seven people each. The individuals had to sign a list, promising that they would be at a certain rostering point at 8 a.m., two hours prior to the start of the rally at 10 a.m. Each factory had a set meeting point, where they were given banners and portraits of Ceausescu, and flowers, too. That each group of people had to turn up at the appointed time was the responsibility of that group's leader. He also had to ensure that no one carried bags or had alcohol with them. Once you were let into the auditorium, most commonly the August 23 Stadium, you could not get out, even to go to the toilet. People got to know the ropes, so they made sure that they would not have to go to the toilet. You had to be very continent.

'At 10 a.m. precisely Ceausescu would appear to mass cheers from the people. Well, in fact the only people actually cheering were at the front. They were the Securitate dressed up in workers' clothes, acting as a barrier between the rest of us and him. The ordinary people didn't cheer or shout much, but the volume was made up by a battery of loudspeakers which produced tape-recorded cheers.

'Everything was incredibly formal. He was so far away you could barely see him, and even then he was surrounded by Securitate bodyguards. He would speak for three hours or so, sometimes longer. At set moments the tape recorders and the Securitate would cheer him.

'Then there might be a spectacle, with tens of thousands of youngsters, children and grown-ups dancing in unison or turning round in circles. That would take an hour and a half. Then she might speak for half an hour or so and the tape recorders applauded her too.'

The rallies went robotically to order. When Ceausescu and Elena were driven off at speed, the ordinary people returned to their rostering points to hand back the poles, banners and photographs of their leader for safekeeping until the next time. The flowers, too, had to be returned. The whole performance took up the best part of a day, but faithful attenders received the perks with which obedience was rewarded: special consideration for a request for a new flat, speedier promotion in the factory or just a couple of days off later in the month with no questions asked. There was only one time on the few occasions Clej attended – to replenish and nurse his cynicism – that anything went wrong. That happened in 1985 on the Romanian national day, 23 August, at the August 23 Stadium:

'There was a short incident just after the start. The power supply went dead. This power cut lasted for about twenty seconds and people started to murmur, but the people who led the applause gave the signal and the Securitate started to clap. There were always some fanatics around who would clap at the drop of a hat.'

Even without the stage-managing and the Securitate, the habit of obeisance to the dictator was deeply ingrained. In the summer of 1986 Gabriel Costache came across the dictator near the building site for the House of the Republic: 'Surprisingly, he was not surrounded by the Securitate. It was not official. But near him there were some pedestrians. When they realised who it was they gathered into a crowd. There were about a hundred people there. Ceausescu started to speak and people began to applaud. When he left they clapped him some more. I was surprised. I studied the pedestrians. They were ordinary people. Why were they clapping him? When I started to walk away I heard them start to insult him. It was extremely shocking. No one forced them to applaud. There was no Securitate around. The incident revealed for me a sort of duplicity. Ceausescu was sort of a monster, but in a way we were his accomplices.'

Public obeisance, private spite. The whole country was locked in a mute, passive sulk against the regime. In the summer of 1985, along with a party of travel journalists, I visited Romania for *The Times*. At the height of summer the country's mood felt chilly and morose. No one who was not in an official position would talk to us – the law was that any off-the-cuff conversation with a foreigner had to be reported to the Securitate within twenty-four hours, so few people dared. There were enough clues to know that something was wrong: petrol queues lasted for two or three miles; our female interpreter, Rodika Gabrila, when asked bluntly what she thought of the regime, burst into sobs and said, 'Oh, my country, my country!'; and the group was nearly arrested *en masse* for taking pictures of a market bereft of produce. Hannah Pakula's book on Queen Marie, as a biography of a much-loved royal, was banned in Romania and therefore extremely sought after. We wanted to give the book to Gabrila, who had been an interpreter for Pakula when she was doing her research in Romania. Lest it fall into the wrong hands, the book, at one point, had to be smuggled down a line of journalists waiting at an airport security check so that Gabrila could keep it. It felt less like a biography than a stick of Semtex. But to write about this incident would risk compromising our interpreter, so we too were caught in the web. It was a classic instance of the difficulties of resisting the regime. To know how terrible it was you had to know a Romanian; once you knew a Romanian you were in the web.

None of the journalism written from Romania on that trip, or later, grasped the enormity of the suffering of the people. The piece I wrote did not begin to reveal the extent of the political and social repression that was going on. Few journalists, to our chagrin and regret today, got anywhere near the horror.

British and other Western tourists, arriving in Romania on extremely cheap package holidays, were vociferously discontented. In 1985, large numbers of the 22,500 British tourists who visited Romania complained of disastrous holidays. Radio Free Europe delightedly reported to Romanian listeners that the BBC consumer programme 'Watchdog' found that Romania was at the very top of the complaints league. They complained about the food, the bad lighting in hotels, the queues, the shortages and the incessant pestering by black marketeers eager to change their feeble Lei into hard currency. Ralph Fewins, a cleaning contractor of Bedfont, Middlesex, who paid £1,400 for a two-week holiday in the Hotel Siret in Mamaia, told the *Daily Telegraph* on returning:

The food was diabolical. One night I found a dehydrated caterpillar, an inch and a half long, in my dinner. Yet they kept saying, 'Eat, is good.' The last week of the holiday we were all ill from food poisoning. We stopped eating at the hotel and just lived on bread and Pepsi Cola. My advice is that if anyone offers you a free holiday, plus spending money, you should decline it.

The tourists were free to leave. The huge majority of Romanians were not. The unfree included the dictator's children, all of whom grappled unhappily with their parents' hegemony. Nicu's attempts to do something were the most dramatic. His behaviour was maniacally antisocial, if Pacepa is to be believed. The car accidents, fights and rapes that 'no one dared complain about' were the stuff of legend, so much so that they must have some basis in fact. According to one product of the Bucharest rumour mill, he was plotting against his parents throughout this period. The plotting came to a head in 1986 in what is known as 'Nicu's pre-coup'. It was discovered and squashed. Nicu was sent off, in disgrace, to the Transylvanian town of Sibiu, where he was to rule the roost until the revolution. Alternatively, he may have been sent off in disgrace because his obnoxious social behaviour finally began to embarrass his parents. They bugged him and had him followed, so they would know the evidence better than anyone. He was probably Romania's only licensed lager lout, but he did genuinely see the rot his parents had created.

Around that time Nicu spoke freely to a Romanian friend whom we shall call Ion. Nicu was speaking openly against his father; he was, perhaps, the one man in the country who was in a position to do so without being arrested. He said: 'This man' – Ceausescu – 'is pushing things to a catastrophe. He's faked the harvest figures, the food-supply system is corrupt and people are really suffering. But what does he care? He doesn't know what's happening. He's got no idea of the reality out there.' 'Ion' said that Nicu complained about the impossibility of speaking rationally to his father. But what depressed 'Ion' was that 'although Nicu was criticising the dictator, he had more or less the same reflexes as his father. He told me: "All we need is more greenhouses." He had worked out all the figures for the energy input on a pocket calculator with his father.' 'Ion' shrugged. 'Everything was clear; everything was solved. The only problem was that there were a lot of fools in charge of the greenhouses.'

Nicu was guarded when asked to discuss his 'pre-coup'. Was there any truth in the rumours? He smiled and closed his eyes: 'There were always a lot of rumours in Bucharest.' And the one about the pre-coup? 'No. To take over power, you need to have lots of elements.' It was not a wholesale denial. Why was he sent to Sibiu? 'It's possible that I was sent to Sibiu because some people were afraid of me. In the late Eighties my relationship with both of them got colder.' He paused, to regain what little strength he could summon. 'From the very beginning I was against involving my mother in politics. It got worse and worse in the Eighties.' At this point another Securitate guard entered the hospital room to have a brief word with Nicu's minder. He gestured to the two of them talking and said: 'You see, I've been running away from them all my life and still I haven't succeeded.'

He returned to his theme: 'My mother's influence became more and more. Towards the end I reached the conclusion. The Tito solution.' He lapsed into silence, his eyes closed, a near-corpse. What? 'I don't want to explain.' Please. Nicu opened one eye: 'So Tito's wife was very close to him and then, one day, she was in total isolation.' Why? 'Ask Tito.' Ionna, my interpreter, cracked a joke in Romanian. What was it? She said in English: 'You need a medium.'

Perhaps I did. Nothing was clear; the murk was deep, but the virtue of giving this snatch of conversation verbatim is to show the way Nicu's mind worked and, given the weakness of his position in post-revolutionary Romania, his sneakily admirable high spirits. Later, I learnt that Tito, alarmed at the increasing political ambition and power of his wife, 'sacked' her. She disappeared from public view immediately. If this was what had been in Nicu's mind, the plan clearly failed with his banishment to Sibiu. He continued: 'In the Seventies I could talk to my father and tell him a lot of things. After this less and less. My father was surrounded by people whom I couldn't understand. People who were closer to my mother than my father because they were more afraid of her. She controlled the sycophants. She ruled them. If my father had used this Tito solution then things would have been OK.'

Valentin throughout this period kept some distance from his parents, though he travelled to China with them on one official visit. But they found ways of, if not bringing him to heel, then at least forcing him to acknowledge the reality of their power. One incident cropped up in a conversation with Gabriel Costache, Valentin's friend. Gabriel said that in 1987 the Securitate were following Valentin and his phone was being tapped. (This was probably done by Postelnicu in his constant trawl for blackmail data on anyone within the magic circle, just in case.) That year the Central Institute of Physics, where both Costache and Valentin worked, organised a small international congress. The Securitate were, as usual, everywhere. And then Valentin disappeared for a few days. After the congress was over, the director of the institute was summoned to go and see Ceausescu. The dictator accused the director and the institute of 'neglecting socialism'. Ceausescu went on: 'All you do is organise congresses.' It was a clear hint that he knew all about the congress and, by implication, about Valentin's brief disappearance. Ceausescu then asked the director to draw up a justification for the institute's existence – a clear hint that the institute's days were numbered. Gabriel said: 'The director told me to ask Valentin about the problem. They didn't dare ask Valentin themselves. I told him the problem. I know he spoke to his mother and in this way succeeding in stopping the threat to the institute. The directors were not asked for the justification. The matter was just dropped.'

Relations between the couple and their daughter, Zoia, were also sour. The mathematics institute where Zoia worked was closed down in 1975 by her mother; one Bucharest rumour said that Zoia was punished for continuing a love affair Elena disapproved of. Both stories show that Ceausescu and Elena disciplined their children by punishing, or threatening to punish, those close around them.

Gabriel said that Valentin for most of the Eighties behaved just like anyone else in the department, but that people came to him for help with medicines, flats and passports; help that he did his best to provide. There was a pool of warmth and light and comparative liberty to criticise the regime around all the members of the Ceausescu clan. Although there is every reason to believe Gabriel, what is fascinating is that there were many similar stories of Valentin using his position for good. Valentin the Good Prince was part of the Ceausescu myth, as well defined a character as Nicu the Bad. Sylvia Karim, a Romanian writer who managed to smuggle veiled anti-Ceausescu references into the children's books she wrote, told me one such Good Prince legend. 'A young couple's car broke down about twenty kilometres short of Bucharest. A young man, driving in a simple Dacia, stopped and picked them up. After a few minutes the woman, fed up, started rubbishing Ceausescu: "How dreadful things are . . ." and so on. When they entered Bucharest they asked to be dropped off near a taxi rank, but the driver insisted on taking them home. As they were parting, they introduced themselves. The couple gave their names and the driver said: "I'm Valentin Ceausescu." The young woman fainted. The next day she got a bouquet of flowers from "V.C." so she knew there was no reason to be afraid.'

A near converse of that version is told about Nicu in Steven Sampson's essay 'Rumours in Socialist Romania' in *Survey, A Journal of East-West Studies*, 1984. Sampson writes:

A peasant who was hitch-hiking was picked up by Nicu Ceausescu in his red jaguar. [He didn't have one.] The peasant did not recognise Nicu and told the driver about a demonstration of ethnic Hungarians in Harghita County, at Lake Saint Anna, singing Magyar songs. Nicu took this information to his father, who disciplined the Harghita County Securitate for failing to inform the chief.

Many other such modern myths were told about Nicu the Bad, some ugly, some poignant. A popular one was that Nicu once ran over and killed a young woman, but her family was too terrified to protest. Pacepa breezily refers to Nicu's bad behaviour: 'At 14 he was praised for attaining manhood by raping a classmate, and he was thereupon given his first car. At 15, he got his first boat. And at 16, he became a drunken rowdy, scandalising all of Bucharest with his car accidents and rapes.' This smacks too much of secret policeman's gossip to be trusted, but it gives something of the flavour of the rumours that enmeshed the youngest son. Another rumour, not in Pacepa, was that Nicu had a real Romeo-and-Juliet love affair when a young man, but this was broken up by Elena who did not judge the Juliet figure suitable because she was part Jewish. The detail given to support the story's authenticity is that against her will the young Juliet was forced to have an abortion. Who knows whether this story was true? Perhaps, given the suppression of abortion and the country's fascination with the 'king's sons', it is a reworking of the everyday horror stories of botched abortions, with which the whole country was grimly familiar, and the Nicu legend into a seamless – but false – whole. Nicu specifically told me that he would not talk about his private life; clearly he knew that it was a subject of controversy.

Another, not dissimilar story about Zoia is given in Pacepa. Again, Elena is placed in the role of wicked stepmother, ruining her children's true love by her scheming and hatreds. Elena disapproves of Zoia's new lover, a young journalist called Mihai, and demands that Pacepa organise for him to be sent off to Guinea Conakry:

'I'm sick of having nightmares about him night after night . . . . Remember when we were in Conakry?' she asked. 'The ambassador told us about one of our tractor technicians whose head had just cracked open like a watermelon. It was found to be full of larvae and worms. Remember, the ambassador said they had some kind of bug that laid its eggs through the skin of your head? I want a picture of Mihai's head cracked open like a melon.'

Like different variations of the granny-on-the-roof-rack modern myth, these stories are too similar for them all to be true. Yet there is no doubt that, as Pacepa, unpleasant as ever, says in a subheading in *Red Horizons*, all three were 'disappointing children' to Ceausescu and Elena. They were intelligent enough: Valentin certainly merited his position in the physics institute; Zoia's reputation was not so high in the mathematics institute where she worked but still she was no fool; Nicu, the least intellectually gifted, had great charm. But none of them married happily or got on well with their parents. At the end, Zoia and Nicu had severe problems with alcohol abuse. Just as Nicu was rumoured to have been a flagrant and sometimes violent womaniser, Bucharest gossip put Zoia down as an unhappy nympho-maniac. Everything the dictator and his wife touched turned to dross. The Ceausescu children, like all the other passive dissidents in the country, were trapped in the prison of their parents' making.

Active dissent, even as the regime creaked and groaned with the burden of reconciling the reality of an ailing ruler in his late sixties with the mythic 'unifying nimbus' of the cult, was still rare in the late Eighties. The numbers of people who put their head over the parapet were small: Doina Cornea, the academic at Cluj University who had 'come out' as early as 1983, and her son, Leontin; Ana Blandiana and Mircea Dinescu, both poets; Andrei Pleshu, a teacher of philosophy; Mihai Botez, the mathematician – though he went into exile in the United States a few years before the end; his wife, Mariana Celac, the architect; Dan Desliu, 'a rather bad poet', former Stalinist but doughty opponent of the Securitate; and, not forgetting, the ferocious old Stalinist Silviu Brucan. As well as being roughed up, arrested and subject to anonymous threats from time to time, the dissidents normally lost their jobs as soon as 'they came out'. They could have starved, had it not been for the Western diplomats who started to invite them on a regular basis to embassy cocktail parties. Although the British and other governments were still shamefully timid in their public stance towards the dictator, their officials on the spot proved up to the human need. The last British ambassador before the revolution, Hugh Arbuthnott, and his deputy, Alan Clarke, showed a signal humanity and courage in giving practical help, such as food parcels, to the embattled dissidents. Arbuthnott, now serving in Portugal, wrote to the author explaining that since he was still working for the Foreign Office he could not elaborate on his experiences. Another diplomat who stood out was the Dutch ambassador, Coen Stork. He told me: 'I took my lead from Hugh Arbuthnott.'

The dissidents lived far more restricted and uncomfortable lives than, say, the Czech or Slovak dissidents. Even in prison Vaclav Havel enjoyed a greater sense of freedom than someone like Doina Cornea, who endured a form of house arrest which was nearer solitary confinement than the almost cosy phrase 'house arrest' would suggest. Havel, in prison, had the respect of many of his fellow convicts. In 1988 in Prague he told me that he was often asked to write the informers' reports on the notorious dissident Vaclav Havel, because, unlike most of the inmates, he could write more than his own name. He willingly accepted the challenge to 'mystify' the authorities and towards the end of one period in prison was dictating reports on himself around the clock. But hardly any of the Romanian dissidents were able to cock such snooks at the Ceausescu regime. Once Havel was told by the Czech secret police, the StB, that no one would care if he disappeared: 'he was a nobody'. On his release he returned to his flat to discover thirty Western reporters on his doorstep: President Reagan had mentioned him in a speech that day. The Romanians should have been so lucky. As late as 1987 Reagan ignored congressional pressure and decided to continue Most Favoured Nation status for Romania–United States trade.

One could fall from a state of grace very sharply for the most gentle dissent. The publication of Ana Blandiana's poem 'A Star from My Street' in a selection of children's verse all but blighted her career as a writer. The 'star' of the title is an alley cat called Scallion:

> He dispenses smiles, pawshakes.
> Sometimes a fine,
> Or, better rather,
> A reprimand.
> And everyone pays attention
> And is grateful to him.
> And I was even told
> That a mouse
> Who waited to be seized
> By His Majesty (in person)
> Squeaked softly
> Among the sighs
> 'What an honour for me
> To be swallowed up by Him!'

The capitalisation of the pronoun and the references to His Majesty led the authorities to suspect the poet's true intent; the poet's editors were reprimanded; her column in a magazine was dropped and the children's poetry book where it appeared was pulped.

A more violent threat to the regime exploded in Brasov in November 1987 when workers at the Red Flag truck factory struck. The workers ransacked the local party headquarters and revealed the luxurious life style of the party 'fat cats' – nothing very special to Westerners but probably Croesus-style wealth to the Romanians – before being crushed by Securitate special troops and the army. (The hero worship of the army after the revolution has blurred the fact that the Army High Command was a wholly reliable instrument for repression for the dictator throughout the endgame.) Agerpress, the official government news agency, poured its scorn on the revolt: 'deeds alien to the socialist system' had been committed by 'some elements of the workforce' who had, therefore, damaged the 'honour of the collective'. The Romanian public knew very well how to read between the lines. A revolt by the heroic workers against the supposedly 'workerist' regime of the RCP led by the great worker himself was bad news for Ceausescu. Silviu Brucan, sensing a change in the air, publicly attcked the regime at the end of November 1987:

A period of crisis was opened up in the relationship between the Communist Party and the working class. . . . We have seen in Poland what such a rupture means and how difficult it is for the Party to regain the confidence of the workers, even when the best of intentions to improve their lot is apparent.

Brucan was briefly put under house arrest for his carefully phrased criticisms, which fell far short of a personal attack on the dictator. He had, as ever, judged his words very well. Too much dissent and he might have followed the Red Flag strike ringleaders into prison for hard labour; too little and he would not have received the publicity in the West that ensured a measure of protection. Even so, such an attack required great mettle.

Inside Ceausescu's head such alarums were noises off. His mad knocking down and rebuilding of Romania became obsessional. Whole villages on the road to Snagov came down, replaced by ugly blocks of flats shoddily built, lacking power, water, working toilets and lifts. To add insult to injury, the new tenants had to pay rent on these unloved homes, whereas their old homes had been theirs by right. Unsurprisingly, people hated Ceausescu's 'systemisation' programme more than anything else. Unlike the cruelties of the dictator's social-engineering policies, where families were understandably not keen or even ashamed to air their grievances about abortions or unwanted 'irrecuperables', the knocking down of a person's home – be it in Bucharest or in the countryside – was a concrete, all-too-visible act.

One old lady whose little wooden home lay on the dictator's route to Snagov was Viorica Ionitsa. Although the *nomenklatura* silently opposed systemisation and did its best to slow the pace of destruction, homes that the dictator passed going to and from his villa were specially endangered. She said: 'He was always passing. The Securitate ordered us not to stand by the fence but to go inside our homes when he came by.' To keep the dictator happy, they knocked down Viorica's home, which she and her husband had built thirty-one years ago. It only had two rooms, but it was their own. This was one of sixty-four houses which were flattened in the small roadside village of Vladiceasa. Did the inhabitants protest? Viorica said: 'We were afraid. We could say nothing. An Englishman came often but it was difficult to tell him anything because there was a Securitate man dressed as a peasant around. I told the Englishman: "Look, there is the Securitate."' Who was the Englishman? 'The ambassador.' It was Hugh Arbuthnott. The conversation triggered Viorica's memories of her loss: 'Ceausescu was a very bad man. He should not have demolished my home. There was no bigger punishment.' She started to cry. Come the revolution, the peasants got their own back on the mayor of the village, who had supervised the demolition. She was stripped and the last they saw of the mayor was her running naked across the snow.

Why did he do it? Systemisation partly stemmed from the communist 'Big Brother' principle that it was easy to monitor the population when they were locked up in blocks, the better to inform one upon the other; partly because of the dictator's banal obsession with tidiness and order. He wanted the real world to match the neat rows and columns of styrofoam blocks he played God with in the attic of the Royal Palace.

Most of all, the new civic centre, with the House of the People as its centrepiece, consumed his attention. As the rise of the new openness –glasnost – under the benign hand of President Gorbachev in the Soviet Union made Ceausescu a less and less popular and necessary figure in the world, the West began to see through his foreign-policy hocus-pocus. The invitations to foreign capitals, in particular to important Western capitals, dropped to a trickle. The Frenzy, trapped at home for longer periods, just whirled round the house that would be his lasting monument faster and faster. It was as if the dictator knew, despite all the shrill protestations of the court poets and Ceausescu cultists, that he did not have long to last.

Ironically, it was the very demolition of Bucharest's city centre to make way for his monument that finally turned the West against him. A tide of anger was rising, fuelled by the brave souls who, risking the wrath of the Securitate, took photographs of the demolished buildings and sent them to the West. One such was a candlestick-maker, Petru Papurica. He worked at the Plumbuita monastery, an old royal palace on the outskirts of Bucharest, made available to the Orthodox church after another, far older and more beautiful monastery was flattened by the bulldozers. Papurica, twenty-nine, used to whistle and tell sly anti-Ceausescu jokes while he carved ornate candlesticks at his workbench; in his time off he took photographs and wrote detailed descriptions of the destruction that Ceausescu was wreaking and sent them to the West, in particular to West German news magazines, so that the world would know.

Meanwhile, the termites worked to build the House of the Republic for the glory of his name. They were egged on by one court poet, Eugen Barbu, who went out into a class of his own, according to Radio Free Europe, by praising the demolition caused by the civic centre. Barbu dedicated an article in *Scinteia* proclaiming the Big House as this new 'Acropolis of Ours'; moreover it was a 'revolution-ary urban achievement' and he declared himself sublimely happy at 'having got rid of dilapidated yet picturesque buildings . . . express-ing and generating social inequality'.

But the very function of the House of the People was just that: to make concrete the social inequality between the dictator's lowly vassals and the pomp and might of His Majesty. The architect of the House had been selected by a competition. There were a lot of interesting and arresting designs, but, to put it rather brusquely, the architect who came up with the most banal, Stalinist pastiche appealed successfully to the Ceausescus' taste. The prizewinner, after the revolution, has disappeared from view because she has been battered by much hostile criticism.

But someone who worked on the project from the start and longed to talk about it was Petre, the civil engineer. An intelligent and sophisticated man who spoke fine English, he described the extra-ordinary atmosphere as they built the House. 'I was in charge of one of the work sections – the house was so big, with 15,000 workers on the site, that we were divided into different sections. I started at 7 a.m. and finished at 7.30 p.m. It was very eerie working there. The House had outside lifts, just covered cages made of steel nets. At the end of the shift, in winter darkness, there was dark inside, dark outside, apart from thousands and thousands of lights on the workers' safety helmets. Tiny spots of light spreading out across the site, people on the way home. From eighty metres above, on the top floor, they looked like ants. It was a very strange feeling. Everyone was so tired, so oppressed. We were practically robots.'

And yet: 'I loved it. There is no way I hated it. I knew that it was my money that was paying for it. I knew that we were having to forgo elemental necessities to build this House but we put so many years of our life into it we couldn't help loving it.'

Ceausescu was, Petre said, an appalling man to work for. 'Ceausescu was shown the plans, but he could not make head or tail of them. He needed to have half-scale models. He was a very simple-minded man with no technical background. It was difficult for him to estimate the scale and form of the House. He would accept and approve the plans we showed him and then would balk at what we built. For his simple mind there were differences between what he imagined and what happened in real life. Then he wanted reality changed.

'We were faced with a man who could not relate plans to real life. Ceausescu came often to the House. Once a week at the beginning, but by December 1989 he came three or four times a week, sometimes twice a day, Saturdays and Sundays included. There was a feeling as though he would never see the House finished. He tried to hurry things up, pushing things along faster than the limits of what was possible. By doing that he was destroying the time we had spent on the details – the beautiful gold work on the ceilings and so on. We were losing quality all the time.

'His behaviour was paranoid. Of course, I didn't know him personally. But I knew his acts, and they were paranoid.' And Elena? 'Her influence was worse, she was more stupid than him. At times she was absolutely unbelievable.'

Celac the interpreter had complained about the dictator's jerky body language and lack of natural coordination. Petre made a parallel complaint: 'He lacked all sense of proportion. Whenever I went to the

House I was oppressed by the size. He was not a tall man. Perhaps he was trying to compensate for his physique by exaggerating the proportions of the House. For example, you needed to be two and a half metres (eight feet) tall to be in normal proportion to the doors and windows. It was madness.'

Like everyone else who came across the dictator and Elena, Petre and his colleagues felt that it was impossible to have any interchange of ideas with them: 'We couldn't talk to them. First of all, we were not asked. We were absolutely neglected. There were 15,000 people on that site. Regardless of how they worked or how badly they were fed, we still needed toilets. They didn't provide any, so the House was full of shit. It stank everywhere.

'So what happened was that there were special "shit teams" who used to clean paths to make sure that when Ceausescu, Elena and the Securitate came on a visit they wouldn't stand on anything unpleasant. One summer, I think it was a Saturday in 1987, he came to make his usual visit, inspect the work and order everybody about. We never spoke when they came into our section, but always used to listen very hard. We would be working twenty-five metres up on the ceiling of a hall and we could hear Ceausescu and Elena talk. They were the only ones who said anything. Of course, we listened to every word they said because sometimes it meant that they wanted the work done differently and we needed to know.

'But on this visit Ceausescu strayed from the specially cleaned-up path and went into a dark place where there were no lights. And we all know that you should never stray from the path.' Petre started to giggle at the memory of it; his wife too started to laugh. 'He went into the dark place and came out with one of his shoes completely covered with one of the biggest turds you ever saw in your life. The workers started to laugh, but then the Securitate looked at them so they shut up. A Securitate man rushed over and started to clean the shoe but there was so much on it was impossible. Normally, he would stand around giving orders, but this time he said nothing and just walked off to his car. With every other step you could see the tidemark the shit left on the floor. Nobody spoke. Nobody dared laugh. It was as if an atomic bomb had gone off.'

Ceausescu, who towards the end was said to be washing his hands twenty times a day in alcohol to stop infection and disease, must have been mortified. But so were the Securitate. 'They came looking for saboteurs. They wanted to know who had left the shit there. Of course, no one owned up and said it was their shit. So they called a meeting and demanded to know who the boss of that section was. It happened to be a friend of mine. They interrogated him, called him a saboteur. He said he didn't know whose shit it was. He came to this house when they let him go. He was absolutely terrified. The Securitate had instructed him not to speak about the shit or ever to talk to Ceausescu ever again.

'A few weeks later Ceausescu came up to him and asked him about some aspect of the work. But my friend had been told by the Securitate, who were watching him, not to say anything to Ceausescu. So he just stood there, silent. And Ceausescu started to get angry and said: "Come on, who are you?" He was trying to disappear, but Ceausescu followed him. After Ceausescu had asked three times, "Who are you?" he had to answer. He came here again that night, terrified. He sat with his head in his hands and said: "That shit. It's going to be the death of me."'

Internationally, a certain edgy distancing from the Romanian regime became more common, as President Gorbachev's rise in the Soviet Union left the dictator casting a bleaker, darker shadow over his own country. To mark his seventieth birthday in 1988, the sycophants had to resort to reheating some of the old porridge. The Queen was quoted as saying: 'You, personally, Mr President, are a statesman of world stature with widely recognised excellence, experience and influence.' True, she had said that, but back in 1978. Her Majesty joined what Michael Simmons of the *Guardian* called 'the royal birthday snub club', Europe's most exclusive club: 'To qualify, monarchs have to deny emphatically having sent to President Nicolae Ceausescu of Romania the greetings for his 70th birthday that the President's officials say they sent.' Other members were King Juan Carlos of Spain and King Carl Gustaf of Sweden, both of whom saw toasts made years earlier at official banquets reprinted in *Scinteia* as new.

The foreign journalists too were filing sharper pieces from Bucharest. Their reward was not to be welcomed back; in fact, not to be allowed back at all. For example, Nick Thorpe, who interviewed Brucan for the *Independent* in 1987, was denied an entry visa when he later applied for one. More sinister methods were used, too. Dr Dennis Deletant of London University's School of Slavonic and East European Studies knew Romania extremely well and had been writing anonymous pieces detailing the awfulness of the regime for some time. They were anonymous because his wife is Romanian and her parents lived in Bucharest: another example of the spider trap which made public outcry for those in the know so difficult. After his last trip to Romania before the revolution in 1988, he wrote an anonymous article in *The Times*. The Securitate worked out who the author of this unusually well-informed critique was and let it be known that Dr Deletant would be unwise to return. They told a friend of the family: 'He's number seven on the list.' Dr Deletant, who is not at all the dry stick he looks like, forms, with Arbuthnott and others, the deceptively fierce spin attack of the international awkward squad which helped to bowl out Ceausescu.

The foreign diplomatic, journalistic and academic toughening emboldened the dissidents, but they never amounted to a life-theatening menace for the regime. Far more worrying was the old dictator's health.

They came for Professor Iulian Mincu on April Fool's Day 1988. A tough, warm, forceful doctor with a thinning mop of silver hair, the professor is one of the world's leading experts in the treatment of diabetics. He was not, however, trusted by the Securitate. Speaking in his office, to be found down winding, ill-lit corridors full of lots of sick Romanians wandering around in hospital pyjamas like lost souls, he said: 'Between 1975 and 1978 the Securitate considered me a scientific spy because I published some of my research work in foreign medical journals. The Securitate said I was betraying Romanian medical secrets. From 1975 to 1981 they would not let me leave the country.'

Even so, in 1988 they came to fetch him. He was rushed to Ceausescu's villa Primavera, where he was taken to the dictator's bedside. He found there sixteen other doctors, some Securitate officers, three other officials and the minister of health, Victor Ciobanu, without whom no consultation could take place. The professor blew out his breath with exasperation: 'It was like a congress.'

How was the patient? The professor expelled spent air. 'He was impossible, absolutely impossible. It was impossible to work with him because he had decided that he knew more about it than anyone else. For example, he was a diabetic. He had been diagnosed a diabetic twelve years before, in 1976. Insulin was a necessity. But he wouldn't take it. When they called for me he was a very sick man. But from 1986 to 1988 he had not allowed his own doctors to take his blood. There had been no blood tests for two and a half years.'

Ceausescu's doctors and the Securitate had required Mincu, despite his poor security record, to see the dictator because he was due to arrive in Australia on 11 April 1988 – and was in no fit state to travel. Mincu took command of the situation: 'That's the moment when Ceausescu asked me my opinion and I said: "Either you go to hospital or you go into a coma."'

One should always by wary of stories which have people standing bravely up to Ceausescu, but Mincu was the only one of Ceausescu's doctors who agreed to see me. (The dictator's personal physician, Dr Paul Nicolau, lost us in a car chase in the back streets of Bucharest.) As Mincu was the only doctor willing to talk about the dictator's health after his death – and in post-revolutionary Romania any admission of a proximity to the dictator requires some nerve – then it seems not unlikely that Mincu was the only doctor who had the guts to order his impossible patient to hospital.

The tests done at the hospital showed that the dictator was a sick man. Readers should be aware that the professor was talking to me through an interpreter and it is possible that some of the medical details may have been garbled in translation. Mincu said that the dictator's blood level was very acidic. He had hyperglycaemia, which meant that the sugar level in his blood stream was very high: at 360 milligrammes per 100 millilitres it was three times higher than normal. He had diabetes, type two, which required insulin treatment, and the heart and kidney problems, in particular macro- and micro-angiopathy, that often come with this diabetic condition. As well as this he had high blood pressure and was taking Adalat, a drug to depress his blood pressure. None of his conditions was necessarily lethal, but what alarmed Professor Mincu was that his diabetes had been untreated for so long. He said: 'They never treated him properly. Ceausescu's doctors were very good, but they never succeeded in doing their duty. There were whole weeks when he wouldn't take Adalat, whole months when he wouldn't take insulin.'

The effect of untreated diabetes over a long time, according to Dr Raj Patel, a British GP, is that it can make you confused. Poorly controlled high blood pressure and poorly controlled diabetes can lead to periods of confusion. From as early as 1976, the year when he was diagnosed diabetic – or even earlier, if the condition existed long before diagosis – Ceausescu may have suffered from two related complaints which would have affected his mental grasp. The first is transient ischaemic attacks, which are short-lived strokes to the brain. The second is multi-infarct dementia, which is very small blood clots that go to the brain. Each one would effectively knock out bits of his brain, leading to bouts of confusion alternating with bouts of clarity. All of this fits with the recollections of people close to the dictator.

Because of the necessity to appear reasonably fit for his visit to Australia, Ceausescu complied with Professor Mincu's instructions, took the insulin, and his health and old vigour started to recover very quickly. The story of the visit was front-page news in the musty copy of *Scinteia*, dated 12 April 1988, found in the garden shed near the old family home at Scornicesti.

But, said Mincu, a month and a half after his return from the Antipodes, Ceausescu, now feeling fit and well, stopped taking the insulin. He felt so well there was obviously no need to take any medicine. Mincu continued: 'Of course, the health balance broke up again. It had been like that since 1976. Ceausescu did not have any dialogue with anyone, except his wife. And she was utterly ignorant.' What was the effect in Mincu's opinion when he stopped the insulin? 'It would affect his metabolic capacities. His judgement would go. In the last period Ceausescu was not able to take any right decisions in the morning. It was a sort of delay in his actions. He was on a rollercoaster.' To illustrate his point the professor wobbled his arm up and down.

Was he mad? The professor replied: 'He was paranoid. He would jump from extreme to extreme. When Ceausescu was timid, he was very afraid of everything. He didn't trust anyone, not even his own doctors. And then he would consider himself better than anyone. He knew more about medicine, about diabetes than anyone. For example, I gave him a strict diet to help his condition, with a set amount of carbohydrates and a set amount of protein. But Ceausescu disagreed with this diet and invented a different one for himself, changing all the amounts. It was absurd. But it was very difficult to talk to him. Ceausescu was convinced that he was the greatest Romanian, that fate chose him. He believed in everything he said. And Elena would back him up. How could you argue with someone like that?'

Check

New Year's Eve with the Ceausescus was never a particularly lively soirée and 1989 was no exception. One of the very few people who attended it and are both alive and at liberty today is Violeta Andrei, the actress wife of Stefan Andrei, the sometime foreign minister and then economic minister in the Ceausescu regime. What was the party like? She pouted her ruby-red lips, tossed back her frothy head of orange hair and lifted up her breasts in a gesture which was profoundly disturbing: 'It was like a burial.

'Ceausescu was on the television, making some tedious speech. We were the eight members of the Political Executive Committee and their wives, all sat around small, separate tables. We didn't talk to anyone else, but only whispered to our partner. We had to look as though we were listening to Ceausescu on the television. He sat behind his desk watching us, his eyes following each couple for a time, to make sure we were all listening to it. Elena sat framed behind a vase of flowers, her face as the centrepiece of the blooms.' What flowers were they? 'Four dead yellow carnations,' Violeta replied tartly. 'The two black labradors were there. I loved these dogs very much and they liked me. They used to come to me as soon as I arrived, something which Ceausescu was not very happy about. It was not the dogs' fault but he didn't like it.' Bobu, she added, was so servile he called the dogs Comrade Corbu and Comrade Sherona.

'It was so dull. At midnight they put the lights out but instead of singing or dancing we had to pass in front of them – they were sitting half asleep in big armchairs – and wish them Happy New Year. I did it, but to myself I wished "Death on you".' Violeta contorted her features, caked in make-up, into a mask of hatred. 'Party? Don't call it a party. It was worse than a funeral. Because at a Romanian funeral people laugh and sing and toast the dead, but on this night you had to whisper quietly and listen to this idiotic programme with Ceausescu making a speech.'

Violeta, like virtually everybody else in *Red Horizons*, does not get a high rating from Pacepa. The secret policeman described her: 'She was a little painted doll, an affected young actress who always paraded around as if she were on stage.' On the day that she met me she had black painted eyebrows, heavy bottle-green mascara, rouge on her cheeks, powder on her forehead, a diaphanous negligée streaked with tinsel, lips drawn into a heart shape and she reeked of some exotic perfume. Most striking of all was her habit of punctuating every point she made by putting her long fingernails to her breasts and lifting them, giving out a little gasp as she did so. It was an act which at times rendered the shorthand in my notebook almost indecipherable. What added a certain sadness to this performance was that she was a lady of a certain age; moreover, she was speaking from the kitchen of her once enormous villa surrounded by packing cases. It may have been a con, but the general impression was that now that her once highly influential husband was in prison, things were pretty bleak for her. And what man could possibily fail to be moved by the plight of this tinsel-clad damsel in distress?

Pacepa, certainly. The passage about Violeta in *Red Horizons* continues:

As soon as Elena had ordered microphone coverage put on Violeta, several years earlier, the first recording of one of her casual love affairs was made. It was with a student. There had been many others since then, always handsome young men with an athletic build. 'Just look at that minx!' Elena burst out that time. 'The party gave her one of its top people as a husband, but she runs around hiking up her skirts at every tarzan who throws her a smile.'

Did she ever meet Pacepa? 'Yes.' Her eyes narrowed. 'I met him in 1977 at the ball of the generals. All of them wanted to dance with me, Pacepa too. Of course, you know that Aesop's fable, the one about the best grapes are the ones you cannot have.' She let that one hang in the air. 'He dedicated a page to me.' Suddenly the thought struck that not being attacked in *Red Horizons* would have been for some in the Ceausescu magic circle like not being attacked in *Private Eye*, the satirical magazine, for British politicians or journalists: to be ignored was the more cruel slight.

Were they bugged? 'All the time. Postelnicu had microphones in the house, my husband, myself and the children followed all the time and our letters opened and censored. When we wanted to talk we used to whisper in each other's ears with the bath taps running or loud music on. In 1989 we knocked eggs at Easter' – an old Romanian tradition which, in the high ranks of the RCP, would have been officially frowned upon as a Christian juju – 'and whispered "Happy Easter" to each other. The next day Postelnicu came up to my husband and said: "You broke eggs last night."'

Violeta then went into a long, involved portrait of her husband, Stefan Andrei, disclosing huskily that he was the only dissident within Ceausescu's Political Executive Committee. On the verge of the revolution, she claimed, it was Andrei who had been plotting against the dictator; if only the revolution had come a few days later, her husband would have been revealed as the heroic anti-Ceausescu force he really was, rather than being locked up in prison as one of the longest-lasting, ablest and most trusted of the dictator's advisers. Tudor Postelnicu, Emil Bobu, Constantin Dascalescu and Ion Dinca were the real villains. When people were sacked or threatened with disgrace or wanted to emigrate, they turned to Andrei for succour. She named the émigré Romanian musician Gheorghe Zamfir, whose distinctive Romanian pipe music formed the soundtrack for the film *Picnic at Hanging Rock*, as one recipient of her husband's kindness. Without knowing whether there is any truth in this particular case, it would not be surprising if Andrei had occasionally helped people out, because every individual within the magic circle enjoyed a measure of power to do a bit of good. Andrei, easily the most intelligent and sophisticated of the long-lasting sycophants, could well have behaved decently – in return for what favours one can only guess. Perhaps he was genuinely a good man. Perhaps.

But such a view does not gel with Sergiu Celac's description of him as the consummate survivor in the Ceausescu court. And it was also clear that Violeta was not going to miss this opportunity with a Western reporter to make some special pleading for her wrongly imprisoned husband. She said, passion almost choking her voice: 'He knows that he's innocent. The conditions inside Rahova are very bad. He's being held underground, with very little light. The food is terrible: he's fed rotting cabbage and gruel.' That Stefan Andrei was not enjoying Rahova was no shock; nor that he spent his time, according to Violeta, weeping ceaselessly. Given that no one with a strong moral sense of himself or herself could last long at Ceausescu's feet, this picture of Andrei behind bars – a broken cry-baby – struck me as being all too likely.

Aside from Violeta's case for Stefan Andrei, unsung dissident and pre-empted plotter, she had a privileged seat at the almost unbeliev-able, over-the-top Victorian melodrama which was to lead up to the revolution. As someone in the presidential box, Violeta is a fascinat-ing, though not objective, spectator of the last scenes of the Ceausescu story. It was the Theatre of Horror, the Theatre of Cruelty and the Theatre of the Absurd, all rolled into one.

On Elena, Violeta is at her most entertainingly subjective: 'Elena was very bad. She hated me very much. Every time I went abroad, she had me followed by the Securitate. When I just went to the country I was followed.' What was Elena's dress sense like? (A not wholly ingenuous question.) 'The clothes she wore were very luxurious, but' – faked pity filled her eyes – 'she did not have the physique or the style to carry them off.' Violeta said that she visited Snagov as the guest of the Ceausescus only once. This may not be true because it is in Violeta's interest to play down the level of intimacy between the two couples; on the other hand, everyone agrees that Elena and Violeta got on together like two geese in a vat of acid. 'At Snagov the atmosphere was like an interminable meeting. All the meeting looked down on me. The only point of being there was to praise Ceausescu and Elena. To talk or to do anything else was not approved of.'

She knew that Nicu had bad relations with his parents and the Securitate. Five years ago, she had been sitting at one of the official villas which clustered around Ceausescu's home at Neptun, when she saw Nicu throw a park bench at the Securitate who were assigned to follow him. (They would have followed him so obviously only on the express orders of Postelnicu, who himself would not have taken such a risk with the heir apparent's sensibilities if he was not acting under the instructions of the dictator or, if he was unwell, Elena.) Violeta said that she once was friendly with Elena's hairdresser, who left the country about four years ago after inventing an illness. The hair-dresser told Violeta that he had overheard Nicu shouting at his father: 'The country will be destroyed. It's freezing cold and no one has anything to eat. You'd better fucking resign!'

The cold was appalling, said Violeta. 'The gas pressure was so low that we put in a wood-burning stove. At the theatre it was so cold you could see your breath when you exhaled. Sometimes it was six degrees below freezing and still we had to act. There were some places in Bucharest where it was not so cold. His office. But where my husband worked was also very cold.' This last sentence may or may not be true, but if the wife of one of Ceausescu's most favoured ministers suffered the cold at home, the lot of those less well placed than Violeta must have been truly grim.

What about Ceausescu's health? 'He was paranoid and had been for a very long time. About ten years ago a doctor, I think his name was Schechter, told Ceausescu that he was paranoid, but like every paranoid he refused to believe this and refused to take the treatment. The story goes that after Ceausescu refused to accept his diagnosis, the doctor committed suicide.' (This was one of many stories which it proved impossible to get to the bottom of.)

Violeta knew Mincu well and asked him some time before the revolution how long Ceausescu and Elena had to live. Violeta said that Mincu told her that Ceausescu's diabetes was bad but that he would live for at least two more years; as for Elena, her health was good, she could live till she was one-hundred-and-twenty. This did not cheer Violeta. She went on: 'All the doctors hated Ceausescu very much because from the moment that they took care of the dictator they were followed all the time, were bugged and were not allowed to go to official congresses abroad. The doctors became prisoners too. Everyone wanted Ceausescu and his wife dead.'

Violeta, who had at first been keen to underline her remoteness from the presidential couple, began to lose her guard as the minutes passed. Some of the details she now gave sat awkwardly with her claim that the Andreis had had very little to do with the Ceausescus. At social gatherings Violeta said that they always brought special food to Ceausescu. He never ate the same as everyone else. Towards the end this may have been because of his diabetes, but since it was never officially admitted, the mystery lingered in people's minds. Violeta, like everyone else, was drawn to watching the dictator closely, to see whether his health was faltering or his diet visibly changing, but, she said: 'I tried not to stare too much.' Too keen an interest in Ceausescu's eating habits could, in the paranoid world at the top of Romania, be taken the wrong way: denoting a potential poisoner or a Western spy; who knows what thought crimes could be committed?

'They used to ask my husband to come over for a chess game and volleyball at the weekend. My husband didn't want to go because he was tired. He used to say: "I can't go on like this – it's madness." I told him to go anyway. Perhaps he [Ceausescu] might have a heart attack while playing volleyball.' How did the dictator play chess with Stefan Andrei? 'My husband always had to make an effort to lose. While they played chess, Stefan Andrei told Ceausescu what was happening in the world. That was how he kept Ceausescu informed – not on paper but in conversations, always keeping it simple and practical.' This is exactly the same method Pacepa describes when he briefed the dictator, often over a chess game.

'He used to cheat at volleyball,' she said. 'The Securitate played on Ceausescu's side. They were all very strong men so that Ceausescu knew he was going to win. Sometimes it would be Ceausescu and the Securitate versus Bobu, Dinca, Stefan Andrei and some others.' (None of these ministers was noted for their sporting prowess.) 'He had to win all the time. He was increasingly megalomaniac.'

Did Violeta have any fond memories of the foreign dignitaries who met Ceausescu? 'We received from Harold Wilson a little Minox camera.' Where was it? 'The prosecutor took it away after the revolution. And the Queen gave Stefan a portrait of her and her husband.' She paused to lift her breasts. 'Margaret Thatcher appreci-ated my husband very much. We have a picture of Stefan with Margaret Thatcher somewhere. She appreciated Stefan because he was an intelligent man who didn't believe in Marxism. They talked about the problems of applying Marxism, because he never shared Ceausescu's politics.'

That last point may be the words of a loyal wife sticking up for her husband, against the grain of the evidence, but what Violeta had to say about the Frenzy backed up all the other witnesses: 'It was chaotic. Ceausescu and Elena would make up their minds without knowing the first thing about something. You can't imagine the hurry, the running around, the lack of any organisation.' Stefan and Violeta Andrei were greatly envied for their prominent position in the hierarchy, and the luxuries that came with it. There would have been many compensations she may not have thought it politic to discuss, now that her husband was weeping in Rahova gaol. Yet the microphones, the constant Securitate surveillance, the possibility of being called away at a moment's notice to flatter and wheedle in front of the dictator, the neurotic edginess which consumed the energies of all those who served Ceausescu must have taken their toll. Few Romanians, if they had known, would have relished the opportunity of spending New Year's Eve with the Ceausescus. Even envied 'fat cats' like Stefan and Violeta Andrei were in a kind of well-appointed psychiatric penitentiary, with no idea how to get out.

Once you hopped on the Frenzy, you could not get off. Zoia

Manescu, the daughter of Constantin Manea, the leader of Ceausescu's cabinet, told me that her father, an elderly man, had long wanted to retire, but Ceausescu would not let him go. Had she read *1984*? 'Yes. I started Orwell's book but I couldn't finish it. There were so many things which were similar.' That is the great drawback of *1984*: Orwell doesn't give much of a clue as how to overthrow Big Brother. It was a question that the Romanians were to resolve before 1989 was over.

Ceausescu's seventy-first and last birthday on 26 January 1989 was celebrated with the usual dreary tosh from the hagiographers. But Radio Free Europe, with something of a spring in its step, produced an 'A to Z' of the personality cult written by Dan Ionescu. Here is a shortened version:

A is for architect (title of book in his honour)
B is for builder (as in 'Builder of everything good and just')
C is for creed (as in 'he is our creed')
D is for the demiurge (as in 'New Romania's demiurge')
E is for epoch (as in 'He – our epoch')
F is for future (as in 'When we say Ceausescu, we say the Future')
G is for god (as in 'our secular god')
H is for honey (as in 'He is the honey in the words')
I – no nonsense available
J – no nonsense available
K is for kissing (as in 'Sweet kissing of the homeland's earth')
L is for light (as in 'He came as pure as light')
M is for miracle (as in 'Ceausescu/The Romanian Miracle')
N is for nimbus (as in 'He is a nimbus of victory')
O is for oak (as in 'Splendid oak of the Romanian glory')
P is for Prince Charming (as in 'Prince Charming's Birthday')
Q – no nonsense available
R is for road (as in 'Our road towards the future')
S is for son (as in 'The sun's son')
T is for truth (as in 'Ceausescu is the warm truth')
U – no nonsense available
V is for visionary (as in 'Visionary scrutinising the future')
W is for worker (as in 'the country's first worker')
X – no nonsense available
Y – no nonsense available
Z is for zodiac (as in 'Nicolae Ceausescu's sign of the zodiac').

As the spring of 1989 arrived all the omens were black for the regime. In February, the Securitate started a diplomatic incident when they stopped Arbuthnott, the British ambassador, from visiting the beleaguered Doina Cornea in Cluj, a long, gruelling drive from Bucharest. The militia enforcing the dissident's house arrest man-handled Arbuthnott. When he protested to the authorities, they said he had been guilty of a traffic offence by driving his car the wrong way down a one-way street. For evidence, they placed one-way signs at either end of the street, making it a 'no-way street'.

In March, six old RCP heavyweights published the hardest-hitting attack on Ceausescu and the regime so far. The letter ranged across the arc of misery, but seemed to touch its deepest chord when it complained of the food crisis in the country that imperilled the country's future. It called for an end to the 'food exports, which are threatening the biological existence of our nation'. The six signatories were an intriguing bunch: Silviu Brucan, foxy as ever at seventy-three; Gheorghe Apostol, seventy-seven, Ceausescu's old, defeated rival hoping at last to see his lifelong enemy down; Constantin Pirvulescu, ninety-four, the ancient communist and the only one who ever had the guts to rubbish Ceausescu in public; Corneliu Manescu, seventy-three, a former foreign minister and chairman of the United Nations general assembly; Alexander Barladeanu, a former Politburo member; and Grigore Raceanu, who was described as a veteran communist. The letter was carefully worded, raising Ceausescu's great foreign-policy successes only to crush them as a thing of the past, since 'all the leaders of the non-Communist nations in Europe refuse to meet with you'. It hit at the Securitate's baleful shadow, too, which hitherto had always been unmentionable in party circles. The signatories wrote that the Securitate had been created 'to defend the socialist order against exploiting classes' – perhaps they had in mind all those who died on the Canal of Death – but that Ceausescu had turned it against the intellectuals and, most important of all, the workers. The signatories were put under various degrees of house arrest, with Silviu Brucan being singled out for close attention by the Securitate. But the genie released by the letter, once out, was hard to put back.

The wind of change from the east was blowing stronger and stronger, so much so that the Romanians read Russian newspapers to discover what was going on in the world. The Riga-based *Soviet Youth* published the full text of the letter by the six. The Russian magazine highlighted the signatories' damning the 'cult of personality' and the 'total control over every person by the Romanian security service'. *Soviet Youth* also ran a Russian translation of an interview by the French paper *Libération* with the Romanian dissident poet Mircea Dinescu, whose 'Absurd Chess', an attack on 'systemisation', is quoted in part at the beginning of this book.

After the Dinescu interview was published in *Libération*, the lid came down on Dinescu. He was expelled from the party, blacklisted as a writer and dismissed from his job as an editor. Without being charged or sentenced for any crime, he was placed under punitive house arrest, guarded by eighteen Securitate men in three shifts so that there was a team of six outside his house at any one time. Dinescu complained about his treatment in a letter to the authorities. He said that his mail, telephone calls, friends and contacts abroad were subject to constant surveillance when not cut off. For one long period his single communication from the outside world, he said, consisted of a 'vulgar and anonymous death threat'. Dinescu added that 'post-humous glory of a certain kind can be achieved' in a country where one interview can change one's life so 'violently', where 'some writers are guarded ever more closely while common thieves and criminals are freed prematurely' and the 'regime responds to the poet's arsenal with real arms'. The letter ended with Dinescu noting that 'suicide was an inefficient form of protest', thus making it clear to anyone that if he was to die, the number-one suspect would be the regime.

The Securitate's hounding of the dissidents was not without its own black humour. Towards the end of the year, when the conditions of his house arrest had softened to allow him to go out, a further letter smuggled out to the West by Dinescu revealed what happened when two dissidents met at the dining table of the Writers' Club:

A week ago at the canteen of the Writers' Club, I lingered at a table with the poet Dan Desliu. After our departure a colleague witnessed a grotesque scene in which three characters were searching frantically in the kitchen for a certain plate with several slices of bread which had been on our table and which the waiter had cleared away together with other, harmless plates. The trouble-some plate was recovered. I returned a few days later with the wicked thought of stealing the plate. As we sat at a table with several colleagues, Dan Desliu and I, the only ones to know about the story of the plate, were surprised when the waitress substituted for the plate with rolls on our table a different plate with slices of bread, under his pretext that they were fresher. Dan Desliu sensed the telegraphic qualities of this piece of crockery and put it in his bag with the aim of studying it at home at leisure. To be candid, I doubted that in a writers' restaurant in the Socialist Republic of Romania, plates with ears could be placed on the tables of the hungry authors. And yet, in broad daylight in the courtyard of the Writers' Club, the poet Dan Desliu was attacked by a man as he was getting into a taxi, his bag being snatched from under his arm, and the culprit ran off with the wretched vinyl bag containing a ballpoint pen, a pretzel, and the precious plate.

Dr Deletant, writing in the *Independent*, noted that the attacker was no common thief by what happened next. Desliu was arrested for stealing the property of the Ministry of the Interior.

Dissidents had been arrested, written letters and given interviews to the foreign press before. But the difference this time was that the Romanians could read all about it in the Soviet press. While the West's newspapers had always been banned, the Romanians had long been allowed to read the Soviet press. Glasnost opened up everything, not just the political scene. Albert Pin of the Moscow-based *New Times* magazine made a number of unflattering comparisons between Bucharest and the North Korean capital. On Bucharest's much-vaunted underground system, Pin had the following sour comment to pass: 'In fact, many more people could use a subway . . . but for the fact that life stops so early in the evening in Bucharest. As in Pyongyang, nightlife in Bucharest ends early. Bars and restaurants work until 9 or 10 p.m., and the last subway train departs at 11.30 p.m.' The gloomy tone was far removed from the fake jollity and upbeat lift that percolated throughout Romania's official media. The impact of Soviet complaints about Romanian night life may well be impossible to gauge, but it was not negligible. Bulgarian TV, not, one would have thought, the world's most enticing news service, enjoyed more and more fans north of the Danube. The Romanian media stood out more starkly than ever as the dog that didn't bark.

None of the Romanian newspapers gave any coverage whatsoever to the most damaging and obvious slap in the face that the Ceausescu regime had so far received from abroad, when Prince Charles savaged the dictator's 'systemisation' programme in a speech in April 1989. The speech was reprinted in *The Times*, under a Peter Brookes cartoon of a bow-tied Ceausescu with two fangs hanging outside his mouth, Dracula-style. It was the royal family's revenge for 1978.

The prince did not mince his words:

We in this country are painfully aware of the trauma caused by uprooting traditional communities. . . . That process should have made us, therefore, all the more sensitive to the awful spectre of an entire society – not just certain districts – losing its roots and its ancient communities, which is what is happening today in a corner of eastern Europe, in Romania. There President Ceausescu has embarked on the wholesale destruction of his country's cultural and human heritage.

What happened here in the 1960s is, of course, not comparable with the policy known as 'systemisation', which aims to transform Romania's rural environment into over 500 urban collectives designated as 'agro-industrial complexes'. The object is to reshape the nation's identity, to create a new type of person, utterly subordinate to its dreams. To achieve this, President Ceausescu has set about destroying the cities and villages of his country and replacing them with blocks of flats which are a repetition of failed 1960s social engineering, mixed with the atmosphere of George Orwell's 1984. . . .

The prince rammed the point home by quoting from an open letter signed by many people in British life opposing 'systemisation':

We call on you to stop the demolition of the country's villages. Driving people from their ancestral settlements, where they have a purpose, where they have houses to meet the needs of life and labour, is a sacrilege. The peasant house is identified with the soul of its builder. By striking at the peasant house, by replacing it with a poky flat in a tower-block, you strike not only at the soul of the people but also at the patrimony which belongs to all mankind.

The text of the open letter may have seemed woolly to those few members of the elite in Bucharest privileged to read the foreign press – pre-eminently the dictator himself – but the thrust of the speech allowed no room for interpretation. It was the straightforward rubbishing of the dictator and his rotten regime that people like Prince Ghica had been longing for. News of the speech was given on the BBC and Radio Free Europe. The whole Ceausescu monolith was beginning to wobble.

But still the British Foreign Office sat on its hands. The Labour MP Paul Flynn asked Sir Geoffrey Howe in April 1989 to take back Ceausescu's knighthood. Sir Geoffrey replied: 'Although there have been occasions in wartime when our enemies in recent conflicts have had their awards taken away, there is no precedent for depriving the holder of an honorary award in peacetime. It is not judged right to depart from the rule in this case.' In the end, his knighthood was snatched back not many hours before he died. The knighthood was gold to the dictator; to have taken it away in the spring would have sent an inspiring signal to the Romanian people, but Her Majesty's government was not big enough to admit that it had been wrong to have him knighted in the first place.

The rising gale from Moscow, the squalls from the dissidents and the Prince Charles speech drowned out the regime's great propaganda stroke of the spring – the announcement by Ceausescu to the Grand National Assembly in early April that Romania had paid off its entire national debt. It had been a pyrrhic victory, achieved at appalling human cost. If it was true. The exiled broadcaster Chris Mititelu said: 'Of course he could be lying – maybe it's down to half a billion, and he's owed half a billion by Sudan and Libya, and says that works out at zero.' No one was inclined to give the dictator the benefit of the doubt.

The Frenzy did not rest. Daily checks on the progress at the House of the People were made. Petre the civil engineer recalls one incident that year that stood out: 'We were working flat out on a ceiling in one of the halls. It should have taken six months, but we had been ordered to complete it in forty days. We were high up on scaffolding working away when they came in, without notice, surrounded by the usual Securitate. As soon as they came in all our talk stopped. There was a complete silence, apart from them. Their voices were amplified by the vastness of the hall. She started to cry: "Why so much scaffolding?" After a crisis for us lasting many seconds, he simply told her: "How can they finish the painting without scaffolding?" You could see from her face that she was crazy.'

Ceausescu that summer put more energy into the creation of the New Man, Romanian style. Radio Free Europe reported that by far the largest section of the 'Theses for the 14th Congress of the RCP' dealt with how 'to step up ideological, political and educational activity in order to mould the New Man'. Of course, there was no more seemly living model for the New Man than Ceausescu himself. But the details of what the New Man would actually look like or how he would behave were hazy. Honesty and courage were two values the radio station picked out as being indicative of the New Man.

A good candidate for the title, if the rhetoric matched reality, would have been thirty-year-old Viorel Mazilu. By summer 1989, he had had enough. An orphan, he had no family to look after. He was fed up with Ceausescu's Romania and wanted out. He had made two previous unsuccessful attempts to escape: in 1987, the first was botched when he was caught by the Securitate in a border town for which he had no papers; the second attempt, a week later, when he planned to swim the fearfully wide Danube failed when he was spotted by border guards not far from the shore. They were under orders to shoot to kill. He was captured and badly beaten up. A few days later a judge gave him six months in prison; he left the court wearing ankle chains, cruelly tight. He was to wear the chains for a month. The conditions in the prison at Turnu Severin were 'medieval' – a hundred men jam-packed in four-tier bunks in a room big enough for half that number. And the food? 'Even the pigs ate better.'

Eventually, he was released and given back his old job at a Bucharest bakery. He waited two years, saved up and then, in June 1989, it was time for another go. For his third attempt, he took a holiday near the Yugoslav border. He had two chances: one on the way to the holiday resort and one on the way back. He planned to jump into the Danube from a railway bridge which crossed a stretch of water not far from the border and swim for his life. For his first chance his nerve failed when he was told that the Securitate had driven submerged wooden stakes into the river bottom to impale would-be escapers. A few days later, on his return to Bucharest, he steeled himself for the jump. But as the train neared the spot, word ran down the train that the Securitate had boarded and were methodically checking everyone. Fearing another arrest which, with his prison record, would mean another longer spell in jail, he jumped before the Securitate got to him. But the moment he picked was not a good one. The train was just going into a tunnel and then everything went black.

He woke up to discover that he was in hospital, his right foot amputated. Mazilu learnt that he had lost three inches of his foot when the train wheels had run over it after his fall. He suspected that the rest of his foot was cut off as punishment. Maybe, but Romanian medicine is a rough and ready affair; there were hardly any drugs around and a would-be escapee and orphan would not be at the top of the list. Whether his amputation was called for or punitive, they did not look after him well. A month after the accident there were maggots in his wound.

After the stream of Amnesty International reports on the repression, the increasingly hard attacks on Ceausescu by the journalists – both Western and Soviet – and the ferocious rubbishing of 'systemisation' by Prince Charles, one would have thought that Western businessmen would have nothing to do with the dictator. Not so. Violeta Andrei recalled in 1990: 'Last summer Rolls-Royce proposed that they and the Romanians should build a plane together. Rolls-

Royce would make the engines and the Romanians would make the rest. Elena didn't accept this and told Stefan: "Don't be absurd. We must make the engines here too." It was impossible to convince them that the engines could not be made in Romania.' She added that the representatives from Rolls-Royce were very surprised that Stefan was arrested after the revolution.

It would seem extraordinary that Britain's prestigious maker of aero-engines was still trying to deal with Ceausescu's Romania after all the problems with the so-called Rombac contract of 1978. The country's hard-currency restrictions reduced production before the revolution to no more than one aeroplane a year, according to a March 1990 report by Jane Renton in the business pages of the *Observer*. The report added that in March 1990 a deal had been signed between a new 'privately-funded UK leasing enterprise' and the new Romanian government. Although Rolls-Royce Tay engines were to be manufactured and the company would benefit from licensing income, neither it nor British Aerospace had any equity in the new deal; a crucial qualification Violeta Andrei clearly had not grasped. By 1989, the British aircraft manufacturers were in fact somewhat wary of Romania. Once bitten, twice shy.

One businessman who helped to ease the deal and had no compunction about meeting the dictator was Francis, Lord Newall. An old Etonian and member of the Cavalry and Guards club, Lord Newall is best known in Britain for being chairman of the British Greyhound Racing Board. No mention was made of the peer's line of business in the coverage by the Romanian news agency, Agerpress, of his tête-à-tête with Ceausescu on 10 October 1989. Agerpress wrote:

On October 10, President Nicolae Ceausescu of Romania received Lord Francis Newall, member of the Defence Commission of the British Parliament, Member of the Parliamentary assembly of the Council of Europe, who is paying a visit to Romania at the invitation of the Grand National assembly.

The guest thanked for the interview granted, for the possibility of visiting Romania and getting acquainted with the achievements of the Romanian people in the economic, social and cultural development of its country. . . .

President Nicolae Ceausescu pointed to the particular significance of strengthening cooperation among the states of the European continent. . . .
In that framework, the need was emphasised for the assertion of a new policy in the world arena, which should exclude the imperialist circles' interference

in the domestic affairs of other people, their actions of destabilising socialist countries, of denigrating socialism, expressing the conviction that these states could not be diverted from their socialist development path.

Even through the fog of Agerpress's prose, it is clear that Ceausescu was rattled by the storm building in Eastern Europe.

One pertinent question was: what was the dog-racing peer doing hobnobbing with the dictator? The peer was unabashed when he met me in a bar at the House of Lords. Lord Newall said: 'I was trying to help BAC and Rolls-Royce'. While working in some unspecified consultancy capacity, the peer had struck up a friendship with the dictator's brother, General Ilie Ceausescu, deputy minister of national defence and, let us not forget, once organiser of the racket where the Romanians sold Western military secrets to the Soviets and Soviet military secrets to the West.

The peer said: 'Ilie was my chum because I used to poke him in the belly and say "General, you are getting too fat". We laughed and giggled. He made lots of dirty jokes, a funny, round little man.'

The friendship dated from 1986 when Lord Newall visited the country at the instigation of an ex-Romanian, George Pop. 'He introduced me to Ilie Ceausescu. Through Ilie we went round ten different towns and villages looking at the ethnic problem.' Lord Newall was referring to the age-old controversy between the Romanian majority and the ethnic Hungarian minority in Transylvania: 'There was a tendency to Romanise everything, but the Hungarians exaggerated it to make their point.' In 1987 Lord Newall returned to Romania with his wife, 'an official visit', as the guest of General Ilie Ceausescu. He said: 'It's a fascinating country. No one ever wrote about it except to say what an awful regime it had. You had to treat them [the regime] like a child. Say something nice, and then they would listen to you.'

Lord Newall said 'something nice' in a House of Lords debate, somewhat obliquely making the argument that the West should not be duped by Hungarian propaganda when considering the Romanian human-rights record. He said on 29 July 1987: 'Is my noble friend aware that in the villages of Transylvania where the Hungarians are in the vast majority they also have a majority in the council? It is not the Hungarians who are being oppressed by the whole county.' When asked to expand on this remark, Lord Newall told me: 'Within the regime, the Hungarians ran their own show.' This was not a view widely held outside the Central Committee building of the RCP and its propaganda organs. For example, the country's ethnic Hungarians were not allowed to have their own political party or to stand in free elections. Their own Hungarian-language university was closed by Ceausescu back in 1956. Those who protested at the community's lack of political rights were, like Ilona Luca, found guilty of 'anti-state agitation', flung into prison and on release diagnosed as suffering from 'political paranoia' and flung into a psychiatric prison. Not quite running your own show.

Lord Newall got to know Romania well. He met Ilie Ceausescu seven times in all. In 1988, he was invited by the president to tour the northwest and southeast corners of the country. He told me: 'By now I was getting much bolder in saying how bad things were.' That is the peer's constant refrain: that he used his access to encourage the regime to improve the lot of the people.

He was happy to conform with the regime's wishes. In the summer of 1989 he had offered to arrange a trip to Romania for the BBC's foreign editor, John Simpson, at the request of the regime – an offer Simpson was not prepared to accept. On his last trip, in October 1989, Lord Newall visited Scornicesti and laid a wreath on the grave of Ceausescu's parents: 'It was a diplomatic thing. I have a photograph of myself where the Ceausescus were born. Ilie Ceausescu came with me. We spent two days in the car, arguing and discussing things. We went round the Dacia car factory, a doorhandle fell off on a brand-new car. I gave away a lot of coffee.' The peer met a number of ministers and senior officials in the regime, including the defence minister, General Vasile Milea: 'He gave me a little dagger, with a woven gold thing. I thought he was a nice man.' General Milea was to perish during the revolution. His deputy, General Victor Stanculescu, came to Newall's last dinner party in Romania. To thank his friend General Ilie Ceausescu, Lord Newall gave him a china plate, decorated with a portcullis, 'worth £40'.

Finally the summons came to meet Nicolae Ceausescu. It was Lord Newall's third meeting with the dictator. 'You must appreciate that there was no sign of any change. That very day Ceausescu had gone into a market at Bucharest. It was quite remarkable. He actually told me: "Statistics of meat-eating show that everyone in Bucharest had seventy-five to eighty kilos of meat a year. He really believed it, he really did. I thought the man was totally bamboozled or he went a bit mad at the end.'

George Pop, who paid the peer's fare on at least one of his trips, made the initial introduction between Lord Newall and his dictator's brother. Pop, an entrepreneur of Romanian origin who now lives in Britain, has been awarded the OBE. He, too, seems to have been involved in easing the progress of the Rombac contract as a consultant. He declined to talk to the author. He did, however, castigate the author in his absence at a dinner party thrown at the British Embassy in Bucharest in the summer of 1990 about the article in the *Observer* which revealed his friend Lord Newall's links with the regime. Many people say that Pop knew the top personalities in Ceausescu's Romania extremely well, but Pop remains a figure in the shadows.

The dictator was happy to walk into the limelight that November, billed as Europe's last Stalinist, for the 14th Party Congress. The Berlin Wall had been shattered, Havel and his mates were on the verge of taking power at the cost of very little blood but a lot of sore throats in Czechoslovakia, but nothing had changed – so it seemed – in Romania. The party cadres still clapped in the approved staccato fashion, leaping up and down and cheering at the very mention of Ceausescu. He looked around, underneath his eyebrows, checking to see who was the first to stop clapping and sit down. My Turkish friend Ali, who drove me across the country on Christmas Eve, had gone along to the Congress in November. During the long drive he acted out the pantomime applause, the hurrahs, the paranoia. 'It was shit,' he said, graphically.

At the Party Congress, Valentin allowed himself to be put forward as a candidate member of the Central Committee, a step which brought a halt to the friendship between him and Gabriel Costache. Gabriel said: 'I was astonished that he accepted. I knew his stand. For such a long time he had been opposed to the regime. He had had no time for it at all. It just didn't make sense. Prior to 1989, he didn't want to get involved in politics. Out of the blue, he joined in the worst period possible. It was obvious that things were unbearable.' It was certainly quite the wrong time to jump on the bandwagon with the rest of Eastern Europe falling apart. Perhaps it was because Valentin subconsciously wanted to be with his parents at the end.

It certainly was a mystery, but that autumn Valentin, now divorced from his wife, had become closer to his parents that he had been for a long time. Through Valentin we have another window on the closing melodrama. He told me: 'I lived with them for a while after I got divorced. We said hello, that sort of thing,' He laughed. 'My address, officially, is still Primavera.' (That is the name of Ceausescu's official villa.) 'I noticed that he was absent-minded and looked tired, even in the morning. He was changed. I got the impression . . .' He paused, to weigh his words. 'I didn't know who was running the country. He wasn't that interested in what was happening in Romania, but much more keen on external affairs, that and the House of the Republic.'

Was he mad? 'He certainly was mad. That was my impression. But he knew certain things. He was not well informed, but my brother said he knew certain things.' Valentin explained that though he had not been close to Nicu at the time, he got to know him better and to like him in prison. While in prison, he had managed to pick up information that changed his perception of his father.

'He lied to himself. We all lie to ourselves, don't we? But he lied to himself more than normally would be the case. In 1989 the harvest figures were published and they were extremely good. My friends said: "These figures are impossible, they're made up". So, it was October 1989, I asked him. I said to my father: "Do you really believe in the harvest figures?" And he replied: "Yes. I believe them." It's not what he said, but the way he said it. He was so proud of these figures. But he was lying to me. Because while I was in prison, Nicu told me that my father knew the figures were bad.

'My brother said they were forced to report good figures. I knew he needed to give good figures to the Congress but I also knew he was very much against the fiddling of statistics. So it was a deliberate lie. And when you lie, you know that you are lying. All the politicians do it, for something good in the end. But what impressed me was the way he looked at me when he said the harvest figures were really good. He was not speaking in public, but to someone close whom he trusted. There was no need to lie to me. He could have brushed it off. Or said: "What's the point?"' Did you believe him? 'Sure – I believed him. That's the point. He was believable. It was close communication. I could see his expression on his face.' He lapsed into a long silence. 'Now I don't know what to believe about my father.'

I asked Nicu about this conversation, but the question was a mistake. To answer it, it required a tacit admission from Nicu that he knew what was going on at the end, when his whole case was based on the fact that he had been cold-shouldered by his parents from at least the mid-Eighties onwards. He was also extremely protective of his brother's reputation. Nicu said: 'My brother didn't know anything.

He was not involved.' A few minutes later there was a knock on the door and a man entered. It was Valentin.

Together, the two brothers – the Bad Prince and the Good Prince – looked much alike. Not just physically, but also in the way they held themselves. Valentin looked at me, annoyed: 'What are you doing here?' He then gave Nicu a crumpled piece of paper on which was written a telephone number. It was a private moment, a scene from the movie *The Godfather* perhaps, the two sons of the boss of bosses meeting after his death. We left them for their family meeting, the Bad Prince and the good one who knew nothing and was not involved.

Checkmate

The fear machine was still in place at the beginning of December 1989. Less than a month later, after the revolution, it was possible to go on a tourist trail of Securitate buildings. The most important was the Ministry of the Interior, the Gothic 'Addams Family' house which was Postelnicu's centre of operations. Not far from the Hotel Inter-Continental was the headquarters of the external branch of the Securitate, the Departmentul de Informatii Externe, or DIE, where Pacepa worked until his defection in 1978. It can be found by turning left out of the lobby of the hotel, crossing the car park till you reach Strada Batiste. On the far, north side of the pavement is, to your left, the office of CSA, the Czechoslovak airlines, and straight in front part of the American embassy. Turn to the right and walk down Strada Batiste, across one set of traffic lights, and the DIE building will loom up above on the other, north side of Strada Batiste. Its distinguishing features are a small gatehouse at the left of the building and ornate street-level irons bars on the windows which deter would-be intruders. The window bars have a fine curve to them, suggesting the slanting stern of a Napoleonic man o'war. One has to retrace one's route, east to west, past the back of the Inter-Continental Hotel for the phone-tapping building. At the hotel across the wide six-lane Boulevard Nicolae Balcescu and immediately in front, on roughly the same latitude, is a small, gloomy street, Strada 13 Decembrie, which leads to the southern end of the Palace Square where the Central Committee building stands. Three quarters of the way along Strada 13 Decembrie on the left-hand, south side is a pizza restaurant, just short of the Union Hotel. Immediately opposite this, on the north side, is a down-at-heel building fronted by unwashed frosted glass. The door is nondescript, steely grey. Set into the door is a small screw, which just stands proud of the door frame. Press the screw. One can hear the ding-dong of a bell. Inside, the Securitate used to monitor much of

Bucharest's telephone conversations using the very latest Western electronic equipment. They probably still do.

After the revolution in early January, with the snow turning to treacherous ice underfoot, Mike Goldwater, the photographer, Andrei and Razvan, our two tough translators, and I spent a day doorstepping these three buildings. We were bustled away from the Interior Ministry building very quickly. We had better luck at the DIE. We waited in our warm Western hire car until individual Securitate officers had left the gatehouse and had walked a short distance from safety. Then we pounced. Four to one: the Securitate usually had six to one. Goldwater, who is both one of Britain's finest magazine photographers and a restless fidget, zoomed in and out on their faces, his bemittened fingers working the apertures of his lenses with a manic intensity; Andrei and Razvan cross-questioned the now not-so-secret policemen; I scribbled importantly in my notebook. As they ran away from us, sometimes slipping on the ice, it was hard to remember they had once been held in utmost terror. One exchange lingers in the mind between Andrei and a Securitate man:

Andrei: Did you work here two weeks ago?

Securitate man: Who, me?

Andrei: Yes, you. Did you work here two weeks ago?

Securitate man: (Looking nervously at Goldwater's camera) I don't know.

Andrei: No. You must not say 'I don't know'. You must say 'No comment'.

They were all so ordinary, so unfrightening and now so afraid of us. We went to the local Bucharest Securitate office following one man out of the office till he went and stood in a queue for bread. He was touchingly timid when we confronted him, explaining that it had been his job to alert the authorities to the suffering of the people. He had been in the economic section, preparing reports on how little food there was in the shops so that the Central Committee would know how bad things were. He had two children. Please, he said, don't take my photograph. It was taken anyway: a poignant portrait of a secret policeman down on his luck, dodging the camera behind the other, curious shoppers in the bread queue.

But, first, a lot of people had to die.

Ceausescu and Elena never knew what hit them. Valentin was adamant about this: 'They were surprised by events, astonished. They couldn't believe what was happening. I think they never realised it. They never realised that they were not loved.' Part of the explanation for their disbelief is the unlikely spark – to use the Marxist-Leninist jargon – of the revolution. The spark crackled not in the capital, or Brasov or the Jiu Valley, previous flashpoints of unrest, but in Timisoara, a city on the western edge of the country nestling on the Hungarian border. The regime had not anticipated trouble there. However, it was not so unlikely. The people of Timisoara could get and understand Hungarian TV and radio, which had given fitting prominence to the breach of the Berlin Wall and the collapse of communism in Czechoslovakia. They were some of the best-informed and therefore most bitter people in the whole country; moreover, the region had enjoyed the more liberal, Western-orientated and sophisticated rule of the Austro-Hungarian Empire which was still, just, within living memory. The whole country was ripe for revolution, but the Hungarian minority living a stone's throw from their greatly richer and freer cousins were the ripest of them all.

Pastor Laszlo Tokes provided the focus for their anger. It is a delicious irony that a godless regime, which had wallowed in the abnegation of morality, had stolen Christian imagery to glorify the director and had pulped Bibles into toilet paper, was brought down by a humble parish priest. (The detail about the toilet paper sounds far-fetched. The World Reformed Alliance sent 20,000 Bibles to Romania in 1972 and 1981. Fewer than 200 were actually delivered to the churches. Instead of being distributed as Ceausescu had promised, the bulk was turned into toilet paper at a factory in Braila in Moldova. Unfortunately, the quality of the Romanian pulping was so poor that words like Esau, Jeremiah and God remained visible. Samples were sent to the West, where the Reverend Dr Alexander Havadtöy of Yale University documented, then publicised the scandal.)

Pastor Tokes, a burly fellow blessed with a rich, deep voice, belonged to the Hungarian Reformed Church. He had originally been sent to Timisoara in disgrace, after being punished for his insubordination against the regime at his previous posting in the town of Dej. The hierarchy of his church – like nearly all the other faiths, including Judaism – was compromised by what can at its best be described as a servile acquiescence to Ceausescu's despotism; at its worst, the church leaders were, like the Securitate, a reliable tool of the repression. Tokes arrived in Timisoara as the number-two priest in a small church; the senior pastor was an old man with a long record of compromise. But when he died, Tokes was appointed in his place and slowly began to question the verities of the Years of Light. Very few people made head-on criticisms and continued in office; Tokes made oblique references in his sermons by invoking God's wrath on such biblical baddies as King Nebuchadnezzar, who, it will be recalled, carried off the children of Israel into captivity in Babylon. He quoted from the Book of Daniel:

To you it is commanded, O peoples, nations, and languages,
    That at what times ye hear the sound of the cornet, flute, harp, sackbut, psaltery, dulcimer, and all kinds of musick, ye fall down and worship the golden image that Nebuchadnezzar the king hath set up:
    And whoso falleth not down and worshippeth shall the same hour be cast into the midst of a burning fiery furnace.

King Nebuchadnezzar sounded all too familiar. His parishioners got the point. Word spread. Soon his congregation numbered more than a thousand people, many of them not of his particular church. In September 1988 Tokes and a fellow minister wrote a letter to the authorities denouncing the 'systemisation' programme. The regime paused, before its creature Bishop Laszlo Papp decided to suspend the turbulent priest on 1 April 1989. The suspension was greeted with such an international uproar that Papp rescinded it, but ordered Tokes to Mineu, a remote farm hamlet accessible only down a rutted wagon track. The neatness of this solution betrays the subtle hand of the Securitate. Tokes would not go. His refusal to move was helped by an accident of geography. The church was only one floor above his flat. He didn't ever have to leave the building to make his sermons, making a snatch arrest that much more inconvenient. The regime got Papp to order Tokes's eviction, but the manoeuvre took time. Meanwhile, his parishioners organised a petition in his defence. Papp refused to accept the petition, but with each round the stakes were getting higher and higher.

On 24 July Hungary's most popular news programme, *Panorama*, screened a secret interview Tokes had made with a Canadian television team in which he threw aside King Nebuchadnezzar and launched into a detailed denunciation of 'systemisation'. The hundreds of thousands of viewers in western Romania who could watch Hungarian TV silently applauded. The stakes were raised again when the corpse of Erno Ujvarossy, a church elder, was found in a forest on the outskirts of Timisoara. No one should underestimate the courage required by Tokes to continue fighting the regime.

On 20 October the Romanian court ruled against Tokes in his case against eviction. He appealed, still keeping his defiance within the law. With the world beginning to watch and take notice, the regime had to be careful to follow the correct legal procedures inside the courtroom. Outside, they were a law unto themselves. One day early in November, four men broke into Tokes's locked flat. They were masked and were armed with clubs and knives. The pastor was beaten and clubbed to the floor while his three-year-old son, Mate, looked on. His pregnant wife, Edit, called out to the uniformed police who had kept the flat under surveillance for months for help. They left their plain-clothes colleagues undisturbed.

In late November Tokes lost his appeal, and Friday 15 December was set as the deadline for his departure. The clock ticked out the last days.

Before the revolution proper came the 'Best Love Angle Story of Europe's Year of Revolutions' when Nadia Comaneci, the former Olympic nymphette, touched down in early December in New York aboard the too-perfectly named Pan Am jet *Liberty Bell*, having made it across the frontier into Hungary – the last defector from Eastern Europe. She made it, the Securitate snapping at her heels with a threat to 'return or die', to find life in the West every bit as complicated as in Romania, but a lot more human. The newspaper headlines made it all sound so simple. The *Daily Mail* ran: 'Nadia: I did it for love' and the *Daily Express*: 'Nadia's Home Free!' The small print in the *Observer* pointed out that her Scarlet Pimpernel who smuggled her out, Constantin Panit, was married with children; she had another boyfriend, Graham Buxton Smither, who had been waiting for her . . . but these are the problems of the free.

Tokes continued to sit it out, his perilous position still, of course, virtually unknown to anyone outside Timisoara. To egg him on his way a gang of thugs armed with beer bottles broke every window in his flat. Tokes sent his son out to stay with his grandmother, boarded up the windows but stayed put. Come the deadline, Tokes was still inside his flat. Word had got around that a forced eviction was to take place. That Friday parishioners came to stop it, singing psalms and reading prayers while the police looked on. It became a street spectacle in a country starved of happenings, unless they were stage-managed by the RCP. A crowd of several hundred built up. The mayor came along and told them to disperse. They did not. The stand-off lasted through all of Friday night and Saturday morning.

On Saturday afternoon the spectacle started to snowball. People who had gone out to find bread, potatoes or *tsuica* started to drift along to see what was happening. They stayed. By doing so, those of them who had been born after 1945 were making the first democratic decision of their lives. The numbers grew one by one by one. The original core of Hungarian Protestants was soon outnumbered by ordinary Romanians. Some were standing up for Tokes's freedom of speech and worship out of Christian belief; some with no great religious conviction, were supporting his struggle against the regime; many others were just drawn to the spectacle and stayed to see what would happen next. Thanks to Gorbachev and the East Germans and the Czechs and Slovaks, there was the smell of change in the air.

By nightfall on Saturday the crowd numbered 5,000: enough people to encircle the block in which Tokes's flat and church were housed; enough people, too, to intimidate the Securitate and the police, who were observing the spectacle with mounting alarm. In the dark they could not be identified. A voice started to cry out: 'We want bread!' The Securitate officers watching probably did not realise that this cry was the tinderbox of the French Revolution of 1789. The cry was picked up, amplified, the crowd's confidence growing with each shout. Another cry sounded: 'Down with ration cards!' From that it was not so far to making the open challenge to the regime which had been locked away in people's minds for more than four decades: 'Down with dictatorship!' and, most daring of all, 'Down with Ceausescu!'

More police squads arrived at 10 p.m. but the people's strength was growing like Topsy. Having the psychological momentum is all-important in this sort of situation; the civil police and even the Securitate had lost it. And perhaps they, too, in their hearts, were sick of him. The crowd marched into the centre of town, throwing the everpresent portraits of Ceausescu into the Bega canal. A new threshold was crossed when the crowd saw a bookshop, stacked with very little else apart from *Romania on the Way of Building Up the Multi-Laterally Developed Socialist Society*. They smashed down the door and set fire to the books in the middle of Opera Square. Then they broke into the offices of the RCP and broke and burnt all the many photographs, pictures and books praising Ceausescu they could find. The erasing of the dictator's spoor had begun. There was another huge shout when the Romanian flag appeared with its hole ripped out where the old communist logo used to be. The revolution had its symbol.

While the crowd enjoyed itself in the main square, the founder of the revolution had been forgotten. The Securitate smashed down the door of his flat at 3 a.m. on Sunday. But he was not there. They raced upstairs and crashed through the church door. Tokes and Edit were praying by the altar. The pastor was wearing his black cassock over his pyjamas, his Bible in his hands. The Securitate gave him a nasty beating, then took the pastor and his wife in separate cars to Mineu. For three days the Securitate grilled Tokes, insisting that he go on television to admit that he had been acting under the command of foreign imperialists. It was the old Ceausescu line: any dissent was bankrolled by alien elements. Outside the isolated farmhouse Securitate troops swaggered about, using floodlights at night to heighten the sense of menace. But, by luck, Tokes had found a radio. By listening to Radio Free Europe, the BBC and the Hungarian radio stations, he knew that the uprising was getting stronger and stronger. He could sense the power drain out of the secret policemen as their demands for him to go on television grew more and more insistent. He graciously declined their offer. It was now his captors' turn to tremble.

Meanwhile, the regime had lost control of Timisoara. After ransacking the RCP headquarters, the crowd had fed on itself, cheerful, almost cocky at its power. For so long accustomed to singing the dictator's praises, they now sang and chanted abuse till their throats were ragged. It was as widespread an uprising as the one at Brasov in 1987, where the rebellious tractor workers had, too, stormed the RCP office; but then none of the other conditions were right. At Timisoara, the other revolutions of 1989 across Eastern Europe were in the back of everyone's mind. It became almost a matter of pride for the Romanians to throw off dictatorship before Europe's great year of revolutions turned. They knew the dangers of standing up to the police, the so-called militia, the Securitate and the army, all still completely loyal to Ceausescu. But Gorbachev's rallying cry for his reforms – 'If not now: when?' – ran through their heads. The Romanians in Timisoara had kicked the habit of submission.

So far, the Securitate and the army had not fired on the crowd.

Overtaken by the speed of events and the ferocity of the crowd's anger, they had not anticipated the uprising. On Sunday morning, Ceausescu called a meeting of the Political Executive Committee in Bucharest. It was by way of an inquest into how the security forces could lose control so utterly that a mob was able to vandalise the offices of the RCP. After the revolution a transcript of the meeting was published in the newspaper *Romania Libera*. Ceausescu, Elena, Interior Minister Tudor Postelnicu, his deputy Iulian Vlad, the chief of the Securitate, and General Vasile Milea, the defence minister, whom Lord Newall thought 'rather a nice man' were present.

Ceausescu: I think the foreign groups outside are involved in the organisation [protecting Pastor Tokes in Timisoara]. It is known that both East and West have said that things in Romania must change. Some elements have come together and caused disorder. [The police and the army] have done a very poor job. I talked to comrades in Timisoara and told them to put on a show of power with tank units in the centre of the city. My impression is that the units of the interior ministry [regular police and the Securitate] were unarmed.

Postelnicu: Except for those who were border guards, the rest were unarmed.

Ceausescu: Why? I have told you that all have got to be armed. Why did you sent them unarmed, who has given this order? When I understand that the Securitate troops are going somewhere it is clear to me that they are going armed. You sent them to beat with fists. What kind of interior units are they? And the militia [police] have to be armed. That's the law.

Postelnicu: Comrade general secretary, the militia is armed.

Ceausescu: If it is armed, it has to shoot, not to let people attack it. How is such a situation [the intrusion of demonstrators into the Timisoara party headquarters] possible? What did your officers do, Milea? Why didn't they intervene? Why didn't they shoot?

Milea: I didn't give them ammunition.

Ceausescu: Why didn't you give them ammunition? If you don't give them ammunition you might as well keep them at home. What kind of a Defence Minister are you? What kind of an Interior Minister are you, Postelnicu?

Elena: The situation is very grave.

Ceausescu: It is very grave and you are all guilty.

Elena: The Minister of Defence and the Minister of Interior did not act properly.

Ceausescu: Some few hooligans want to destroy socialism and you are making it child's play for them. Fidel Castro is right. You do not quieten your enemy by talking to him like a priest, but by burning him.

Elena: They are cowards.

Ceausescu: They are more than cowards. As supreme commander, I consider that you have committed treason against the country's supreme interests and against the people's interests and against the interests of socialism.

Vlad: You are right, comrade general secretary, that is so. [Vlad tells Ceausescu his troops have batons and tear gas.]

Ceausescu: Why were they unarmed?

Vlad: We believed that was not the case.

Ceausescu: In this moment, if the executive committee agrees, we are dismissing the Defence Minister, the Interior Minister and the chief of the Securitate troops. From this moment, I'll take command of the army. Prepare the decree to take force this evening. They've got to kill the hooligans, not to beat them. [To the three officials] Do you know what I'm going to do with you? Send you to the firing squad. I have realised now that you cannot create order with batons. I will give right now the order that all will have guns and ammunition.

Elena: You should shoot them so they fall and put them in [Securitate] basements. Not even one of them should see the light of day again. We've got to take radical measures, we can't be indulgent.

Ceausescu: We'll fight to the last.

Vlad: We thought it was a limited problem and we could solve it without ammunition.

Ceausescu: I didn't think that we would shoot with blanks. Those who entered the party building should not leave the building alive.

Later, when General Milea promised to carry out the orders to shoot to kill, the dictator had second thoughts about the dismissals. He said: 'Let's delay this decision.'

That afternoon he despatched the killers, who, led by General Ion Coman, the secretary to the Central Committee for Military and Security Affairs, were given the order to shoot by Ceausescu in person at two o'clock on Sunday afternoon. They boarded a plane at Otopeni airport which flew directly to Timisoara, an hour-long flight at the most. On board were Coman and two deputy ministers of defence, General Victor Stanculescu – who had dined with Lord Newall a few weeks before – and General Stefan Gushe, and Lieutenant General

Mihai Chitsac, head of the Bucharest military garrison, who was in charge of Romania's chemical weapons, including the regime's stocks of tear gas. General Milea, still under a cloud, was not sent to Timisoara.

That same afternoon a mob had looted the city centre. The soldiers held their ground, but did not use live ammunition. Not very long after Coman and Stanculescu's plane landed in Timisoara, at around 5 p.m., the troops used tear gas and water cannon against the people while tanks and armoured cars wheeled in through the streets. Around about 6 p.m. the guns finally spoke. The soldiers shot indiscriminately, machine guns spraying the crowd standing in Opera Square, killing and wounding men, women and children. According to four Bulgarians who later escaped southwards: 'The police, security men and soldiers first used water cannons and truncheons against the crowd. Helicopters appeared over the square, tanks and armoured personnel carriers rolled into the streets. . . . The real tragedy began at 6 p.m. We heard long automatic rifle and machine-gun fire. We saw bleeding people running in the streets. A Romanian wounded in the arm hid with us and told us that the public garden close to the square was strewn with corpses. It seemed incredible. Up to that point we thought that only warning shots were being fired in the air. Then we saw the soldier bayonet the woman. When the shooting subsided late in the night, we were about 300 metres from the square and heard groans.'

The gunning-down of unarmed civilians protesting against Ceausescu's dictatorship was a watershed for the regime. It put the events in Timisoara into a different category from the revolts in the Jiu Valley in 1977 and Brasov a decade later. But the killing was not out of character. Merely, the cold oppression with which the regime had subjugated an entire country suddenly became hot. The world, roused from its too long apathy, woke up. For many Romanians in the next few days, in the words of Petru Dumitriu, the world's 'awareness always comes late, nearly always too late'.

No journalists or diplomats were in Timisoara when the regime opened fire. No one had a clear idea of how many had been killed. Only the degree of horror and panic that the people in that crowd felt was accurately reflected by the word of mouth which reached the borders, now sealed on Ceausescu's orders. Lorry drivers, foreign medical students and other travellers who had passed through

Timisoara and emerged at checkpoints in Hungary, Bulgaria and Yugoslavia told of a massacre that had claimed 1,000 – no, 5,000 dead in the first few days. In the complete, eerie silence from the regime over what had happened at Timisoara, the rumour machine went to work: 10,000, 20,000, 30,000. These imaginary figures were passed on to frustrated reporters, all refused access to Romania. When two people answer the question 'How many dead?', one with 'I don't know' and the other with 'Someone told me 40,000', the second answer is printed. The Yugoslav news agency Tanjug printed 60,000 and still there was no honest account from the regime.

The effect of soldiers firing blindly into an unarmed crowd would devastate the morale of a city, but it is not a very efficient way of killing people. The numbers of dead would easily be exaggerated by people mistaking frightened for wounded, and wounded for dead. In the end, the official post-revolutionary tally from Timisoara numbered 97 dead and 210 injured. Those statistics cover the whole of the revolution, not just that Sunday.

After the massacre, Coman, Stanculescu and the Securitate commanders in Timisoara were faced with an immediate problem. What to do with the dead? They were heaped together and thrown into the back of an army lorry under the cover of the night. The truck was driven to a remote army/Securitate base. The plan was for the lorry to be driven to Bucharest where the dead would be incinerated, leaving no trace. After the revolution, the lorry with its macabre load was discovered. But before that the revolutionaries in Timisoara went to the city cemetery to find their dead. They were in a frantic, almost manic state, prepared to believe the vilest about the regime they had successfully overthrown in their city. Fuelled by reports aired by foreign radio and TV stations, they were looking for 60,000 dead, not realising that those broadcasts were based on the same wild rumours they had heard.

They went to the freshest earth in the cemetery. It was a mass grave for paupers, people who could not afford their own plot, still less a proper gravestone, but the revolutionaries hunting for the dead in their wild despair did not realise their mistake. The real victims of the massacre were in the back of an army lorry at a military depot. The revolutionaries dug up the paupers, many of them long dead, so that the world could see the evil they had been fighting. And that was what confronted the stunned Western journalists arriving in Timisoara as dawn broke on the morning of Saturday 23 December. The wrong dead.

For the regime, the operation on the Sunday night, 17 December, had been a success. The people of Timisoara, terrified, retreated behind their doors to weep for the unnumbered dead. The dictator was informed that things had gone sweetly. Reassured, he appointed Elena and a senior Political Executive Committee member, Manea Manescu, to take charge of the emergency, but decided to go ahead with his planned trip to Iran the following day. He flew out of Otopeni on Monday. The fact that Ceausescu left the country for three crucial days even though the regime was up against its worst domestic crisis in twenty-four years supports Valentin's contention that he never realised how hated he was.

The trip was not a happy one. No reporters were allowed access to the Romanian president during the trip, but official photographers captured some of the moments for posterity. On Tuesday 19 December he was photographed signing the visitors' book at a carpet museum in Tehran; on the same day, he was pictured with the Iranian foreign minister, Dr Ali Akbar Velayati, the two men seated at either end of an ornate, gilded sofa which looks suspiciously like a hangover from the Shah's time. The same sofa featured the next day when Ceausescu was pictured with the Iranian president, Hashemi Rafsanjani. The latter looks distinctly ill at ease, but there is no obvious indication of the worries that must have been afflicting Ceausescu.

A few days later he flew home. He had been in constant touch with Bucharest via the embassy in Tehran. The news was all bad. Far from knuckling under, the rebels in Timisoara had returned to the streets every night in mounting numbers – 50,000 by Wednesday 20 December – and mounting revulsion at the massacre. On Monday and Tuesday nights the police and soldiers had stood by. On Wednesday morning the rebels had succeeded in forcing the troops to withdraw from the city centre. Workers at a local petrochemical plant said they had to pull out by 11 a.m. or they would blow up the plant and the city with it. A Romanian who crossed the border into Yugoslavia told reporters that the rebels had commandeered two tanks. The tanks were driving up and down outside the Hotel Continental, manned by rebels waving flags and yelling: 'Down with Ceausescu.' The numbers killed in the massacre, according to foreign news agencies, was growing with each news bulletin. Other cities, mainly in the west of the country, had seen angry anti-Ceausescu demonstrations in sympathy with the dead of Timisoara. The regime had to make a response.

Spitting with rage, the dictator called a crisis meeting at six o'clock that evening of his closest advisers, the army chiefs and the Securitate. He heaped more scorn on General Milea, the disgraced minister of defence, and the idiots who had allowed things to reach this state. He decided that he would make a direct appeal to the people, as he had done so successfully back in 1968. He made orders to make a broadcast to the nation that night and told the RCP machine to arrange a public rally in the Palace Square for the following day, where party members would show their support. He was completely out of touch. A man less surrounded by hollow men would have received strong advice that this path was suicidal. But there was no one who dared contradict the dictator.

That night Ceausescu made his broadcast on television and radio to read the riot act. He blamed 'international and terrorist actions' by 'imperialist circles and foreign espionage agencies' for the Timisoara rebellion, which was designed to 'provoke disorder and destroy the institutions' [of the country]. 'The military units were obliged to defend themselves and to protect order,' he said, adding that the army 'had shown great patience' and had 'fully fulfilled their duty towards the homeland, the people and the socialist achievements'.

Far more important than what he actually said – that was pretty predictable – was how he said it and how he looked. The dictator's delivery was a disaster. He shouted for most of the twenty-four minutes he was on air, his voice hoarse with the strain, occasionally pausing inexplicably, as if for air. He rambled incoherently, repeating identical phrases such as 'imperialist reactionary elements threatening the independence of socialist Romania' at least ten times. And his appearance was no better. It was as if the Romanian viewers saw the dictator as he really was for the first time, a frail, bad-tempered old man, lacking the energy to finish his sentences or think straight. He did not look like a strong man any more.

Even though the content was less important than the image, that too alerted the entire country to the enormity of what had happened in Timisoara. Having castigated the traitors who 'are ready to sell our country for a handful of dollars', he went on to praise the fallen heroes: 'We salute the martyrs who have fallen in defence of the unity of our country.' That meant to the viewers, highly skilled in reading between the lines, that the rebels had struck back, killing members of the security forces. It was a huge admission that the revolt was far more serious than the Jiu Valley strike and the Brasov uprising. The broadcast detonated across the country like a thunderclap.

That night Ceausescu and Elena slept at Primavera, by their bed a Christmas card 'to my dearly beloved parents' from Zoia. The next day, Thursday 21 December, Ceausescu had demanded that the RCP pull out all the stops. He wanted 100,000 people to sing the old songs. The organisation for the rally worked as smoothly as Petr Clej described for the one he attended back in 1985. The party members met at prearranged rostering points, collected their banners and photographs, and trooped off to the Palace Square. At the front the Securitate cheerleaders; the tape recorders were set to whirr their chants. The television cameras were there to broadcast the speech live. The whole apparatus was in place as it had been countless times before. But something went wrong.

Ceausescu had only begun to get into his stride, thanking the Bucharest Party Committee for organising this impromptu rally, when it started. It was not a shout or a heckle or a hiss, but more timid than any of those. It came from the back, where the ordinary people stood, who normally only came to these rallies so they could get a couple of days off work or thought that it might help them get a better flat. They were murmuring.

The murmur grew. Another, keener sound came in, discernible on the TV soundtrack. The crowd were whistling, too. The volume of the protest grew, new instruments of the orchestra of abuse started to play – boos, shouts, cries – until the square was full of discord. Ceausescu ploughed on, spewing out the old dogma, but looking hesitantly over to his right, near the Athenée Palace Hotel, where the volume of abuse was loudest. They began to rip up the banners and smash his photograph. Slowly, he sputtered to a stop. The Securitate cheerleaders, waiting to take their lead from the dictator stopped, too. He had lost the momentum.

He held up his hand and shooed away the wasp as he had done outside hundreds of people's homes, but the discord did not die. Rather, it got rowdier and rowdier. Others around him on the balcony of the Central Committee building started to twitch. The dictator's personal bodyguard, General Neagoe, walked into the screen and whispered, sotto voce, 'They're getting in.' He was wrong on both counts. No one was getting in and it wasn't sotto voce. The TV microphone picked up every word. The general scarpered for the doors back into the safety of the Central Committee building. The other attendants started to drift backwards, leaving the old man on his own but for Elena. Her voice could be heard saying: 'Stay calm, please'. The dictator carried on, berating 'foreign imperialists', but the people were no longer afraid.

It was like the scene in *The Wizard of Oz* when Dorothy's dog goes backstage to reveal a tired old quack turning and turning the fire-wheels and roaring into the microphone. The fear had gone.

Then someone at the TV station cut the transmission and the screen went blank. This was the moment of revolution. Thousands and thousands of ordinary Romanians across the city decided right then to head for the Palace Square and vote with their voices against the dictator.

In Plumbuita monastery, the candlestick-makers were watching the rally when the transmission went dead. One of Petru Papurica's workmates said: 'When he heard the crowd booing Ceausescu he just ran off, there and then. That was the last time we saw him.' Another to run was Marian Neagu, an under-butcher at the special abattoir for the party. He and his wife Paraschiva lived in a shack in the Anti-Aircraft district of Bucharest, which is as lovely as it sounds. They were *flotants,* 'floaters', people without the required permit to live in Bucharest and therefore some of the poorest of the poor. In summer they baked inside their tiny two-room hut with a roof of corrugated iron; in winter they froze. After the revolution, when the snow came, icicles as thick as beer bottles hung from the roof, while inside each breath was made foggily visible. Paraschiva said: 'He was a simple worker, but he wanted revenge in some way. He wanted revenge for the conditions he had to live in. He shouted out loud for his family back home, who couldn't shout. He told me he was going to fight for the children, and if he died he would die for the children, for the way we lived, with no food and rations.' They were just two drops in a tide of people that was to wash the dictator away.

In the square, people hardly dared to believe that they had made Ceausescu falter. Adrian Donea, a taxi-driver, was there. He said that even while everybody was yelling and screaming, they all were shielding their heads because the Securitate used to film the crowd.

But at the moment: 'We had the feeling and the sensation that maybe we win. We can see they're scared, and in that moment we see we can do something and that we're really a force.'

The TV picture returned within a few minutes to show the composed dictator being applauded in the time-honoured way, but the break had been long enough. Ceausescu still continued to rant. In a hoarse voice he threw sops to the people – 100-Lei (£7) wage increase for everyone, a 1000-Lei benefit for pregnant women. He returned again and again to the 'foreign imperialists acting in Timisoara', the old magic formula of resisting foreign interference which, in this very spot, had once worked so well. This time, the people started to walk away.

Once the paralysing fear of the dictator had gone, the regime was finished. But, as Ceausescu told his Political Executive Committee, he was going to fight to the last man. The Securitate troops – much better paid, trained and equipped than the inefficient conscript army – waited till nightfall before they opened fire. The order was probably made by General Ion Coman, now back in Bucharest, and General Nicolae Andrutsa Ceausescu, the dictator's brother, who was in charge of the Securitate training school.

This time gap was to prove a great mistake, for the crowds took over the streets, burning cars and overturning Ceausescu posters and photographs, waving the new flag with the hole in it, all the time infecting passers-by with the revolutionary fever. The people had a symbol; they had a cause, too – they sang 'Timisoara, Timisoara' over and over again, taunting the regime and its armed killers. If the Securitate had struck straight away at the crowd that booed Ceausescu, they might have won the day, but there were, after all, party workers and Securitate men too in the crowd.

As the borders had been sealed against anyone coming in, the world had to rely on Soviet and 'Communist' journalists for their news. Tass, the Soviet news agency, reported that some of those killed were shot as they tried to rescue people from beneath the wheels of an armoured vehicle. Two Tass reporters, filing in a joint dispatch, said that troops fired 'dense volleys' of tear gas in the city's University Square.

The whole square was filled with thick, suffocating gas. Some of the demonstrators withdrew into narrow side streets, but the square promptly filled again with people as soon as the gas began to disperse. The demonstrators began to chant 'We won't leave'. Tanks and fire trucks moved into the square several times in an apparent attempt to intimidate the demonstrators. But the people on the square shouted at the security forces "We are the people", "We are not terrorists" and "You eat the people's bread". Fire engines are trying to douse some burning lorries and huge volleys of tear-gas shells are continuing.

Tanjug, the Yugoslav news agency, claimed that at least twenty students had died as police sprayed demonstrators with bullets and fired rockets from helicopters. The Tanjug correspondent filed: 'A massacre is taking place in Bucharest. Tanks are crushing students in the streets and the police are firing on everyone who's moving.'

Yet the people stayed on the streets to roar their long-gagged anger at the dictator and his works. The students of Bucharest University were an example to many. Gabriel Costache, the physicist friend of Valentin Ceausescu, recalled: 'I was scared. I had been in trouble myself when I was a student in the 1960s and I had not forgotten my arrest. So I was afraid. But a girl made me feel ashamed. It was near the Inter-Continental Hotel. She was sitting on a boy's shoulders, handing out flowers to the police. I was watching her. From that moment my fear went away.'

The shooting continued throughout the night. On the morning of Friday 22 December Petre the civil engineer as usual drove to work at the House of the Republic. He recalled: 'As I drove through the city centre I saw blood on the ground. It was everywhere.' An hour or so later the butcher Marian Neagu set off for the city centre again. He had arrived home covered in blood late on Thursday night. His wife thought he had been wounded, but the blood belonged to a young student who died in his arms. Paraschiva asked him why was he going into danger again. He replied: 'I'm going to the square to fight because a sixteen-year-old died in front of me last night and I am sick of being a coward.'

He was not alone. Despite all the menace the regime could summon to its side, that morning the people returned to throng the streets in their thousands. The regime had, for the moment, lost the battle.

That morning Gabriel Costache telephoned Valentin Ceausescu at the dictator's house Primavera. They hadn't been in close contact since Valentin moved back in with his parents. Gabriel recalled: 'I begged him to use every bit of influence he had to stop the killing by the police and the army. He replied that it was very hard to get in touch with his father. Valentin told me that I should not be scared about people getting shot because there were strict orders for the troops not to shoot people. I told him, listen, you've known me for twenty years – he said, "Yes, twenty years" – and when I say people are being killed by the police and the army, I know what I am talking about.' According to Gabriel, Valentin was convinced that what was happening in Romania was some kind of foreign invasion. He told his old friend that he hadn't heard the shooting on the previous night – an impossibility. The firing had been so loud and prolonged that it had kept the whole city awake.

Gabriel said: 'I am sure he didn't lie to me. He was convinced that the orders not to open fire had been obeyed. But I knew there had been shooting. I don't know what to make of it.' Gabriel continued: 'I told him that the people only wanted one thing. He asked: "What?" His resignation. "But that is almost done. My father is about to resign." '

Valentin must have been hiding from reality. Far from being about to resign, the dictator was still snarling at anyone who came near him. The recriminations inside the Central Committee buildings were swift and absolute. Ceausescu had already threatened Postelnicu, Vlad and Milea with dismissal at the meeting of the Political Executive Committee the previous Sunday, but this order had not been put into immediate effect. But, come Friday morning, Ceausescu was convinced that Milea had been refusing to convey his orders to shoot to kill to the army. That was why the regime was losing the battle on the streets. Around ten o'clock that morning Milea was taken upstairs by members of the dictator's bodyguard, where they shot him dead. An hour later Radio Bucharest announced that Milea was a traitor and had committed suicide. When Gabriel heard the news, he knew that Valentin was wrong and that the dictator was never going to resign.

It is almost irrelevant whether Milea had been a traitor or a hero until then. The army high command, Milea included, could not deliver their troops' loyalty to the regime. The conscripts knew who was in the crowd: it was made up of their brothers and sisters. Unlike the Securitate troops, which had been specially nurtured by Ceausescu because he didn't trust the army, the ordinary soldiers did not lead a privileged existence. For the first days discipline and tradition held good, but by Thursday the soldiers on the ground were beginning to have second thoughts about whether Ceausescu was worth killing for. The ordinary squaddies started to ignore their officers; some turned their guns on the regime. The crowd's cries reflected this – 'The army is with us' – and so did the news-agency reports that some soldiers had been publicly executed for not carrying out orders to shoot to kill.

Once dead, however, Milea attained the status of a martyr. Like Timisoara, he became a holy cause. More important, his killing – for no one believed the suicide story – became a reason for the army officers to do what their troops were already doing in increasing numbers: to switch sides. Across the country, the power was draining from the regime at a bewildering pace. Stalwart technicians of the repression were switching sides in the blink of an eye, desperate not to be caught on the losing side. The most important weathervane was General Stanculescu, who had spent most of the week in Timisoara after personally supervising the massacre on Sunday. But while Ceausescu was in Iran, the situation had changed. The size of the crowd in Timisoara on the Wednesday night had impressed Stanculescu. The general was beginning to realise that something had to give and it was not going to be the people, but such thinking was treason. Perhaps the general, a tall, stocky man with an easy, Bob Monkhouse smile and a reasonable command of colloquial English, knew Sir John Harington's epigram:

> Treason doth never prosper: what's the reason?
> For if it prosper, none dare call it treason.

Certainly the general's actions over the next few, crucial days reveal a man steeped in realpolitik. He arrived back in Bucharest very early on Friday morning and was immediately summoned by telephone to go to the dictator. Stanculescu said he could not go to the Central Committee building. The dictator himself came on the line. The conversation, allegedly, went something like this:

Ceausescu: (shouting) I want you here Stanculescu, now!

Stanculescu: (wheedling) I can't, Comrade General Secretary. I can't come.

Ceausescu: (apoplectic) What! Why on earth not?

Stanculescu: My leg's in plaster.

The dictator was not impressed. He saw through Stanculescu's somewhat transparent ruse of a convenient wound and demanded that Stanculescu show up, on pain of death. He duly turned up with his perfectly unharmed leg in plaster, in time to see his boss, General Milea, being taken to his death *'pour encourager les autres'*. Stanculescu ws not the only one to contrive ill health that day. Violeta Andrei told me that her husband, Stefan, Ceausescu's economics minister, had thought of getting Professor Mincu, a friend, to arrange a heart attack severe enough to get him out of the frame. In the confusion, however, the heart attack scam did not come off. The rats were jumping ship.

The old master still didn't recognise what was happening. His sick, paranoia-heavy mind was full of plots and 'foreign agents'. Again, he decided to place his faith in the people. It was a mistake piled on the mistake of the previous day. He went outside the doors of his office, on to the balcony of the Central Committee building, with a loud hailer in his hand. The mob was out there, swirling around. It was a predictable catastrophe. The dictator did not win over the people; instead, he acted as a focus for their formless rage. They threw sticks and pieces of wood at him; then they charged the building.

His Securitate minders dragged him back inside. What happened next is uncertain. One story goes that his minders pushed him into fleeing by helicopter. Another story is that Stanculescu took charge. He offered the dictator an alternative: resign on the spot, or take the helicopter. Both stories require one to believe that Ceausescu was now a pawn, someone who could be pushed around at whim. It does not match his later, tough behaviour at his trial. The Army High Command, now under Stanculescu's control, did order the helicopter. So it is most likely that a combination of all three explanations occurred: his bodyguards were pushing for him to go, Stanculescu made sure there was a helicopter, but Ceausescu decided himself to flee, the better to regroup and launch the counter revolution. Stanculescu would have known well that the best way to get things done in Ceausescu's Romania was to make any idea seem as if it was the dictator's own.

Once the helicopter was ordered and the dictator was safely – so it was thought – in the lift for the roof, Stanculescu left for the safety of the Ministry of National Defence. Once in his car, he would have radioed orders for the troops to stop defending the building. And that, shortly before noon, is what happened. The soldiers guarding the front pulled out, leaving the Central Committee building defenceless. The revolutionaries surged in.

One of them, the taxi driver Adrian Donea, raced out on the balcony and waved to the crowd below, where Ceausescu had stood not many minutes ago. The crowd cheered, ecstatic. What the revolutionaries in their transport of joy did not realise was that the dictator was still in the building. The lift had stuck, the doors jammed at the top of the shaft, just short of the landing pad where the helicopter was waiting. It was (a sweet irony, this) caused by a power failure, perhaps because of the gunfire, perhaps because the departing officers had killed the building's power supply as a precaution. The crowd outside the building could be heard roaring: 'Death! Death!' Inside the jammed lift, the power gone, the atmosphere, as the minutes ticked by, must have been a trifle tense.

On the roof of the Central Committee building was the white, French-made Ecureuil helicopter piloted by Lieutenant Colonel Vasile Malutanu of the Presidential Flight and four decoy helicopters. As the empty chopper sat on the roof while a riotous crowd celebrated the overthrow of the dictator, the pilot's nerves were getting increasingly frayed. Where was Ceausescu? Malutanu said: 'The rotor blades were turning, and we could hear the angry shouts of the crowd. My colleagues and I were terrified. Our mission was secret. The Army High Command had just given me orders to go and find the president, but I had no idea what the situation was. The revolutionaries had managed to block the lift' – this was wrong, it was either by accident or by the army – 'which was carrying Ceausescu, his wife, Emil Bobu, Manea Manescu and two bodyguards from the Securitate.'

One of Ceausescu's bodyguards succeeded in smashing a window to raise the alarm. The helicopter crew forced the doors of the lift open to get them out. The six passengers piled into the helicopter as the first of the revolutionaries burst on to the roof. The revolutionaries stopped again to wave to the throng below, a crowd-pleasing gesture which meant they were just too late to stop the dictator. But it was touch and go. The helicopter was so crowded that the mechanic had to perch on the dictator's knee like a dummy on a ventriloquist. With Elena in tears and the dictator whey-faced, the chopper slowly whirred away, only just clearing the Central Committee building rooftop, and then up, up, up as the mob that had brought about his doom dwindled into dots.

Eight months after the revolution, Silviu Brucan – the 'Squealer' of the Gheorghiu-Dej regime – gave the fullest yet version of the 'plot' theory to the *Adevarul* newspaper in Bucharest, the linear descendant of *Scinteia* (in which he once so eloquently argued the cause of high Stalinism). Brucan and the former General Nicolae Militaru told the newspaper that they had participated in a coup plot which had sealed Ceausescu's fate. They said the plot, prepared long in advance, involved army units, many generals and a section of the Securitate. They said that the conspirators plotted to 'neutralise' Ceausescu's main aides and to take over the broadcasting stations in order to appeal to the population. They said the coup should have been carried out last October but that it was set back after somebody betrayed the conspiracy.

Brucan and Militaru said it was untrue that the army, as popularly believed, had suddenly taken the side of the people in the revolution. The army was turned against Ceausescu by the plotters. They hinted also that until that point soldiers loyal to Ceausescu had been shooting civilian demonstrators. They said they had 'managed to avoid a civil war by a very small margin because of the specific situation within the army'. By this time, in late August, both men, who had at first been prominent in the post-revolution government, had been dimissed.

But just a few days after the revolution, on Friday 29 December, Brucan told a somewhat different story to John Lloyd and Judy Dempsey of the *Financial Times*. Brucan, one of the six signatories of the letter published in March 1989, had given the two reporters a brief curriculum vitae. After the letter, he told the reporters, he had been closely watched by the regime. They wrote:

Since then, Mr Brucan had been under house arrest and subjected to interrogations lasting up to 22 hours. He was evicted from his home and sent to a village with his wife and daughter. There, without heating or light, he was constantly watched, prevented from visiting his friends, receiving foreign newspapers, or meeting colleagues. When the uprising began on Thursday night he was still under house arrest. But then, 'I looked out the window and saw that the Securitate had left. A neighbour then gave me a lift into town.'

Brucan's December account does not tally with the story he told in August. But it fits with the stories of all the other regime's enemies that Friday morning. They woke up to find the creatures who had kept them captive suddenly scuttling under the stones. In his small, obscure hamlet Pastor Tokes discovered that his Securitate tormentors had fled. The Securitate bosses in Timisoara ran for the frontier, almost bumping into the first Western journalists flooding in as the borders opened. The poet Mircea Dinescu found his guards gone that Friday, so he was free to go to the TV station to declaim his verse, the very first signal to the country and the world that the dictator had definitely been overthrown.

No plot sparked the revolution. A plot, a coup d'état, would not have started in out-of-the-way Timisoara but in Bucharest. How does the plot theory reconcile the heroism of a Hungarian-speaking pastor and his congregation? What about Erno Ujvarossy, the church elder whose body was found in the forest? The people who started it were not generals or members of the RCP old guard, but village Hampdens driven to resist the tyrant. There is, moreover, a disgusting elitism about any plot theory. It plays up the importance of a tiny band of politically far-sighted men – the classic Leninist cell – and plays down the importance of that sea of humanity who shouted down the dictator. What about the unknown student who made Gabriel ashamed when he saw her give out flowers to the soldiers? What about the soldiers who ignored their officers and did not fire? What about the butcher, the baker and the candlestick-maker who went out into the streets and cried 'Down with the dictator'? Up to the moment when Ceausescu fled, it was a revolution won by the ordinary people.

Then, as the presidential helicopter clattered off, the moment of democratic triumph had peaked. First, the revolution was hijacked by a group of politicians whose principal qualification for political power was frustrated subservience under Ceausescu; then, the counter revolution erupted, staged by the forces still loyal to the dictator.

The counter revolution was savage. The Securitate opened fire as Friday night fell on the celebrations across the country. In Bucharest, Timisoara, Arad, Sibiu, Cluj and Brasov, the gunmen opened up. There were never very many of them, but they had night-sights on their rifles, sole use and knowledge of the echoing system of tunnels built under Bucharest by the dictator, and a motive: if they were found and identified by the people, they would be torn apart by bare hands.

That night in Bucharest the butcher Marian Neagu was shot dead, a neat hole in his head. It took his widow Paraschiva a week of trailing round hospitals and morgues before she found his corpse. The next morning the candlestick-maker Petru Papurica was killed as he moved around his flat, not far from the Central Committee buildings, at eight in the morning. He too was shot through the head, blood spurting on the floor. When the news of his death was broken to a friend, an old man, with whom he played cards from time to time, the old man wept and said: 'And now the scoundrels are shooting the bridge players.'

The killing continued over the Saturday, 23 December, Sunday, Christmas Eve, and Monday, Christmas Day. Such was the level of terror and confusion that many people died, not by a Securitate bullet, but because they were caught in cross-fire or brought down by a ricochet or were simply blasted away by mistake by a jumpy finger on a trigger. This almost happened to Ali and me on the road to Bucharest.

The official death toll of the revolution was published by the new government on 10 June 1990:

Bucharest:	540 dead,	1,040 injured.
Timisoara:	97 dead,	210 injured.
Sibiu:	91 dead,	208 injured.
Brasov:	61 dead,	108 injured.
Braila:	40 dead,	97 injured.
Cluj:	26 dead,	50 injured.
Buzau:	25 dead,	26 injured.
Tirgoviste:	13 dead,	28 injured.
Others:	138 dead,	401 injured.

A little over one thousand dead and two thousand injured in all.

Among the injured was Nicu Ceausescu, stabbed in the stomach shortly after he was arrested. Zoia and Valentin came quietly. A television crew did a version of 'Through the keyhole' with Zoia's apartment. To gasps of envy, they showed that she ate meat specially imported from abroad, weighed on scales made of gold.

While the conscript army blazed away – sometimes with their eyes shut – at any target that presented itself, including the old Royal Palace, the National Art Gallery and the National Library in Bucharest, the hijacking of the revolution was made official. For the first few, terrible hours after the helicopter flew off, Stanculescu locked himself up in the Ministry of National Defence and did not return any telephone calls. The politicians led by Ion Iliescu, out of favour but never in disgrace with Ceausescu, sweated it out in the Central Committee building. It was only when the news came that the dictator had definitely been arrested that Stanculescu came on the line. Iliescu was made president of the interim government headed by the new National Salvation Front. The dissident Doina Cornea, who had spent years being hounded by the dictator, became a dissident all over again: 'Dubious elements – profiteers, lackeys and liars – had infiltrated the interim government,' she said.

Iliescu had been made the new leader, not by popular acclamation but by the only effective, organised structure in the country, the Army

High Command. The Army High Command was with the revolution. In fact, the Army High Command had been with the revolution from the very first moment. Stanculescu's mission to Timisoara was swiftly forgotten. The air-brushing of history had begun again.

One of the last moves of the mad king was to fly to Snagov, the resting place of Vlad the Impaler. They arrived near the big villa at around 12.30 p.m. It was a shock for the staff. They knew nothing of the momentous happenings in Bucharest that morning; they only feared that they would get a carpeting from Elena for having nothing prepared. They had been expecting the Ceausescus on Christmas Eve, not two days earlier. The chief of security at Snagov, Sergeant Major Lalescu, watched the dictator and Elena run into the villa and climb up to their bedroom on the first floor. He recalled: 'They went searching through all the cupboards, emptied the drawers and turned over the mattresses. They put everthing into two big blue bags. On top, I could see blankets and loaves of bread. I've got no idea what was under them.'

It may have been a hoard of Ceausescu gold; more likely it was more bread and blankets. They were peasants on the run, after all. They made two phone calls: one to the head of an air-force base, one to a party secretary in a mountain fastness. They were keeping their options open. They hurried back to the helicopter to find that Manea Manescu and Emil Bobu, the bouncing sycophant, had gone off. There had been no farewells. So then the six were four.

They took off, but the pilot had been in touch with his base. The dictator caught the pilot's disapproving look. 'Whose side are you on?' he asked. The pilot replied: 'Where are you going? You give the orders.' The dictator told him to head for Pitesti, the town nearest to Scornicesti. Perhaps, in the back of his mind, he wanted to go home. It was not to be. The pilot lied that he did not have enough fuel and besides they were being tracked by air-traffic control. He set the helicopter gently down next to a quiet country road. As Ceausescu got out, he sensed that the pilot had let him down. He asked: 'Why are you abandoning the cause like this?' The pilot says that before he took off he replied: 'What cause?' Perhaps he did.

Dr Nicolae Deca, a hospital doctor, had been following the events closely with the rest of the country. He heard on the radio at the hospital that the dictator had fled Bucharest. As he was about to leave for home he joked with his workmates: 'I'll go and catch the bastard by his arse' – which is what he unwittingly proceeded to do. He said:

'I was looking forward to being alone in the car to think quietly about this new liberty of ours. As I drove along, deep in thought, I suddenly saw a big man by the side of the road.' It was the second bodyguard. He ordered the doctor to stop and pick up two old people, whom he recognised, not without a certain discomfort: Nicolae and Elena Ceausescu.

Then the second bodyguard, Marian Rusu, who had been Elena's personal detective for years, went away. The four became three.

The doctor observed his extraordinary passengers closely: 'They were completely dumbfounded by the situation they were in. There was disbelief written all over their faces. I think they were terrified and close to despair. They seemed to get smaller and smaller as they sat in the car. We continued down the road, Ceausescu contemplating his situation and me trying to think what to do next. Ceausescu asked me if I knew what had happened. I replied that I had been on duty at the hospital all night and had no idea. He said: "There was a coup." '

At this, the dictator lasped into silence. The doctor, too, supports Valentin's belief that Ceausescu never realised that he had been overthrown because of the hatred of the people. He had always feared a takeover by the army, but as events were to unfold, he could be forgiven for that misunderstanding. A few miles passed in the car, each one absorbed in their own thoughts. Then the dictator turned to the doctor and said: 'We're going to organise the resistance. Are you coming with us?'

The question caught the doctor cold. If he answered yes, he would be trapped with them for longer; if he said no, the remaining bodyguard (Nicolae Rats), might shoot him. Like Stanculescu and Stefan Andrei, the doctor came up with the excuse of ill health: 'I tried to tell him that I wasn't young any more, my constitution was frail, and so on. I ended up by saying, "Anyway I'm not even a party member".' The remark killed the conversation in the car. More miles rolled by.

The doctor was sweating with worry. How could he get rid of his unlikely hitchhikers? He saw a man he knew washing his car by the side of the road; the doctor claimed that his carburettor was giving out and pulled to a stop. The car-washer, Nicolae Petrisor, shouted to his wife: 'It's the Ceausescus!' The remaining bodyguard waved his gun at Petrisor to shut him up and ordered him to drive them on.

Petrisor said that the dictator looked all washed up; Elena seemed more businesslike. Throughout the journey she held a gun to his head.

Ceausescu switched on the car radio. Loud and clear came the quirky cadences of Mircea Dinescu, the poet, freshly released from his six-a-shift house arrest. Petrisor said: 'When Ceausescu heard what Dinescu was saying his head slumped forwards on to the dashboard. He stayed like that for a few seconds. Then he said to me; "Turn it off".'

The bodyguard suggested that they drive to Tirgoviste – the Impaler's old capital – where he knew the security men at the steelworks. The car passed a group of striking workers protesting against the dictator. They recognised the old man and started to stone the car. Petrisor was not just worried about his Dacia's paintwork. He drove down the back streets of the town with Ceausescu and Elena keeping their heads down.

The dictator suggested that they should hole up in a village called Ulmi, where he had taken refuge from Antonescu's secret police during the war. Elena sneered at the suggestion, pointing out that the old woman he had stayed with would have been long dead. They stopped so that Rats could ask the way; perhaps it was a ruse by the bodyguard. While they were waiting for him, some children came along and spotted the two most identifiable faces in the whole country. They started jeering, so Elena pulled out her gun and commanded Petrisor to 'Get going!' Now he was alone with them in the car.

They went to a nunnery and asked for sanctuary. The nuns said no. They went to a hotel for party officials: the porter said there was no room. Power, will, energy had all drained from the couple. The driver took the situation into his own hands and pulled up at an agricultural institute where he knew the staff. The director, Victor Seinescu, was later to suffer a nervous breakdown because he could never get over the stress of what happened that day. Petrisor told him who his hitchhikers were; Seinescu knew he wasn't joking because his face was as white as a sheet. What upset him was that he had just heard on the radio that the Ceausescus had been arrrested in the Tirgoviste area. The media were jumping the gun on reality.

They came in to Seinescu's office without saying hello. He recalled: 'They were terrified.' Either the disaster had finally broken the last ragged remnant of Ceausescu's sanity or he was play-acting brilliantly, because he started to scare Seinescu witless by repeatedly looking at his watch and looking at the sky, as if his rescuers were about to appear. According to Seinescu, he asked why they were there.

'Traitors and foreign agents have got together to overthrow me. Why do you want to hand me over?' said the dictator.

'So you can be tried by the people, you bastard!'

Two police officers came at 3.20 p.m. They didn't know what to do with the Ceausescus either. They were told by headquarters to go and drive out into the country, while arrangements were made at an old cavalry school which had become an army barracks. The officers went and parked in a quiet wood. As the four of them sat in the car, waiting, waiting, waiting, a fox peeped out of the undergrowth and watched them. Meanwhile telephone calls were made to Bucharest; Stanculescu and the others could now breathe more easily. If Ceausescu had been still at large, who knows what would have happened? Now that he and Elena were in the new regime's hands, they could relax. The Army High Command was with the revolution. The fox ran off.

Ceausescu and Elena spent the night in the barracks. They were not agreeable guests, once they found their voices. They complained about being locked up and they complained about the food. The next day the dictator tried to bribe one of the officers appointed to guard them with $1 million and any rank in the army he fancied. The officer, realising the new, post-revolutionary realities more clearly than his captives, said: 'Nothing doing.' As the events of the last few days retreated, the revolution was beginning to take on the shape of a nightmare. At one point Ceausescu heard his name being shouted; he rushed forward to the window, only to be pulled back by the guard. It was not a rescue party but a crowd of ordinary people singing the revolutionary song:

'Olé, Olé, Olé,
Ceausescu's gone away.'

On Christmas Eve, the Securitate special troops found the barracks and opened up. The bullets pockmarked the building. The couple were squeezed inside an armoured car, which drove around to a spot of comparative safety, where they passed an uncomfortable, probably sleepless night.

The trial began in the afternoon of Christmas Day. It should go down as one of the most transparent kangaroo courts in history. The old couple were hemmed in behind two school desks in the corner of the room, faced by the regicides. The chairman of the bench was General Popa Ghica. There were five judges and two assessors, two defence lawyers and a video-camera operator. They included Colonel Lucescu, wearing the navy-blue uniform of the Military Judiciary; the bearded Gelu Voican, the new deputy prime mimister; Magureanu, a Securitate colonel who was a top aide to the acting president, Ion Iliescu, and later became the head of the Securitate, unhappily retitled the Romanian Information Service; and General Stanculescu, who eight days before had flown out to Timisoara to do the dictator's bidding.

The judges had one mission: to deliver a death sentence that day. Only the death of the dictator and his wife would stop the Securitate fanatics who, though the counter revolution was spluttering out, were still out there, killing. Secondly, the new regime needed the dictator out of the way lest he embarrass them at a public trial with revelations of their previous loyal behaviour. Ceausescu cried 'Traitors!' at the judges. With Stanculescu among them, well he might.

But the judges needed at least to obey the formalities. They asked questions, many of them the right ones, about, for example, the Timisoara uprising. But no evidence was produced. Proof might have made the case more clear cut, but such an approach would have taken much longer and stained the good name of people other than the defendants. A defence lawyer was procured from Bucharest, Nicu Teodorescu. He told Paul Martin of *The Times* afterwards: 'I do not believe the court was instructed in advance to sentence them to death. But I had no doubt there would be no other outcome. If they had called for witnesses I believe the court would have refused – the case against them was too strong.' There had been no time to prepare a defence. The court was already sitting when Teodorescu arrived. Thinking on his feet, he tried to explain to his two clients that their only hope of avoiding the death sentence was to plead mental instability. He recalled: 'But when I suggested it, Elena in particular said it was an outrageous set-up. They felt deeply insulted, unable or unwilling to grasp their only lifeline.' Their defence lawyer added with unconscious humour: 'They rejected my help after that.'

Teodorescu was struck by the strong partnership of the couple. 'I had always thought Elena was the dominant force in their partnership, but I soon came to realise Nicolae was in command. They complemented each other perfectly – like a monster with two heads.'

The Ceausescus were charged with corruption, embezzlement of funds, economic impoverishment of the nation and the murder of 65,000 people: a figure wrong by about 64,000. At the end of the trial even Teodorescu, their lawyer, said they were guilty. Given the appalling odds against them, the old couple stood up rather bravely to their ordeal, Ceausescu hoarsely croaking his defiance, patting his wife on the shoulder from time to time for reassurance. Watching the long version of the farce, which was screened on French television, it was hard not to feel a sympathy for these two frightened, tormented pensioners. Hard, too, to remember the fear they once generated and the misery they wrought: the smudged lives, the butcher's widow left with three children in her icy shack, the baker with maggots in his amputated leg, the candlestick-maker's blood on the floor by the broken window pane, the flattened homes, the demolished cherry trees, the milk-skinned creatures who spend their day grinding their teeth . . . . But remember it one must.

The tone was set by the prosecutor. Before he read out the charges, he heaped scorn on Ceausescu.

Prosecutor: For twenty-five years you humiliated the population. For twenty-five years all you did was talk.

Ceausescu: I do not recognise any court. I recognise only the Grand National Assembly. This is a coup d'état.

Prosecutor: We are judging you in accordance with the constitution of the country.

Ceausescu: I will not reply to any question.

Prosecutor: The accused and his wife had luxurious personal arrangements, gave extravagant receptions and the people had only 200 grams of salami on presentation of an identity card. You pillaged the people and even today you deny it. He doesn't want to speak; he is a coward.

Ceausescu deliberately kept mum; his body turned as tightly as it could away from the speaker, his eyes black spots of rage.

Prosecutor: We know everything. For the crimes which he perpetrated against his victims, I urge the death sentence.

Only then did the prosecutor read the charges. Ceausescu replied that he would not sign anything.

Prosecutor: Have you heard this, accused? Please stand up.

Ceausescu: Everything that has been said is a lie. I recognise only the

Grand National Assembly. I do not recognise this tribunal.

Prosecutor: You know the disastrous situation that prevailed in the country up to 22 December 1989. You are aware of the lack of medicine, of heating –

[Elena interrupts, indistinctly.]

Prosecutor: I am talking now to Nicolae Ceausescu, not to Elena. Who gave the order to shoot young people in Timisoara? Do you know about the bloodbath in Bucharest, which is still going on? Women and children are being killed by fanatics? Who trained these fanatics? We, the people, or you?

Ceausescu: I will not reply. Nobody has been shot in Palace Square. No one has been killed.

Second Prosecutor: Today there are more than 64,000 victims in all the towns. Who ordered the shooting in Bucharest and in every large town? You have reduced the people to poverty. There are educated people, true geniuses, who have left the country to escape you. Who are the foreign mercenaries who are shooting? Who paid these mercenaries? Who ordered those mercenaries who are carrying out this bloodbath?

The second prosecutor was referring to the widely believed rumour that Libyan and North Korean terrorists were doing the killing. No hard evidence to stand up this rumour was ever brought to bear, either at the trial or later.

Ceausescu: I will only answer questions in front of the Grand National Assembly.

Prosecutor: Who directs the mercenaries who are carrying out terrorist actions? Elena Ceausescu, doctor engineer, academician, you usually have a lot to say. Why are you silent now?

Elena: This is a provocation.

Prosecutor: Who is stopping you from talking?

Ceausescu: I will speak only in front of the Grand National Assembly and the Representatives of the working class. I do not recognise those who lead a coup.

Another voice: The Grand National Assembly has been dismantled. Through the unflinching will of the people we have another body in power, the Council of the National Salvation Front.

Ceausescu: [snarling] The people will fight against this gang of traitors who, with foreign help, succeeded in this coup.

Another voice: Who are these people fighting throughout the country?

Ceausescu: For their existence, independence and sovereignty . . .

Prosecutor: Do you know that you have been dismissed from your position as head of the party and president of the country, and that you have lost all your other positions? Are the accused aware of the fact, are they aware that they face trial as two ordinary citizens?

Ceausescu: I am president of the country and supreme commander of the army. I do not recognise you. You are ordinary citizens and I answer only to the Grand National Assembly. I do not answer those who, with the assistance of foreign organisations, carried out this coup.

Prosecutor: Why did you take these measures of bringing the Romanian people to this state of humiliation today? To export everything that they have produced? Why did you starve the people?

Ceausescu: I will not answer your question, but I will tell you that for the first time a cooperative worker received 200 kilograms of wheat per person, not per family, but per person. These are lies that you are saying, and you are not patriots.

Prosecutor: You wrote one thing on paper, but the reality was something else. And what about systemisation, which actually meant the destruction of our villages?

Ceausescu: There has never been such a level of development in the villages as there is today. We have built schools, ensured that there are doctors, ensured that there is everything for a dignified life.

Prosecution: A last question. Since we are supposed to be equal, all of us, why did we see on television that your daughter was weighing meat from abroad on gold scales at her villa? Wasn't the meat from your own country good enough?

Elena: Which villa? She lives in a flat like everyone else. Extraordinary. How can you say such a thing?

Prosecutor: Nicolae Ceausescu, tell us about the money that was transferred to Swiss banks.

Elena: [contemptuous] Proof! Proof!

Ceausescu: [patting his hand on Elena to restrain her anger] I do not answer the questions of a gang which carried out a coup.

Prosecutor: Nevertheless, if it is proved that there is money in foreign banks in your name, do you agree that it should be brought back to the Romanian state?

(In fact, no hard evidence has ever been brought forward that the Ceausescus had secret millions stashed away in banks abroad. It is not uninteresting, however, that revolutionaries who stormed the Presidential Palace found a pen bearing the initials of a firm of well-known British bullion dealers and paperwork indicating business dealings with them.)

Ceausescu: We will discuss [indistinct] with the Grand National Assembly. I will not sign anything. What is this National Salvation Council? It is impossible to set up a body without the state power, without the approval of the Grand National Assembly. As happened hundred of years ago, people like you will have to answer to the people.

Prosecutor, to Elena: You, who have always been your husband's primary collaborator, do you know who gave the order to fire in Timisoara?

Elena: How should we know what the military did in Timisoara?

The question could well have been asked of General Stanculescu, sitting in the room.

Prosecutor: What do you know about the Securitate?

Elena: They are sitting across from us here.

Someone cut in quickly, to change the subject.

Another voice: Who demoted General Milea [the executed defence minister, shot on 22 December] and accused him of being a traitor? Why did you not try him properly?

Ceausescu: I heard about his betrayal that day. He did not do his duty in making the army carry out its tasks. The traitor Milea went out with a group of people and somebody shot him. I can't stop a military unit from carrying out its duty.

Prosecutor: What kind of order did Milea refuse to obey?

Ceausescu: I'm going to answer to the Grand National Assembly.

Prosecutor: Are you suffering from some psychological problem?

Elena: You are rhinoceroses who are suffering from psychological problems.

The cold text does not properly convey the atmosphere discernible on the video. The prosecutor was clearly failing to crack the two defendants, whose sharp and pointed retorts were beginning to dent his attack. The video reflects a sort of gloom among the judges as they realise they will never succeed in getting Ceausescu and Elena to admit to anything. Appreciating this, the prosecutor launched into a long tirade, which the Ceausescus sat out, oozing contempt.

Prosecutor: The two accused don't understand what's happening to them and are unwilling to cooperate with the court. Their behaviour is beyond comprehension. It is very difficult to take a decision when, even before the law, the accused refuse to admit genocide, not only in Timisoara and Bucharest, but twenty-five years of crimes. Crimes committed by starving the people, by depriving them of heating and electricity and, above all, crimes against the mind. Innocent children have been crushed by tanks. You have dressed Securitate officers in army uniforms to raise the people against the army. You have ripped out oxygen pipes in hospitals, you have blown up the blood-plasma depot. [Ceausescu smiles] You went to Iran to prostrate yourself before the Ayatollah. You had the opportunity to seek political asylum in Iran, to keep all your accounts in Swiss banks. [Ceausescu laughs again]

Elena: Yes, yes.

Prosecutor: And now you mock the court.

[Ceausescu looks at his watch in what appears to be an attempt to worry the judges that his rescuers may be arriving soon.]

Prosecutor, to Elena: Who paid for the publication of your husband's volumes abroad?

Elena: Leave me alone. How can you say such things?

Prosecutor: You have behaved just like you always did. Have you learnt nothing today?

Elena: I have fought since I was fourteen years old. How can we betray the people?

Second Prosecutor: For the atrocities committed by these two accused, we ask you to sentence them to death and order the confiscation of their wealth.

Teodorescu: I want you to understand that we, as lawyers, want to defend everybody in accordance with the valid laws. Only a president can ask for the Grand National Assembly to be called, but you are not president any longer. You are ordinary citizens. It is a mistake of the two accused that they still have power and try to act accordingly.

Prosecutor: You have killed young people in Timisoara and your security forces were disguised in soldier's uniforms.

This was a remark to blend in with the airbrushing of history that the army had always been with the revolution. In fact it only switched sides on 21 December.

Prosecutor: You were shooting at hospitals, at the wounded . . . .

Elena: Who?

Prosecutor: You say you do not recognise our organisations of the people's power. You do not have to recognise them, Mr Ex- President. King Michael had more dignity than you.

The prosecutor was referring to the recognition the new government had just received from the exiled King. The rest of the world, too, with the exception of North Korea, had rushed to welcome the new regime. He then asked if the accused wished to say anything in their own defence. The dictator's reply is sad testament to his belief in his own propaganda.

Ceausescu: I am not an accused person. I will only answer to the Romanian people. Have you not seen how the people cheered when I went to the factories?
Prosecutor: It is not possible to discuss with you, we are going to deliberate. [The sound of chairs moving]
Another voice: Stand up!
Elena [to her husband]: No, dear, don't stand up. We are human beings . . . .

The judges retired to consider their verdict. They returned. Judge Ghica announced the inevitable.

Judge Ghica: The sentence is pronounced today, 25 December 1989, in a public gathering. We consider that the accused are guilty, and the court announces the sentence sought: confiscation of all property and capital punishment.
Ceausescu: I recognise neither defeat nor anything.
Elena: No court. I sign nothing. I have struggled for the people since I was fourteen, and the people are our people.
Judge Ghica: This decision is final.

Only now, as their hands were roughly tied behind their backs, did they begin to realise what was happening. Elena cried: 'What are you doing?' An echo, this, of the execution of Louis XVI during the French Revolution. 'What are you doing?' said the King. 'Binding your hands,' said the soldiers, before escorting him to the guillotine where he pardoned his executioners.

With the Ceausescus, the whole thing was not so elegant. One of the soldiers was clumsy with Elena. She sneered: 'You're in big trouble now,' to which he demurred. She replied: 'Go fuck your mother.' The obscenity struck the soldiers dumb. The Ceausescus were led, struggling, down a corridor and into a yard where a ragged firing squad was waiting. No one had told the Ceausescus that the sentence was to be carried out immediately. They didn't know they were going to die.

The video goes dead. The moment of death was not captured, or if it was, it was erased. This has given rise to a series of rumours: that Ceausescu was not really killed but replaced by a double, and that he sang the first few bars of the Internationale. It was all more tawdry than that. Colonel Lucescu, the military judge, hotly denied the Internationale story: 'That's an indecent and stupid lie. The trial ended with their death. People shouldn't make stupid jokes. The whole trial and their deaths was a terrible thing. I don't want to go through those moments ever again.' The anger at the falseness of the rumours and the cheapness of the trial struck me as an honest reaction from a man who had no reason to lie.

The firing squad had opened up too soon, clipping the video camerman and peppering the wall behind the Ceausescus with badly aimed bullets. They were not professionally trained killers, after all. The two corpses fell to the ground. The video camera was working now, and showed a ghastly close-up of the dictator and his wife. In death, he seemed once more to be snarling. On the soundtrack, the video picked up a whirring noise. It was the helicopter that would take Stanculescu and Magureanu back to President Iliescu in Bucharest, to tell him the good news.

They were buried in secret a few days later in a Bucharest cemetery as snow fell thickly. False names were placed on their wooden crosses, for him: 'Lt Col Popa Dan'; for her, buried nearby: 'Lt Col Enescu Vasile'. Their execution, announced the evening of Christmas Day, brought an end to most of the killing, but a few unfortunates continued to die, victims of isolated sniper fire by madmen loyal to the dead dictator or – perhaps more common – by mistake. The trial and summary execution gave a sour taste to the revolution which never went away thereafter.

Ill luck starred some of those involved in the trial. The defence counsel, Teodorescu, was ambushed by Securitate loyalists on his drive back to Bucharest. The man next to him was shot dead; Teodorescu escaped with a wound to his neck. While he was recovering in hospital he heard that his nineteen-year-old son, an army conscript, had been killed by Securitate gunmen in the fighting a few days before the Ceausescus died. Two months later, the chairman of the judges, Popa Ghica, committed suicide. He had been threatened by telephone and couldn't take the strain.

No one mourned the dictator or his wife, not even their two sons. Nicu told me: 'That's complicated. It's difficult to understand. I was just recovering from the operation after I had been wounded and I was still drowsy with the effects of the drugs. I heard about it then. Because of the drugs I didn't have a shock. After that, when I came out of the drugs, I had got used to the idea. So, because of the drugs, it was a special situation. The reality was that I could have died before they did.'

Valentin was equally passionless. He told me: 'I was not upset when I heard that they had been executed. I was in prison, with time on my hands, so I was able to study the situation without emotion.' He smiled at some private amusement, which he then shared: 'The execution was a political mistake. They should have said that they were shot while trying to escape.'

It would have been a more convenient way of dispatching the dictator and his wife. It is unlikely that the verdict of history will be any less bleak than the verdict of their two sons.

Epilogue: June 1990

They came in an arrowhead, their hobnailed boots thundering down the Boulevard Nicolae Balcescu in the heart of Bucharest. One man in a grey suit walked out from the pavement, where the long bread queue afforded a weak, anonymous safety, into the middle of the street and tried to stop the arrow. He had no chance. The first miner swung his wooden club – the width of a man's fist – and the grey suit was down. A second miner kicked him in the head repeatedly; a third brought down a rubber cosh. In an instant grey suit had disappeared, hidden by the boots and sticks pumping up and down like a demented threshing machine.

It is a peculiarly nasty experience – far more frightening than the random menace of gunfire – to see a man being beaten almost to death in front of your eyes and know that to intervene would be suicide. It must have been like this in the Thirties, when the Brown Shirts stomped around Berlin.

One man was brave enough to try. He was an ox of a fellow – at six foot six inches and weighing not much less than twenty stone, he towered above the dirty-faced runts in their pit helmets and boots. This man showed a card to the new cluster of miners, but they were not in talking mood. A wooden stave smashed down on his head and the ox, wounded, ran to the safety of a building, pursued. More miners arrived, jumping down from a lorry, and charged the bread queue. Everyone, youths, old women with bags of shopping, children, ran for it squealing like pigs in a slaughterhouse. A man in front of me lost a shoe but kept on half running, half hopping, desperate to flee.

Later the ox turned up at the emergency hospital to get his head bandaged. He turned out to be Gheorghe Daraban, former captain of the national rugby team and a major in the police. Daraban is something of a national hero, but this had not helped him. His jersey, a gift from a touring British rugby team, was dappled with blood. He said, with a bruised grin: 'I was afraid I was going to lose my teeth.'

The first man, in the grey suit, was by some miracle still alive but so unwell that we were not allowed to see him. He too was a police officer.

A third victim of the miners, a Bulgarian Gypsy, was wheeled by on a trolley, her head bandaged, her kidneys in danger of failing. Her crime, for the miners, was her skin tone: dark enough to be one of the 'anti-government Gypsies' who were allegedly allied with the pro-testers against the new regime in Bucharest.

Later that day – Friday, 15 June – viewers of Romanian TV saw President Ion Iliescu appear at a mass meeting of the miners – their flashlights twinkling in the gloom – to thank them for 'saving democracy'. For anyone who witnessed the miners' behaviour, when even police officers were savaged, such warm thanks marks out a man wretchedly imprisoned in the ways of his late, unlamented pre-decessor. That week, when they were not beating people up, you could see them pinning up colour photographs of President Iliescu.

Not just the fear machine but the cult of personality is making a comeback. For people who witnessed the bloody sweetness of the Christmas revolution, the week in mid-June gave bitter proof that the monster that Ceausescu created, though decapitated, is still clumping around the streets of Bucharest.

The explanation – but no excuse – for this state-licensed terror was that the government got the shock of its life two days before. Flushed with its landslide majority in the fairly held elections, the National Salvation Front decided to act against the *golani* (tramps), whose anti-Iliescu hunger strike in a peace camp outside the Inter-Continental was a blot on the landscape. In the middle of the night, the *golani* were beaten up and about 230 arrested and taken into police custody. The move broke the prickly calm. That afternoon, students, teenagers and a job lot of hooligans outside the *golani*'s control went looking for their friends, to liberate them. They torched the lower floors of the main Bucharest police station and smashed up the TV station.

It was only when the protesters took on the Interior Ministry building – the headquarters of the Securitate in the not so old days – that they started to lose. Photographers saw shots coming from inside. One man was killed instantly. Another man was shot in the act of throwing a petrol bomb and died later of a stomach wound. What was curious about his case was that when hospital doctors checked his

ID they found that he was an employee of the Ministry of Internal Affairs. Four others died and 462 were injured.

Although the authorities now had the upper hand, they panicked and pressed the button of the fear machine. The miners came in specially commissioned trains from towns like Hunedoara, hundreds of miles from Bucharest, arriving at four in the morning. The government has said they came spontaneously, yet they were paid, fed and watered and put up in government-owned sports halls.

One of their first victims was the leader of the *golani*, Marian Munteanu, a bearded Christlike figure swathed in bandages at the hospital with a broken left leg, broken left hand and an ugly head wound. A doctor wiped his brow as he spoke in a low whisper. What did he think of Iliescu? 'Who? Which Iliescu? Which president?' It took a moment to realise he was joking. Why did the government do this? 'For power. They did it with fear. You are seeing a new dictator now.'

He went on: 'I wouldn't want to be in his place because you know I believe in God and all of us must answer God's question for what we have done.' And the miners? 'Poor miners.' And then the doctors wheeled him away. To the National Salvation Front, this man is a fascist. Later, they had him arrested and imprisoned.

Next, the miners smashed up the home of the Peasant Party presidential candidate, Ion Ratiu – the man who had been arrested outside Claridges in 1978. To its credit, Romanian TV did show pictures of the damage and a brief clip with Ratiu. There were no pictures, however, of the Liberal Party's devastated headquarters; none either of the offices of *Romania Libera*, an anti-government newspaper, utterly trashed by the miners, or of the three other anti-Iliescu newspapers, *22* (after 22 December) *Baricada* and *Dreptatea* (Justice), closed by government diktat. No pictures either of the miners' violence, their sexual molestation of young women, their unprovoked attacks on anyone looking remotely like a student, while the police walked the other way.

None of the scenes described could fully convey the mood in Bucharest that week, a city fizzing with fear. Most depressing of all was the re-emergence of the Securitate. In the days immediately after the revolution it was they who were afraid, running from our cameras, avoiding our questions. It would have been madness to doorstep the Securitate now. They swaggered around the streets demanding papers but refusing to show their own. In the middle of the night they donned fancy dress, wearing clean, freshly pressed miners' jerkins and spotless gumboots. The staves they stopped you with to check your ID were, however, real enough.

Who else but the Securitate showed Ratiu's house to the miners? Who bused them in, organised their keep? Who pointed out the newspaper offices to wreck? The miners left as smoothly as they had come, packed on to trains which left Bucharest on Friday evening, the good order of their departure suggesting that it had all been stage-managed from above. They left, but not before President Iliescu had thanked them (at a sports hall Ceausescu had used for his rallies), and spoken of an 'attempted coup by a force of extreme rightist elements, a coup of Iron Guardist and fascist character'. The distortions whereby the miners became, in Iliescu's words, 'a powerful force for democracy' were worthy of his predecessor.

In Czechoslovakia, the newspapers have been full of the struggle to get rid of their secret police, the StB, and how the secret policemen fought to maintain their privileges. No such stories have appeared in Romania, for the simple reason that Iliescu and his right-hand man, defence minister General Stanculescu, have made no attempt to take apart the fear machine.

Fear distorts everything in Romania. One example: a doctor at the hospital, sick of tending the broken and the dying with obsolete equipment, showed me his museum piece of an X-ray machine. 'They have all the best equipment at the military hospital but we cannot have it.' He was too frightened to give his name. Not hospitals, but military spending had been the new regime's priority. General Stanculescu has been wined and dined in London by the City's bankers and been the guest of the British armaments industry at the Farnborough air show. George Pop was back in Bucharest; Lord Newall still cropped up in dinner-party conversation. It was just like the good old days.

The government's official response to that grim week in June was shameful and absurd. At a press conference, Petre Roman, Iliescu's prime minister, uttered the old communist imprecations against a 'political infection' and 'hostile forces' and talked of 'concrete aspects' of the situation when he should have been apologising. When asked – given the miners' mob rule – who was in charge of Romania, he replied: 'I must have a smile on my face at that.'

No. The smile was on the face of Nicolae Ceausescu, shot dead on christmas Day 1989 but for the poor, wretched Romanians still very much alive.

Select Bibliography

Bellow, Saul, *The Dean's December*, 1982.

Catchlove, Donald, *Romania's Ceausescu*, 1972.

Dumitriu, Petru, *Incognito*, 1964.

Fermor, Patrick Leigh, *Between the Woods and the Water*, 1986.

Fischer, Mary Ellen, *Nicolae Ceausescu: a study in political leadership*, 1989.

Florescu, Redu, and Raymond McNally, *In Search of Dracula*, 1973.

Funderburk, David B., *Pinstripes and Reds*, 1987.

Govender, Robert, *Nicolae Ceausescu: Statesman and Fighter for Detente, Disarmament and World Peace*, 1988.

Hale, Julian, *Ceausescu's Romania*, 1971.

Mackenzie, Andrew, *A Concise History of Romania*, 1985.

Manning, Olivia, *The Balkan Trilogy*, 1960–65.

Maxwell, Robert (general editor), *Nicolae Ceausescu: Builder of Modern Romania and International Statesman*, 1983.

Newens, Stan, *Nicolae Ceausescu: The Man, his Ideas and his Socialist Achievements*, 1972.

Observer, 'Tearing Down the Curtain', 1990.

Pacepa, Ion, *Red Horizons*, 1988.

Pakula, Hannah, *Queen of Roumania*, 1984.

Porter, Ivor, *Operation Autonomous*, 1989.

Richardson, Dan, and Jill Denton, *The Rough Guide to Eastern Europe*, 1988.

Samuelli, Annie, *The Wall Between*, 1967.

Schopflin, George, *The Hungarians of Rumania*, 1990.

Seton-Watson, R. W. *A History of the Roumanians*, 1933.

Shafir, Michael, *Romania: Politics, Economics and Society*, 1985.

Simpson, John, *Despatches from the Barricades*, 1990.

Stoker, Bram, *Dracula*, 1897.

Index